DEAD DAY ™

RYAN PARROTT

EVGENIY BORNYAKOV

JUANCHO!

CHARLES PRITCHETT

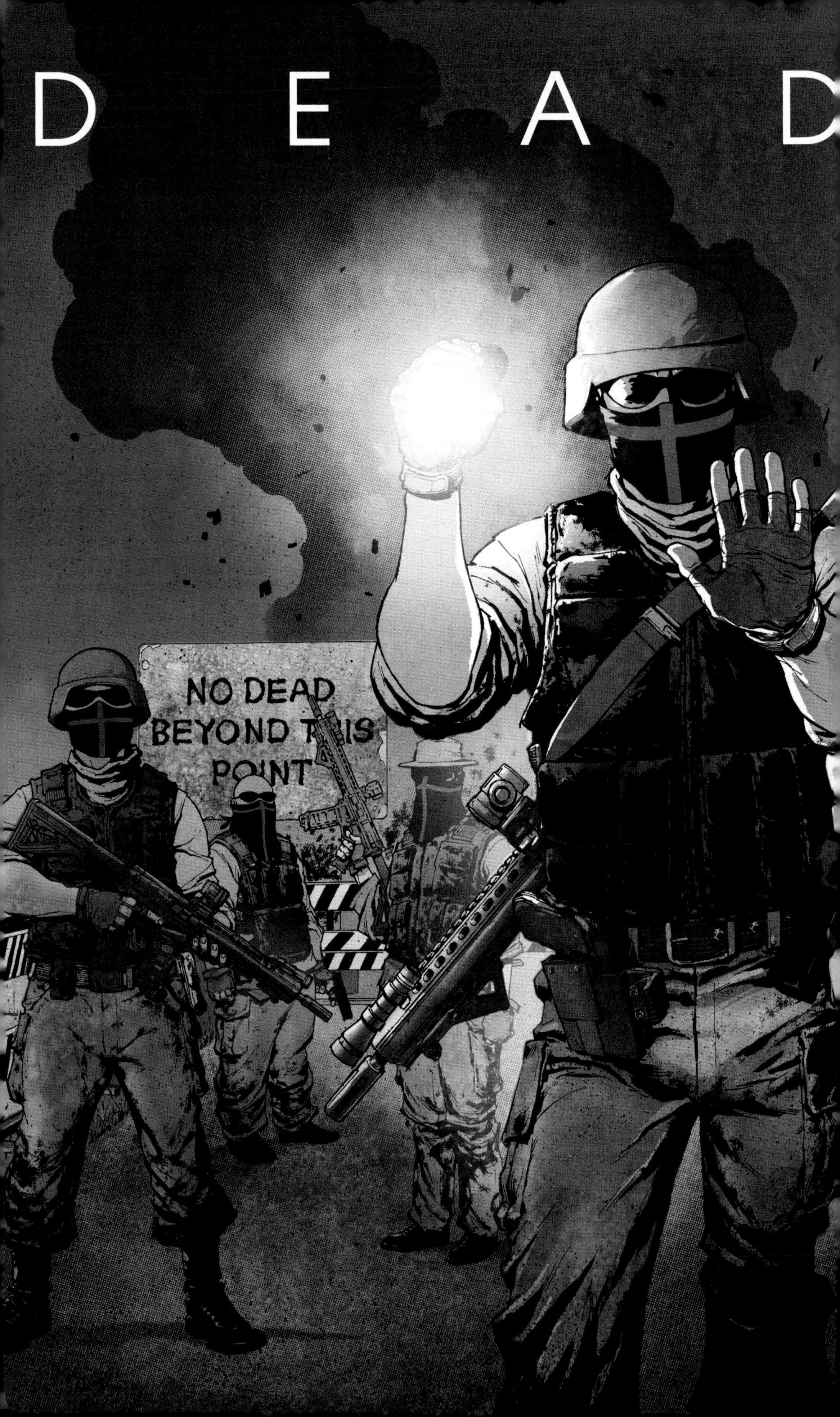
D E A D
NO DEAD
BEYOND T IS
POINT

D A Y ™

RYAN PARROTT writer

EVGENIY BORNYAKOV artist

JUANCHO! colorist

CHARLES PRITCHETT letterer

ANDY CLARKE w/ **JOSE VILLARRUBIA** front & original covers

FRANCESCO FRANCAVILLA, SZYMON KUDRANSKI, ALAN QUAH and **HUGH ROOKWOOD** variant covers

CHARLES PRITCHETT logo designer

COREY BREEN book designer

MIKE MARTS editor

created by **RYAN PARROTT**

AFTERSHOCK™

MIKE MARTS - Editor-in-Chief • **JOE PRUETT** - Publisher/CCO • **LEE KRAMER** - President • **JON KRAMER** - Chief Executive Officer
STEVE ROTTERDAM - SVP, Sales & Marketing • **DAN SHIRES** - VP, Film & Television UK • **CHRISTINA HARRINGTON** - Managing Editor
MARC HAMMOND - Sr. Retail Sales Development Manager • **RUTHANN THOMPSON** - Sr. Retailer Relations Manager
KATHERINE JAMISON - Marketing Manager • **KELLY DIODATI** - Ambassador Outreach Manager • **BLAKE STOCKER** - Director of Finance
AARON MARION - Publicist • **LISA MOODY** - Finance • **RYAN CARROLL** - Development Coordinator • **JAWAD QURESHI** - Technology Advisor/Strategist
RACHEL PINNELAS - Social Community Manager • **CHARLES PRITCHETT** - Design & Production Manager • **COREY BREEN** - Collections Production
TEDDY LEO - Editorial Assistant • **STEPHANIE CASEBIER** & **SARAH PRUETT** - Publishing Assistants

AfterShock Logo Design by **COMICRAFT**
Publicity: contact **AARON MARION** (aaron@publichausagency.com) & **RYAN CROY** (ryan@publichausagency.com) at **PUBLICHAUS**
Special thanks to: **ATOM! FREEMAN, IRA KURGAN, MARINE KSADZHIKYAN, KEITH MANZZELLA, STEPHANIE MEADOR, ANTONIA LIANOS** & **ED ZAREMBA**

AFTERSHOCKCOMICS.COM Follow us on social media 🐦 📷 f

I N T R O D U C T I O N

Just so we're clear from the beginning...DEAD DAY isn't a zombie story. Yes, judging by the cover I know it looks like one, and people do rise from the grave in the series, but oddly enough, most zombie stories are about only the living. They're a form of wish fulfillment where, free from the restrictions of society, people get to reinvent themselves into who they were always meant to be in a simplified, violent new world. So, this story is a little different because...it's about *both* the living and the dead.

You see, my life changed forever on August 8th, 2008. My grandparents, two of the loveliest, most compassionate and generous people I'd ever known, were killed in a random home invasion. It rocked my family to the core, and even though the criminals were eventually apprehended and sentenced to life in prison, none of us were ever really quite the same after that.

In the years that followed, we would routinely lament my grandparents' absence at every major family get-together, all of which ultimately ended with someone wishing, "Wouldn't it be great if we could have them back for just one night, even just to say goodbye?" And as I'm sure all writers do, I began to imagine the possibility...

"What would that night look like?"

For my grandmother, I'm certain she would simply want to host a fabulous dinner party, where we could gossip, trade stories and catch up, just like all the Thanksgiving and Christmas dinners of the past. There would be no sadness or melancholy allowed. But at the same time, what if my grandfather pulled me aside at some point during the evening and wanted to go after those responsible? Could anything in the world possibly stop me from going with him? And should that be how we spend our last few hours together? Suddenly, the idea of a simple night of reconnection felt so much more complicated. And that got me to ask a much larger question...

"What if this night wasn't just for my family...but the entire world?"

So, yes, as much as I love barbed wire-wrapped baseball bats and hordes of moaning, mindless corpses walking the earth, this story is more about the human desire for closure, both for those who were taken too early and those who were left behind to lament their departure. It doesn't provide answers about what happens after you die, but more asks a single question...

"What would you do if the dead could come back for one day?"

RYAN PARROTT
November 2020

1

CHAPTER ONE

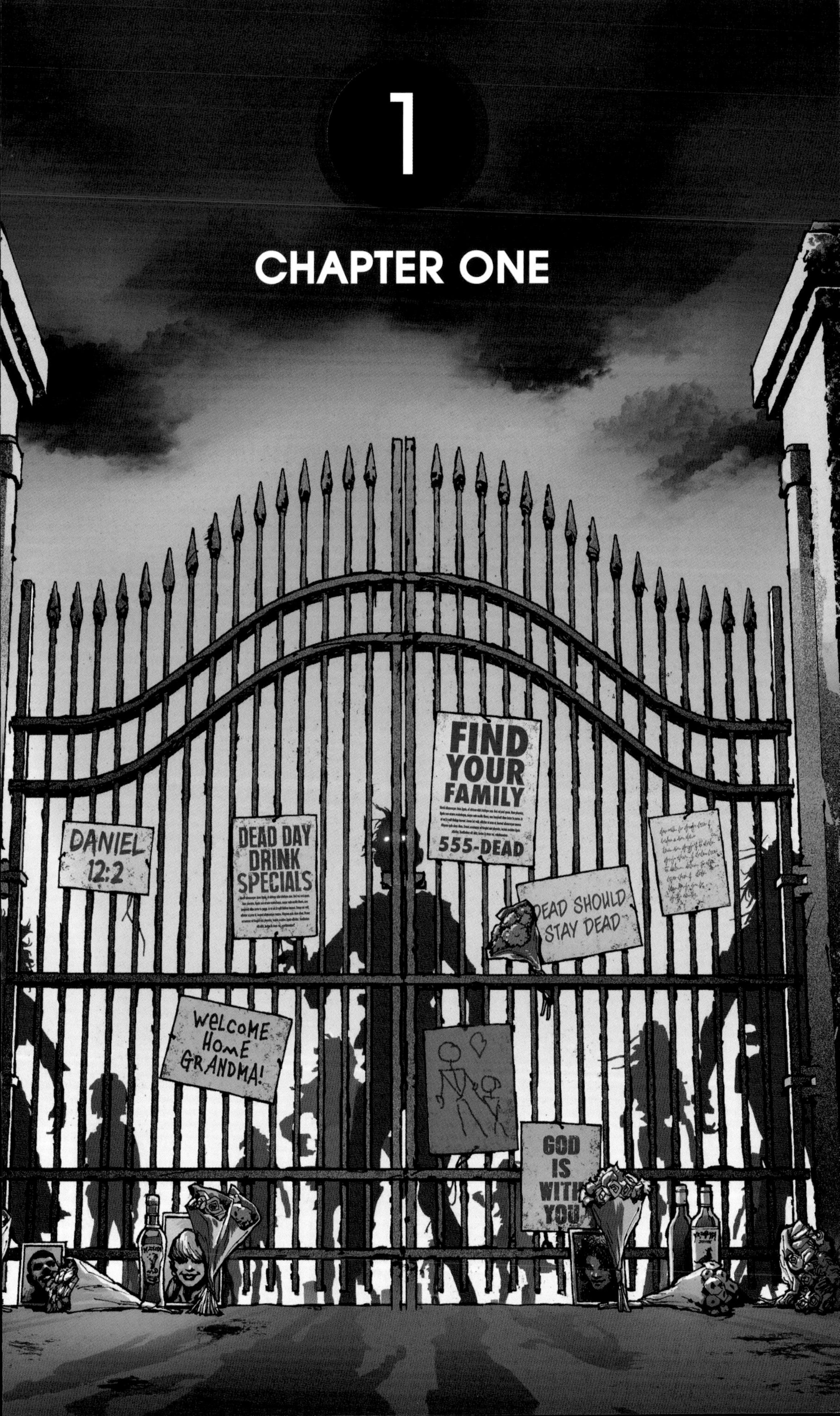

DANIEL 12:2
DEAD DAY DRINK SPECIALS
FIND YOUR FAMILY
555-DEAD
EAD SHOULD STAY DEAD
WELCOME HOME GRANDMA!
GOD IS WITH YOU

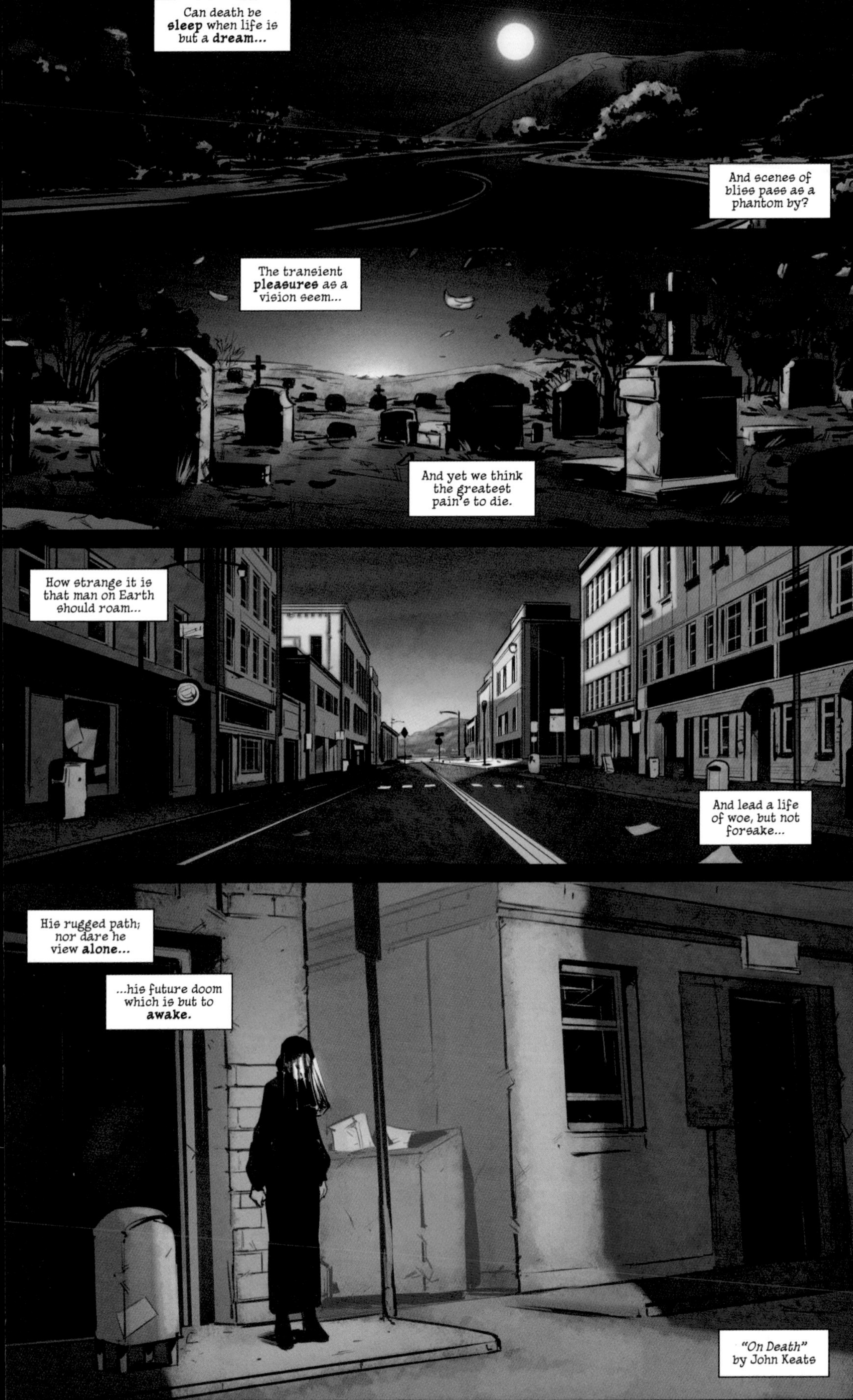
Can death be **sleep** when life is but a **dream...**
And scenes of bliss pass as a phantom by?
The transient **pleasures** as a vision seem...
And yet we think the greatest pain's to die.
How strange it is that man on Earth should roam...
And lead a life of woe, but not forsake...
His rugged path; nor dare he view **alone...**
...his future doom which is but to **awake.**
"On Death" by John Keats

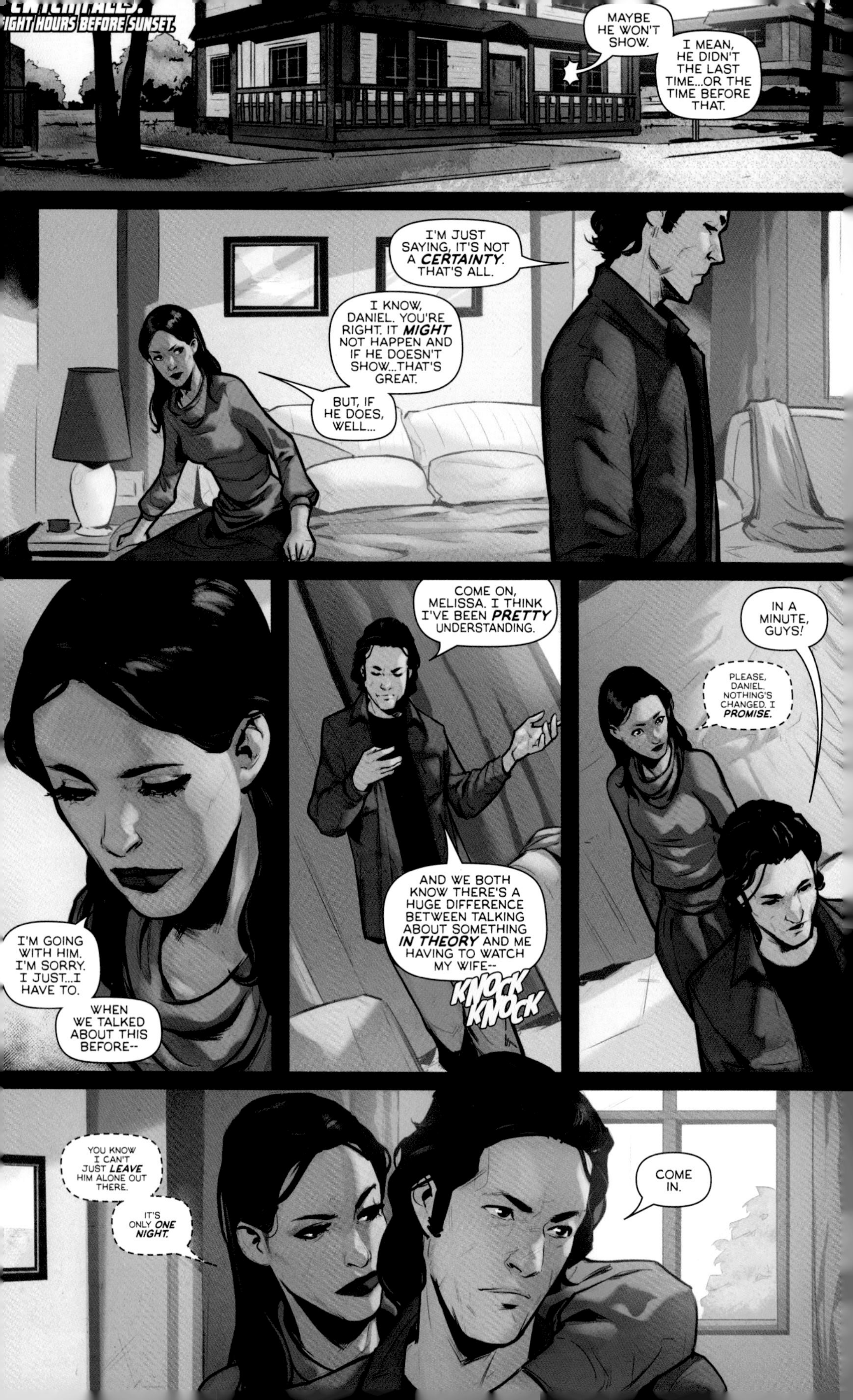
IGHT HOURS BEFORE SUNSET.
MAYBE HE WON'T SHOW.
I MEAN, HE DIDN'T THE LAST TIME...OR THE TIME BEFORE THAT.
I'M JUST SAYING, IT'S NOT A CERTAINTY. THAT'S ALL.
I KNOW, DANIEL. YOU'RE RIGHT. IT MIGHT NOT HAPPEN AND IF HE DOESN'T SHOW...THAT'S GREAT.
BUT, IF HE DOES, WELL...
I'M GOING WITH HIM. I'M SORRY. I JUST...I HAVE TO.
WHEN WE TALKED ABOUT THIS BEFORE--
COME ON, MELISSA. I THINK I'VE BEEN PRETTY UNDERSTANDING.
AND WE BOTH KNOW THERE'S A HUGE DIFFERENCE BETWEEN TALKING ABOUT SOMETHING IN THEORY AND ME HAVING TO WATCH MY WIFE--
KNOCK KNOCK
IN A MINUTE, GUYS!
PLEASE, DANIEL. NOTHING'S CHANGED. I PROMISE.
YOU KNOW I CAN'T JUST LEAVE HIM ALONE OUT THERE.
IT'S ONLY ONE NIGHT.
COME IN.

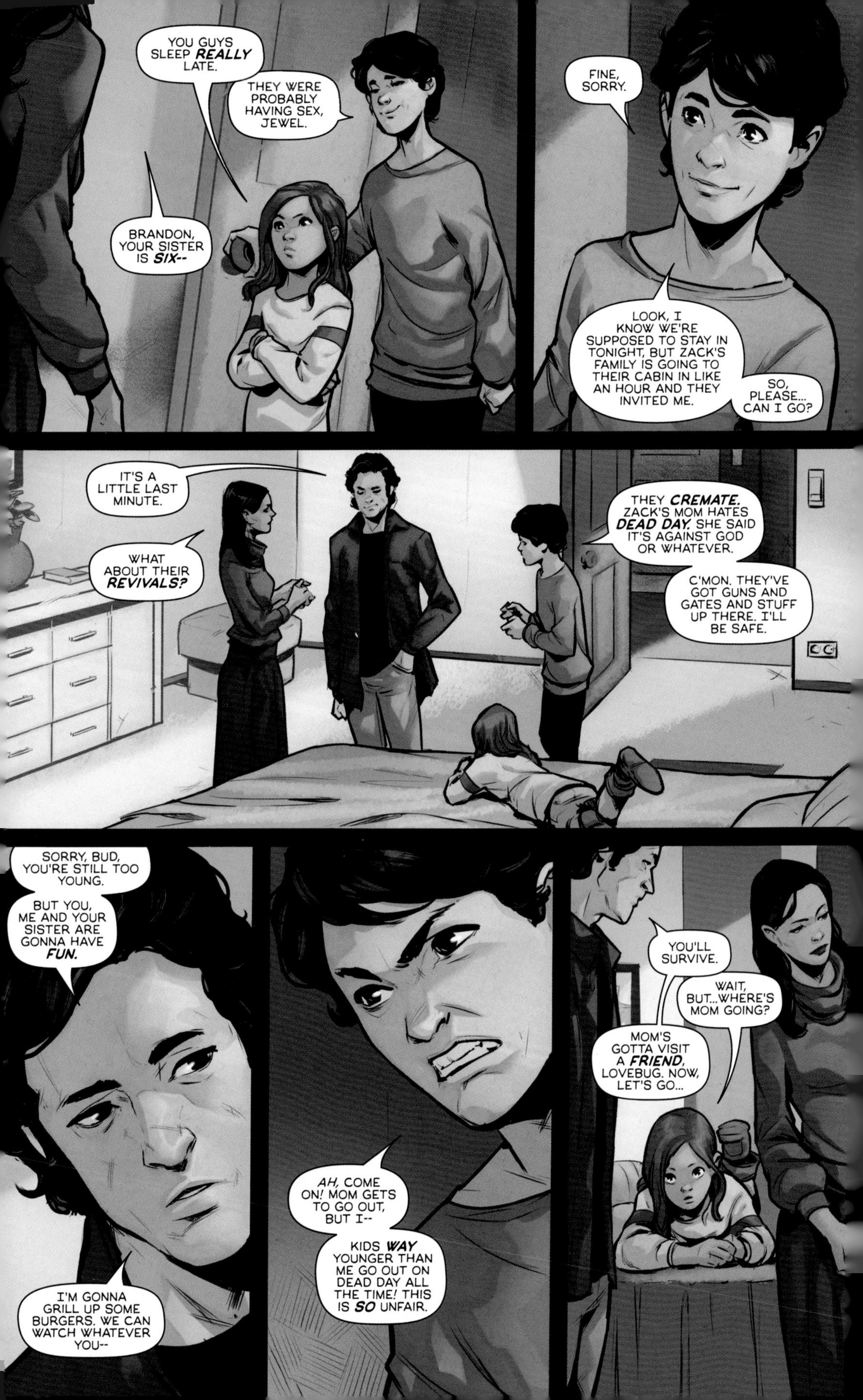
YOU GUYS SLEEP REALLY LATE.
THEY WERE PROBABLY HAVING SEX, JEWEL.
BRANDON, YOUR SISTER IS SIX--
FINE, SORRY.
LOOK, I KNOW WE'RE SUPPOSED TO STAY IN TONIGHT, BUT ZACK'S FAMILY IS GOING TO THEIR CABIN IN LIKE AN HOUR AND THEY INVITED ME.
SO, PLEASE... CAN I GO?
IT'S A LITTLE LAST MINUTE.
WHAT ABOUT THEIR REVIVALS?
THEY CREMATE. ZACK'S MOM HATES DEAD DAY. SHE SAID IT'S AGAINST GOD OR WHATEVER.
C'MON. THEY'VE GOT GUNS AND GATES AND STUFF UP THERE. I'LL BE SAFE.
SORRY, BUD, YOU'RE STILL TOO YOUNG.
BUT YOU, ME AND YOUR SISTER ARE GONNA HAVE FUN.
I'M GONNA GRILL UP SOME BURGERS. WE CAN WATCH WHATEVER YOU--
AH, COME ON! MOM GETS TO GO OUT, BUT I--
KIDS WAY YOUNGER THAN ME GO OUT ON DEAD DAY ALL THE TIME! THIS IS SO UNFAIR.
YOU'LL SURVIVE.
WAIT, BUT...WHERE'S MOM GOING?
MOM'S GOTTA VISIT A FRIEND, LOVEBUG. NOW, LET'S GO...

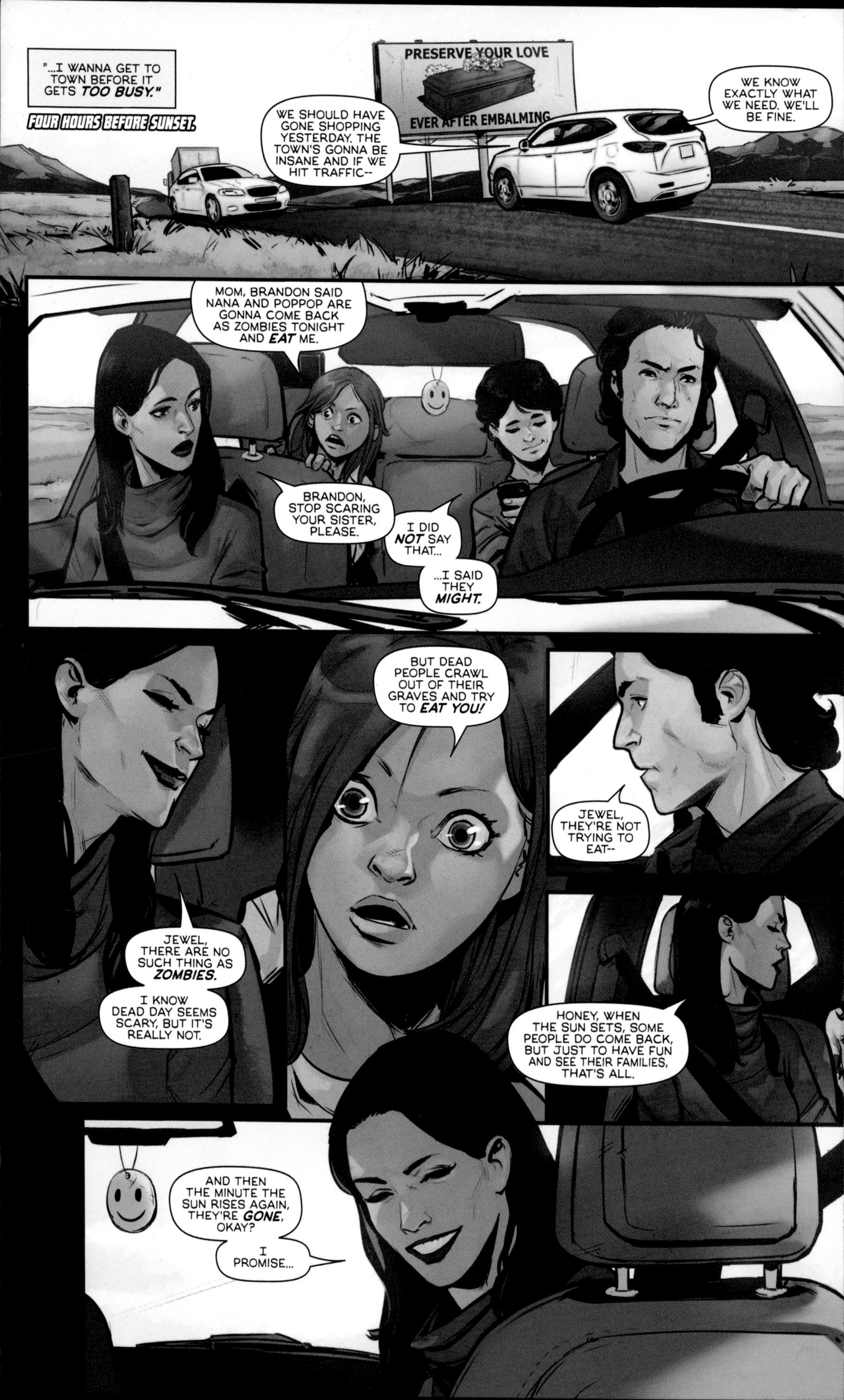
"...I WANNA GET TO TOWN BEFORE IT GETS *TOO BUSY.*"
FOUR HOURS BEFORE SUNSET.
PRESERVE YOUR LOVE
EVER AFTER EMBALMING
WE SHOULD HAVE GONE SHOPPING YESTERDAY. THE TOWN'S GONNA BE INSANE AND IF WE HIT TRAFFIC--
WE KNOW EXACTLY WHAT WE NEED. WE'LL BE FINE.
MOM, BRANDON SAID NANA AND POPPOP ARE GONNA COME BACK AS ZOMBIES TONIGHT AND *EAT* ME.
BRANDON, STOP SCARING YOUR SISTER, PLEASE.
I DID *NOT* SAY THAT...
...I SAID THEY *MIGHT.*
BUT DEAD PEOPLE CRAWL OUT OF THEIR GRAVES AND TRY TO *EAT YOU!*
JEWEL, THERE ARE NO SUCH THING AS *ZOMBIES.*
I KNOW DEAD DAY SEEMS SCARY, BUT IT'S REALLY NOT.
JEWEL, THEY'RE NOT TRYING TO EAT--
HONEY, WHEN THE SUN SETS, SOME PEOPLE DO COME BACK, BUT JUST TO HAVE FUN AND SEE THEIR FAMILIES, THAT'S ALL.
AND THEN THE MINUTE THE SUN RISES AGAIN, THEY'RE *GONE*, OKAY?
I PROMISE...

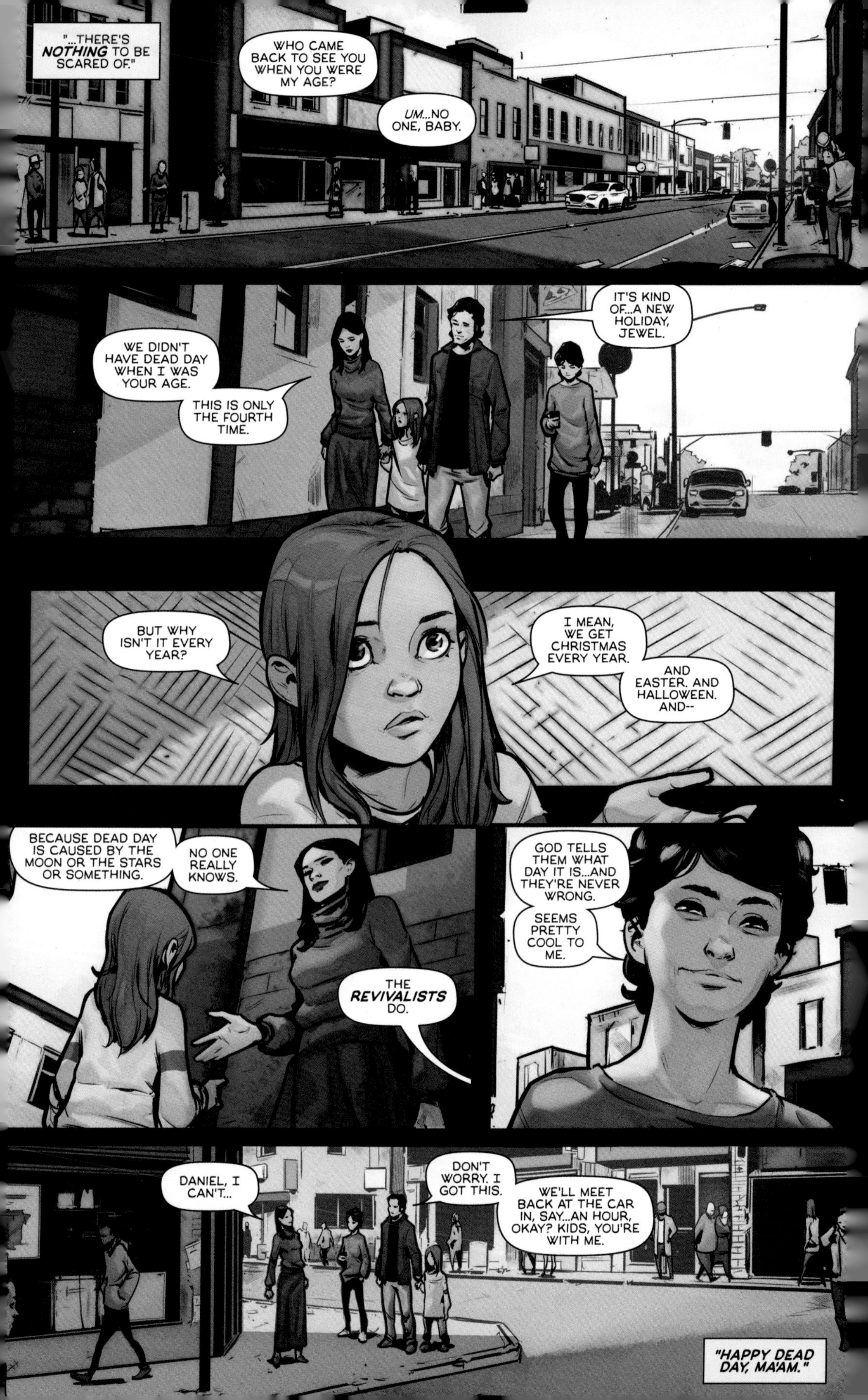
"...THERE'S NOTHING TO BE SCARED OF."
WHO CAME BACK TO SEE YOU WHEN YOU WERE MY AGE?
UM...NO ONE, BABY.
WE DIDN'T HAVE DEAD DAY WHEN I WAS YOUR AGE.
THIS IS ONLY THE FOURTH TIME.
IT'S KIND OF...A NEW HOLIDAY, JEWEL.
BUT WHY ISN'T IT EVERY YEAR?
I MEAN, WE GET CHRISTMAS EVERY YEAR.
AND EASTER. AND HALLOWEEN. AND--
BECAUSE DEAD DAY IS CAUSED BY THE MOON OR THE STARS OR SOMETHING.
NO ONE REALLY KNOWS.
THE REVIVALISTS DO.
GOD TELLS THEM WHAT DAY IT IS...AND THEY'RE NEVER WRONG.
SEEMS PRETTY COOL TO ME.
DANIEL, I CAN'T...
DON'T WORRY. I GOT THIS.
WE'LL MEET BACK AT THE CAR IN, SAY...AN HOUR, OKAY? KIDS, YOU'RE WITH ME.
"HAPPY DEAD DAY, MA'AM."

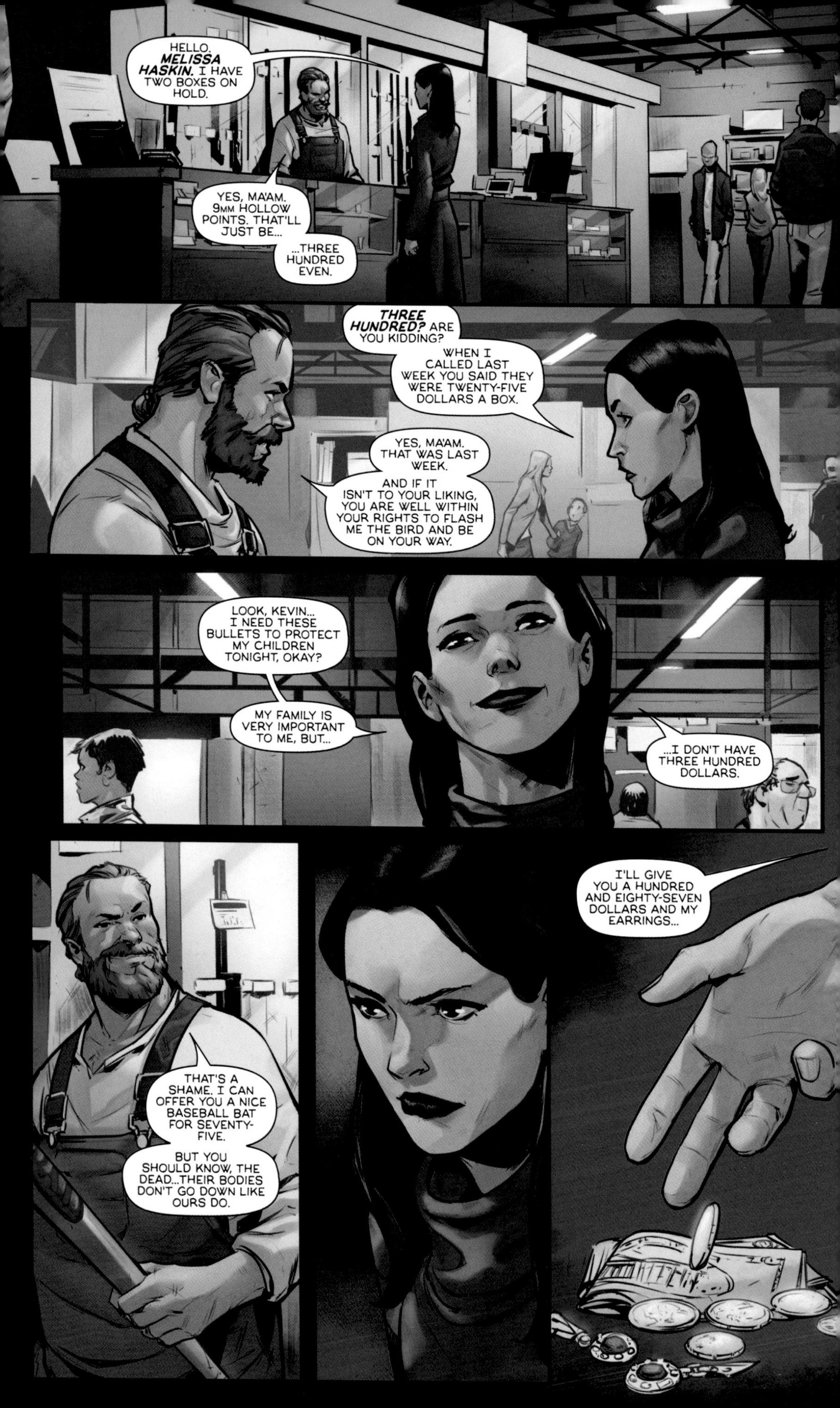

HELLO. MELISSA HASKIN. I HAVE TWO BOXES ON HOLD.
YES, MA'AM. 9MM HOLLOW POINTS. THAT'LL JUST BE...
...THREE HUNDRED EVEN.
THREE HUNDRED? ARE YOU KIDDING?
WHEN I CALLED LAST WEEK YOU SAID THEY WERE TWENTY-FIVE DOLLARS A BOX.
YES, MA'AM. THAT WAS LAST WEEK.
AND IF IT ISN'T TO YOUR LIKING, YOU ARE WELL WITHIN YOUR RIGHTS TO FLASH ME THE BIRD AND BE ON YOUR WAY.
LOOK, KEVIN... I NEED THESE BULLETS TO PROTECT MY CHILDREN TONIGHT, OKAY?
MY FAMILY IS VERY IMPORTANT TO ME, BUT...
...I DON'T HAVE THREE HUNDRED DOLLARS.
THAT'S A SHAME. I CAN OFFER YOU A NICE BASEBALL BAT FOR SEVENTY-FIVE.
BUT YOU SHOULD KNOW, THE DEAD...THEIR BODIES DON'T GO DOWN LIKE OURS DO.
I'LL GIVE YOU A HUNDRED AND EIGHTY-SEVEN DOLLARS AND MY EARRINGS...

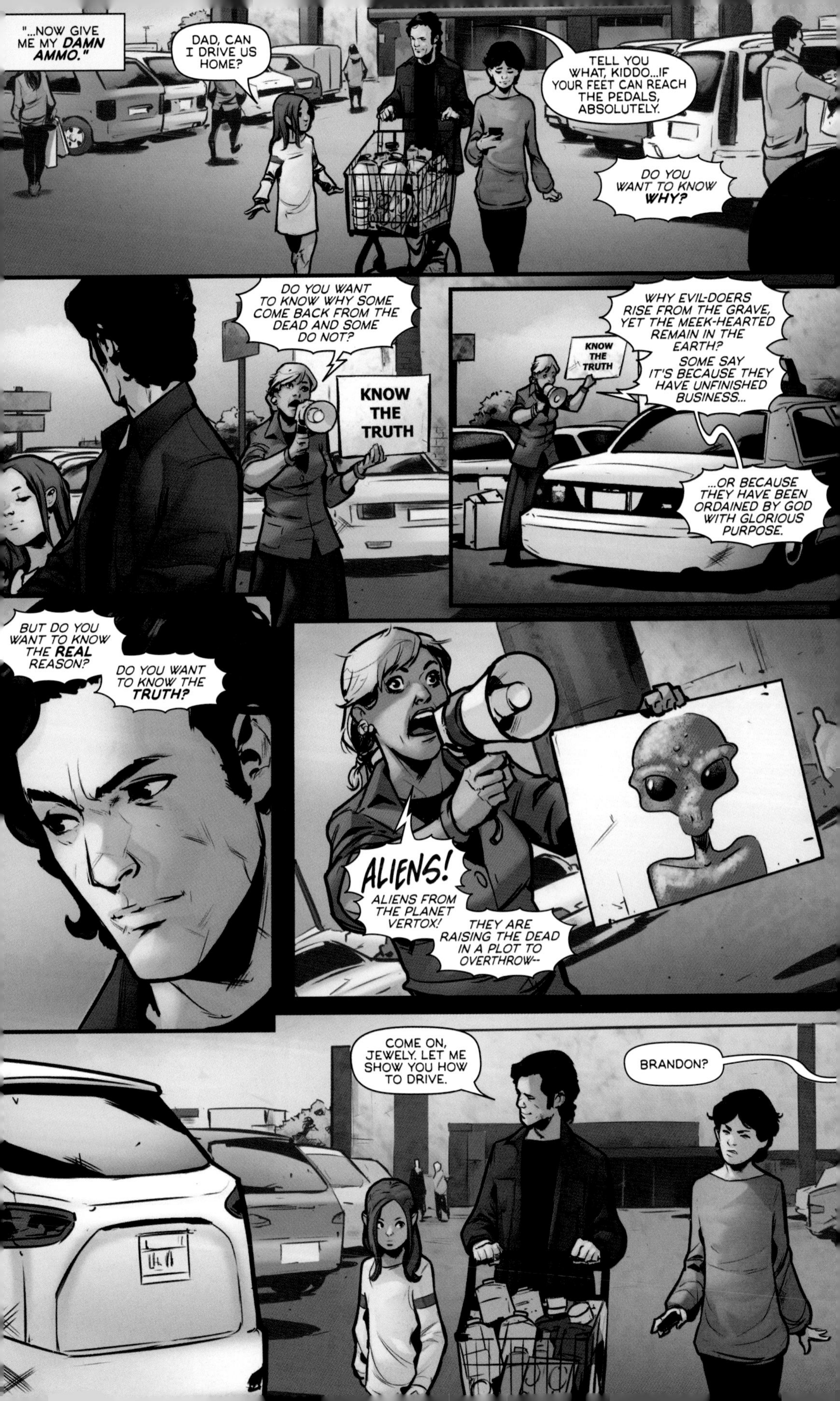
"...NOW GIVE ME MY **DAMN AMMO."**
DAD, CAN I DRIVE US HOME?
TELL YOU WHAT, KIDDO...IF YOUR FEET CAN REACH THE PEDALS, ABSOLUTELY.
DO YOU WANT TO KNOW **WHY?**
DO YOU WANT TO KNOW WHY SOME COME BACK FROM THE DEAD AND SOME DO NOT?
KNOW THE TRUTH
KNOW THE TRUTH
WHY EVIL-DOERS RISE FROM THE GRAVE, YET THE MEEK-HEARTED REMAIN IN THE EARTH?
SOME SAY IT'S BECAUSE THEY HAVE UNFINISHED BUSINESS...
...OR BECAUSE THEY HAVE BEEN ORDAINED BY GOD WITH GLORIOUS PURPOSE.
BUT DO YOU WANT TO KNOW THE **REAL** REASON?
DO YOU WANT TO KNOW THE **TRUTH?**
ALIENS!
ALIENS FROM THE PLANET VERTOX!
THEY ARE RAISING THE DEAD IN A PLOT TO OVERTHROW--
COME ON, JEWELY. LET ME SHOW YOU HOW TO DRIVE.
BRANDON?

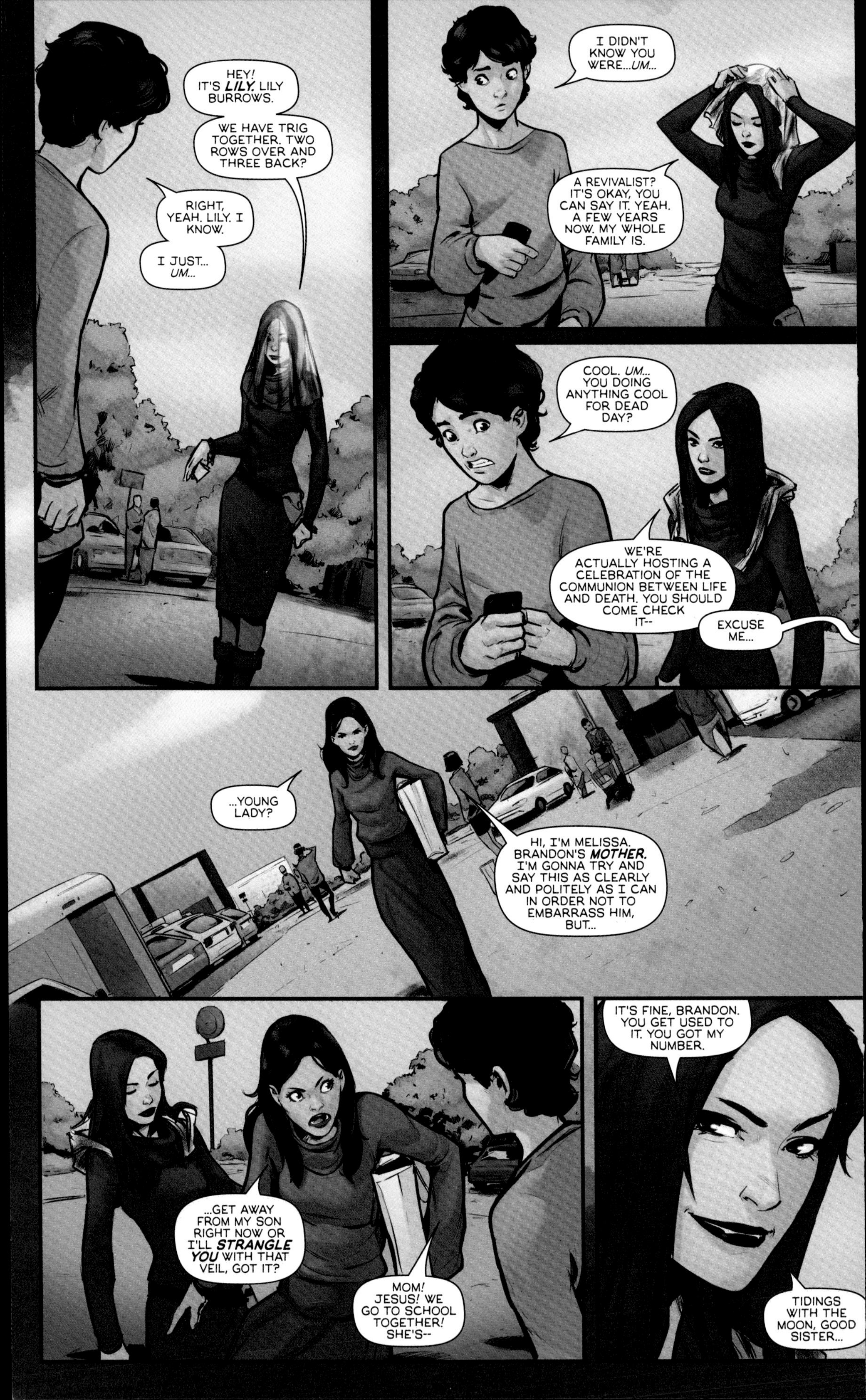
HEY! IT'S LILY. LILY BURROWS.
WE HAVE TRIG TOGETHER. TWO ROWS OVER AND THREE BACK?
RIGHT, YEAH. LILY. I KNOW.
I JUST... UM...
I DIDN'T KNOW YOU WERE...UM...
A REVIVALIST? IT'S OKAY, YOU CAN SAY IT. YEAH. A FEW YEARS NOW. MY WHOLE FAMILY IS.
COOL. UM... YOU DOING ANYTHING COOL FOR DEAD DAY?
WE'RE ACTUALLY HOSTING A CELEBRATION OF THE COMMUNION BETWEEN LIFE AND DEATH. YOU SHOULD COME CHECK IT--
EXCUSE ME...
...YOUNG LADY?
HI, I'M MELISSA. BRANDON'S MOTHER. I'M GONNA TRY AND SAY THIS AS CLEARLY AND POLITELY AS I CAN IN ORDER NOT TO EMBARRASS HIM, BUT...
...GET AWAY FROM MY SON RIGHT NOW OR I'LL STRANGLE YOU WITH THAT VEIL, GOT IT?
MOM! JESUS! WE GO TO SCHOOL TOGETHER! SHE'S--
IT'S FINE, BRANDON. YOU GET USED TO IT. YOU GOT MY NUMBER.
TIDINGS WITH THE MOON, GOOD SISTER...

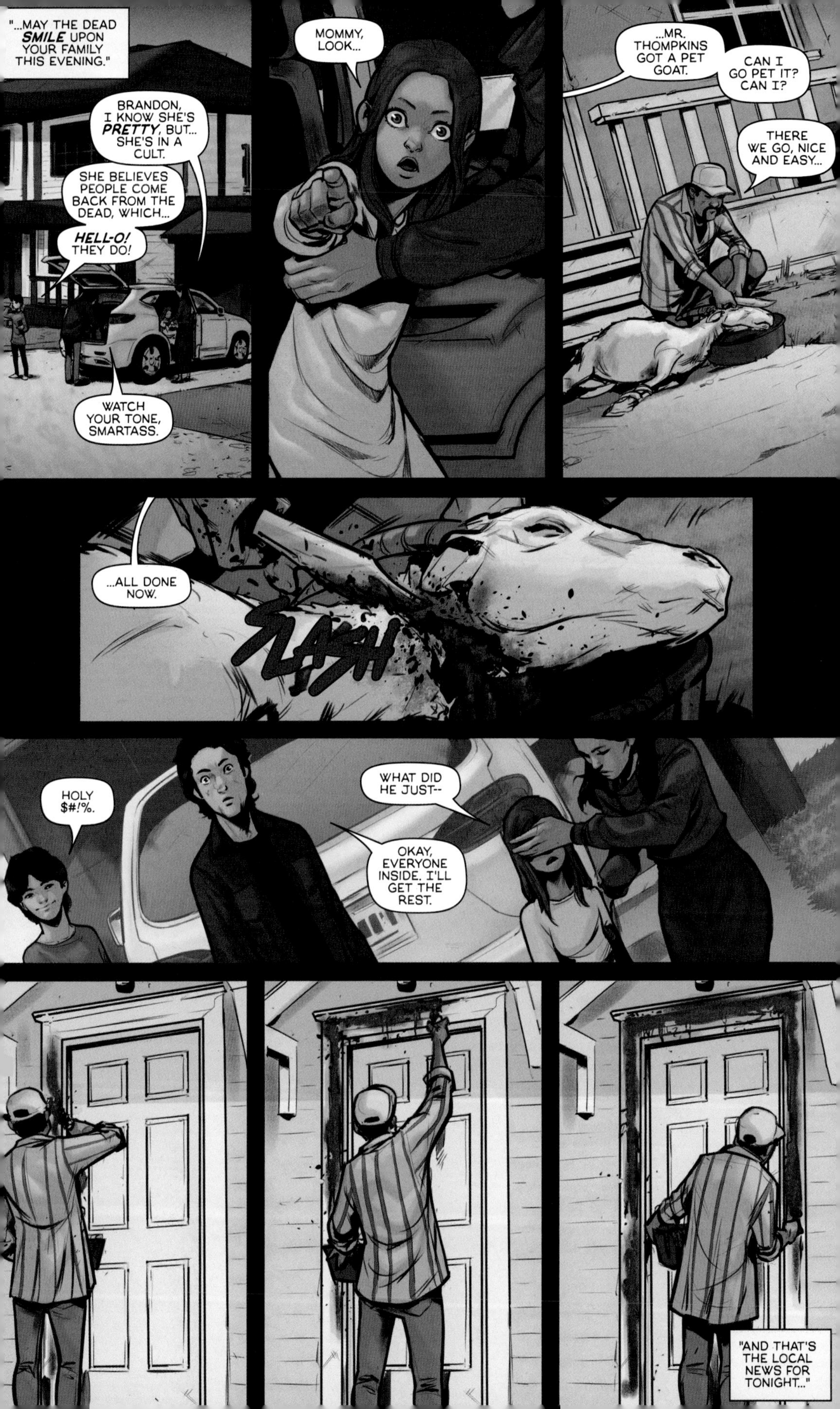
"...MAY THE DEAD SMILE UPON YOUR FAMILY THIS EVENING."
BRANDON, I KNOW SHE'S PRETTY, BUT... SHE'S IN A CULT.
SHE BELIEVES PEOPLE COME BACK FROM THE DEAD, WHICH...
HELL-O! THEY DO!
WATCH YOUR TONE, SMARTASS.
MOMMY, LOOK...
...MR. THOMPKINS GOT A PET GOAT.
CAN I GO PET IT? CAN I?
THERE WE GO, NICE AND EASY...
...ALL DONE NOW.
SLASH
HOLY $#!%.
WHAT DID HE JUST--
OKAY, EVERYONE INSIDE. I'LL GET THE REST.
"AND THAT'S THE LOCAL NEWS FOR TONIGHT..."

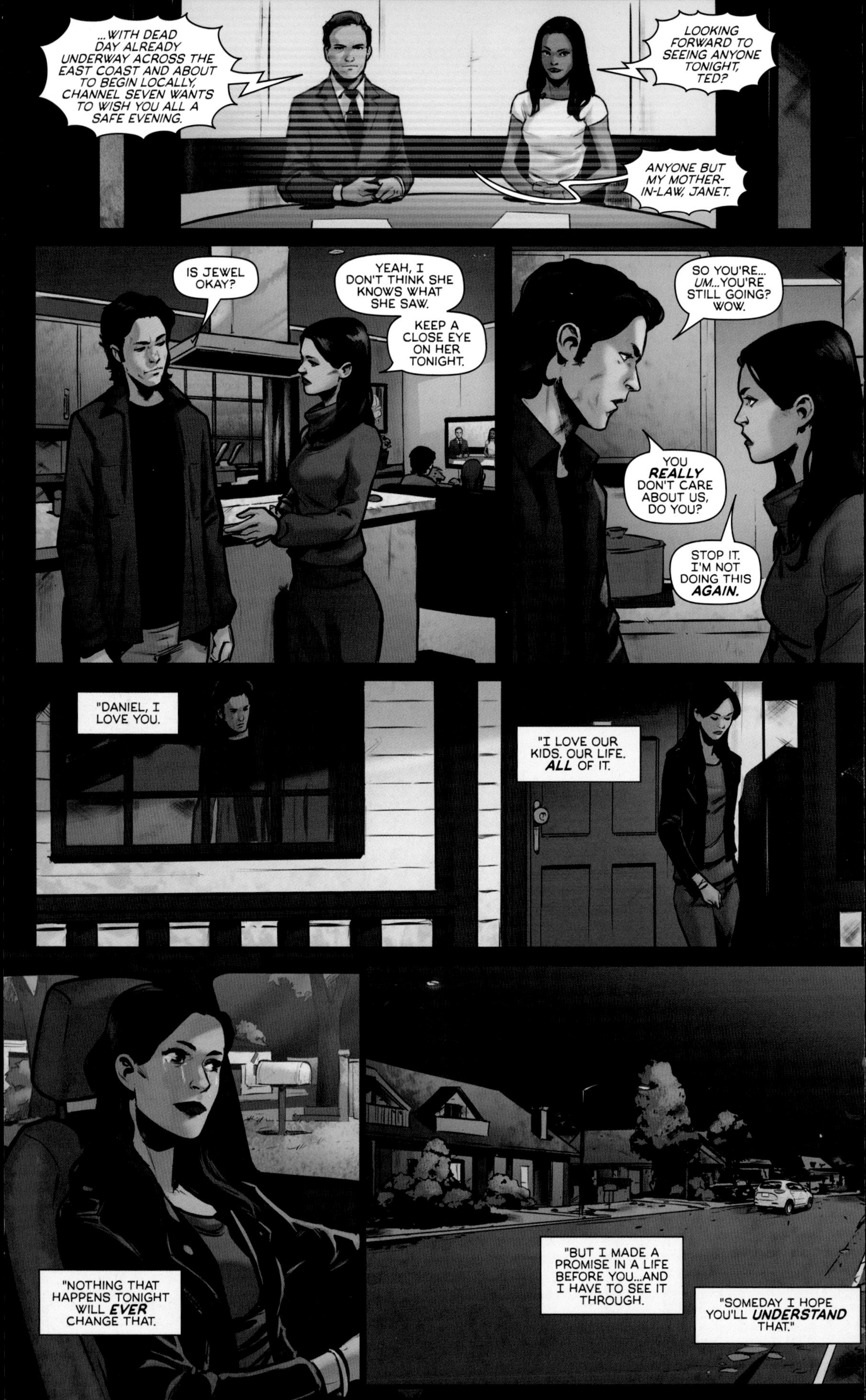
...WITH DEAD DAY ALREADY UNDERWAY ACROSS THE EAST COAST AND ABOUT TO BEGIN LOCALLY, CHANNEL SEVEN WANTS TO WISH YOU ALL A SAFE EVENING.
LOOKING FORWARD TO SEEING ANYONE TONIGHT, TED?
ANYONE BUT MY MOTHER-IN-LAW, JANET.
IS JEWEL OKAY?
YEAH, I DON'T THINK SHE KNOWS WHAT SHE SAW.
KEEP A CLOSE EYE ON HER TONIGHT.
SO YOU'RE... UM...YOU'RE STILL GOING? WOW.
YOU REALLY DON'T CARE ABOUT US, DO YOU?
STOP IT. I'M NOT DOING THIS AGAIN.
"DANIEL, I LOVE YOU.
"I LOVE OUR KIDS. OUR LIFE. ALL OF IT.
"NOTHING THAT HAPPENS TONIGHT WILL EVER CHANGE THAT.
"BUT I MADE A PROMISE IN A LIFE BEFORE YOU...AND I HAVE TO SEE IT THROUGH.
"SOMEDAY I HOPE YOU'LL UNDERSTAND THAT."

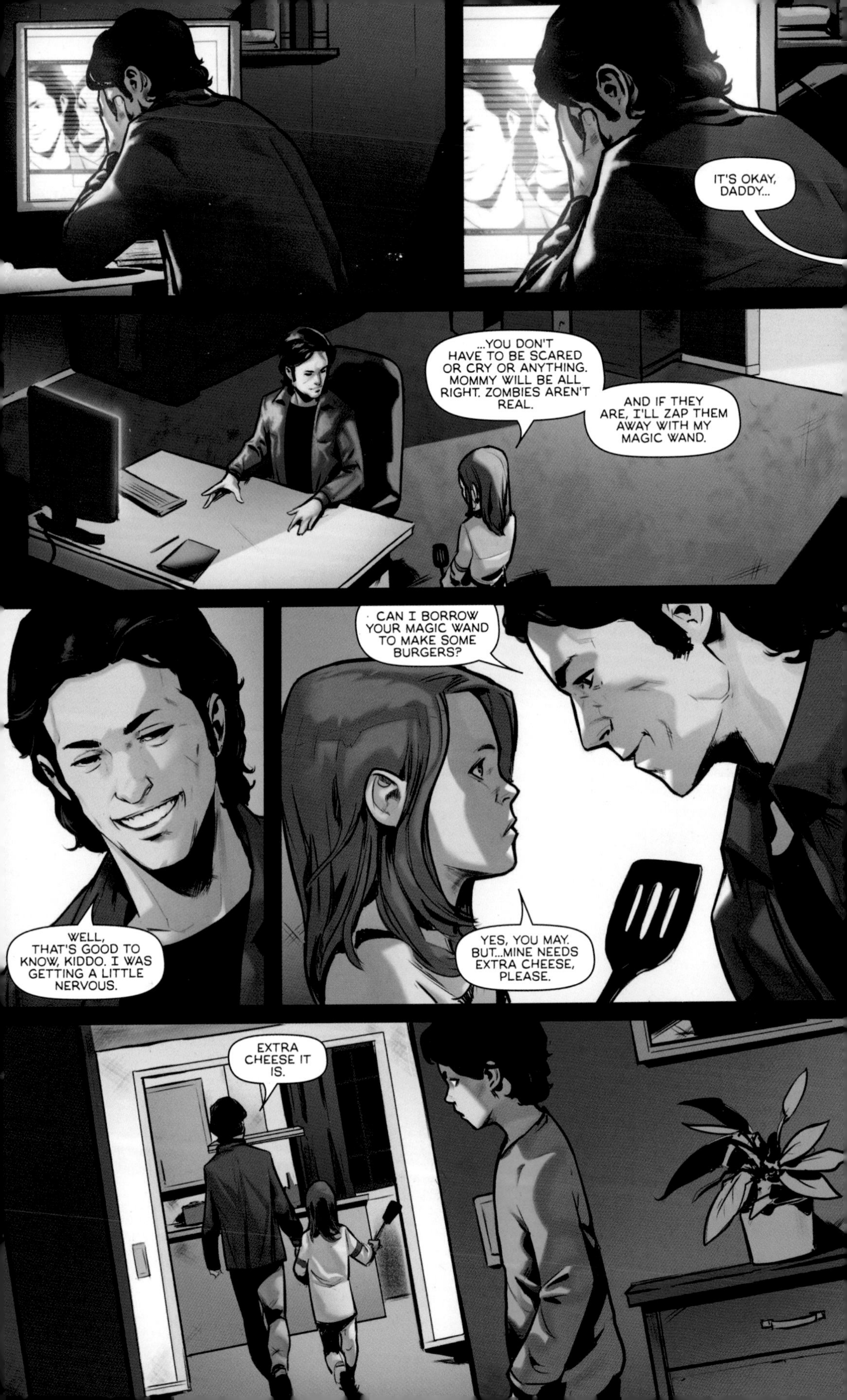
IT'S OKAY, DADDY...
...YOU DON'T HAVE TO BE SCARED OR CRY OR ANYTHING. MOMMY WILL BE ALL RIGHT. ZOMBIES AREN'T REAL.
AND IF THEY ARE, I'LL ZAP THEM AWAY WITH MY MAGIC WAND.
WELL, THAT'S GOOD TO KNOW, KIDDO. I WAS GETTING A LITTLE NERVOUS.
CAN I BORROW YOUR MAGIC WAND TO MAKE SOME BURGERS?
YES, YOU MAY. BUT...MINE NEEDS EXTRA CHEESE, PLEASE.
EXTRA CHEESE IT IS.

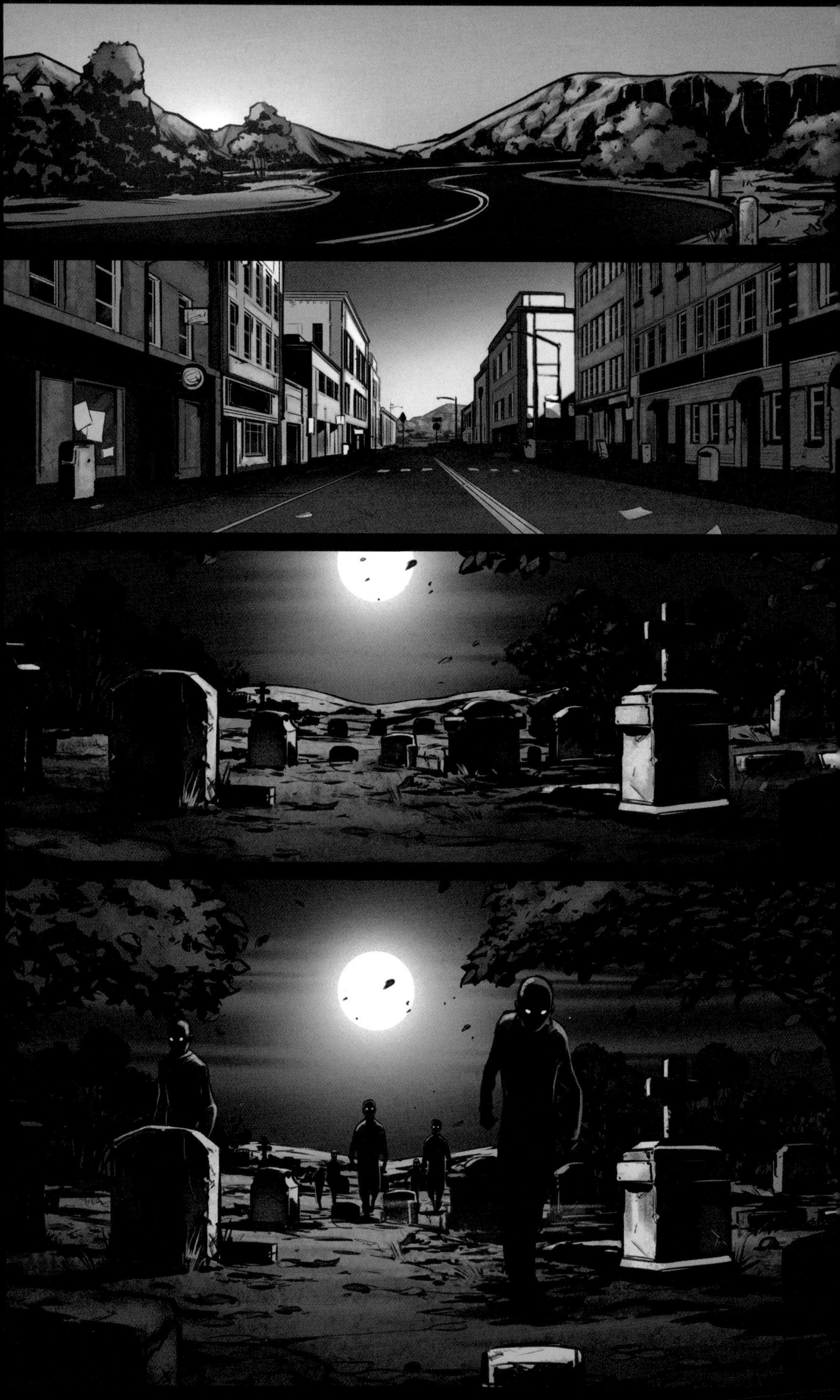

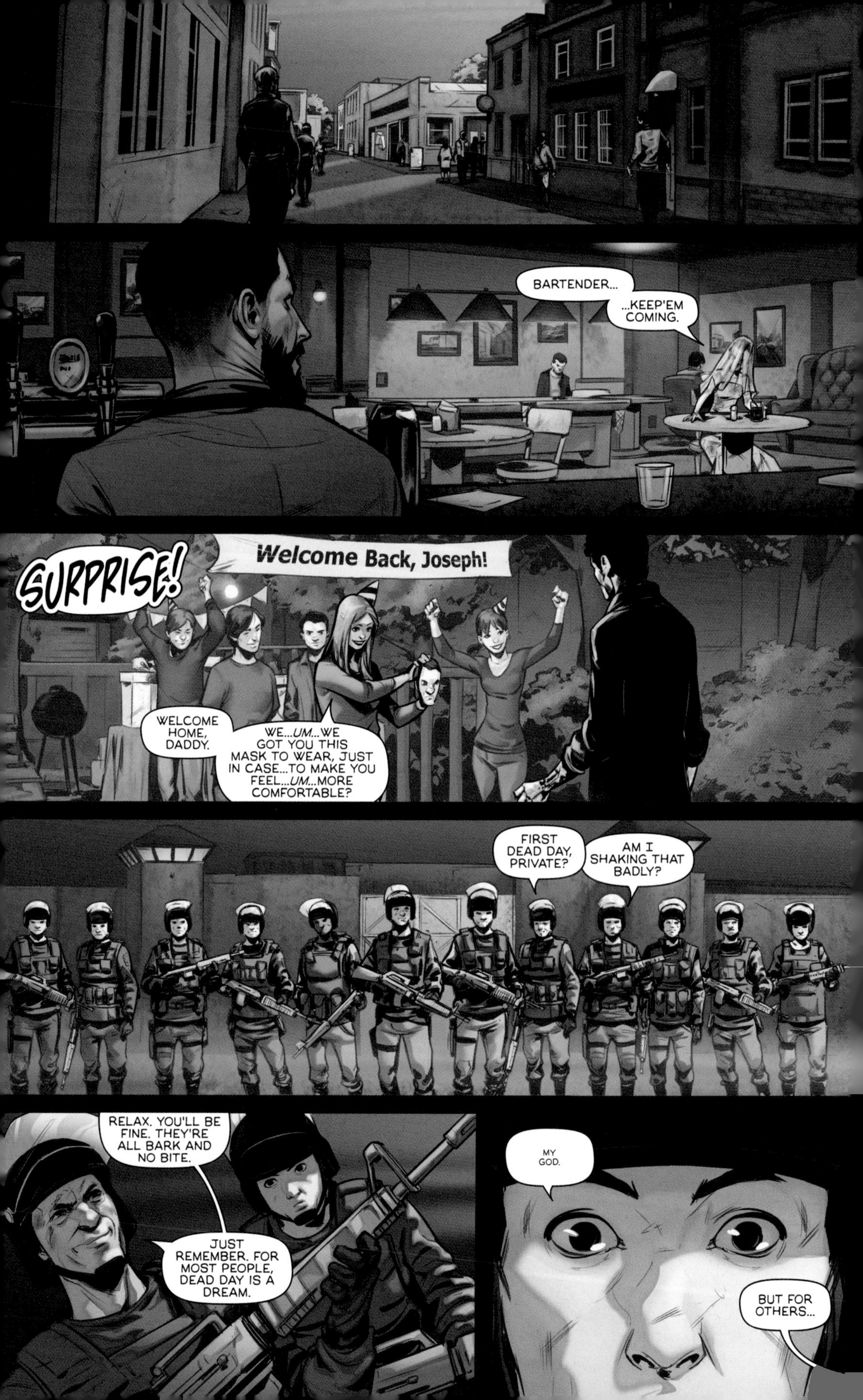
BARTENDER...
...KEEP'EM COMING.
Welcome Back, Joseph!
SURPRISE!
WELCOME HOME, DADDY.
WE...UM...WE GOT YOU THIS MASK TO WEAR, JUST IN CASE...TO MAKE YOU FEEL...UM...MORE COMFORTABLE?
FIRST DEAD DAY, PRIVATE?
AM I SHAKING THAT BADLY?
RELAX. YOU'LL BE FINE. THEY'RE ALL BARK AND NO BITE.
JUST REMEMBER. FOR MOST PEOPLE, DEAD DAY IS A DREAM.
MY GOD.
BUT FOR OTHERS...

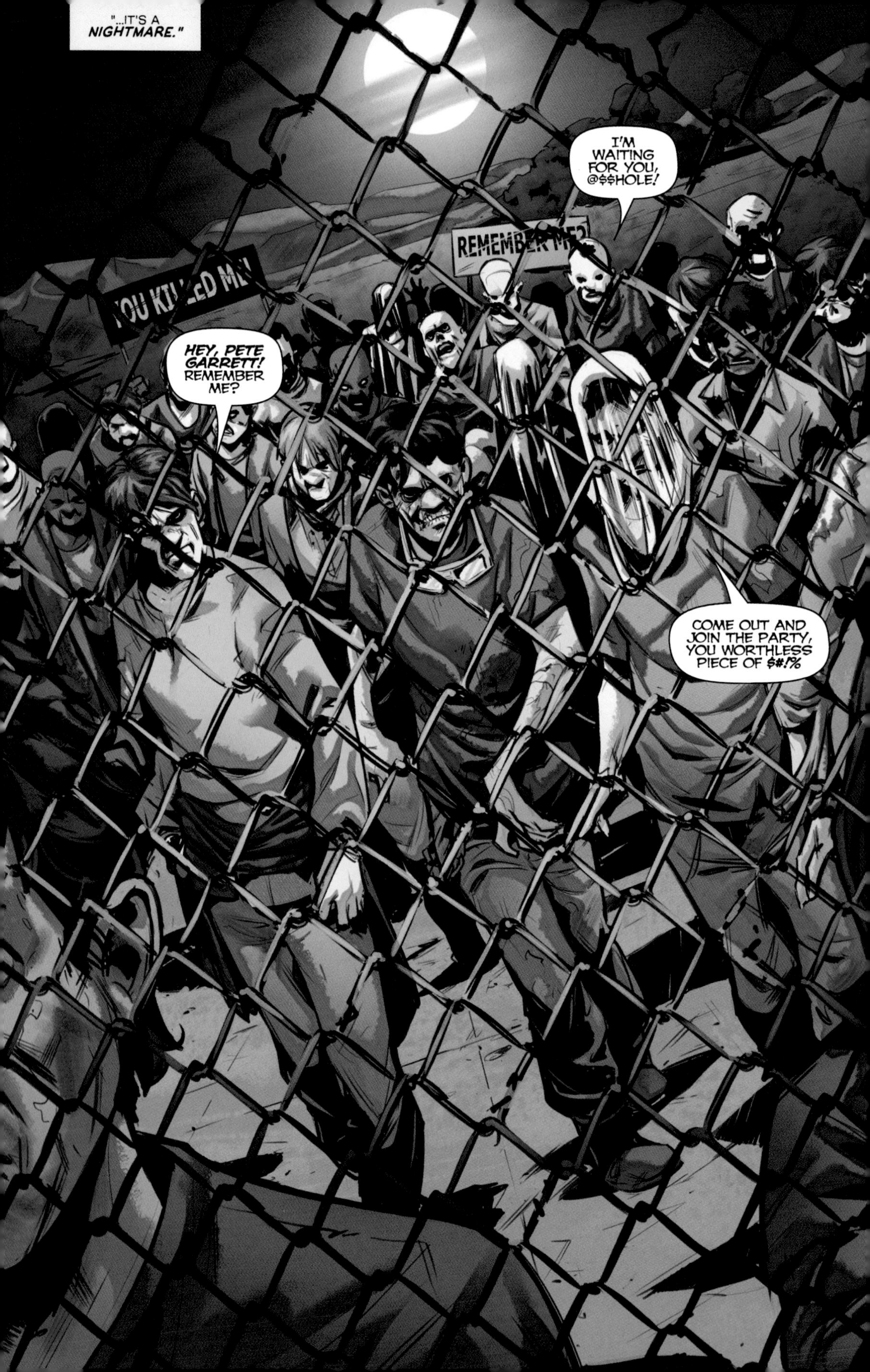
"...IT'S A NIGHTMARE."
YOU KILLED ME!
REMEMBER ME?
I'M WAITING FOR YOU, @$$HOLE!
HEY, PETE GARRETT! REMEMBER ME?
COME OUT AND JOIN THE PARTY, YOU WORTHLESS PIECE OF $#!%

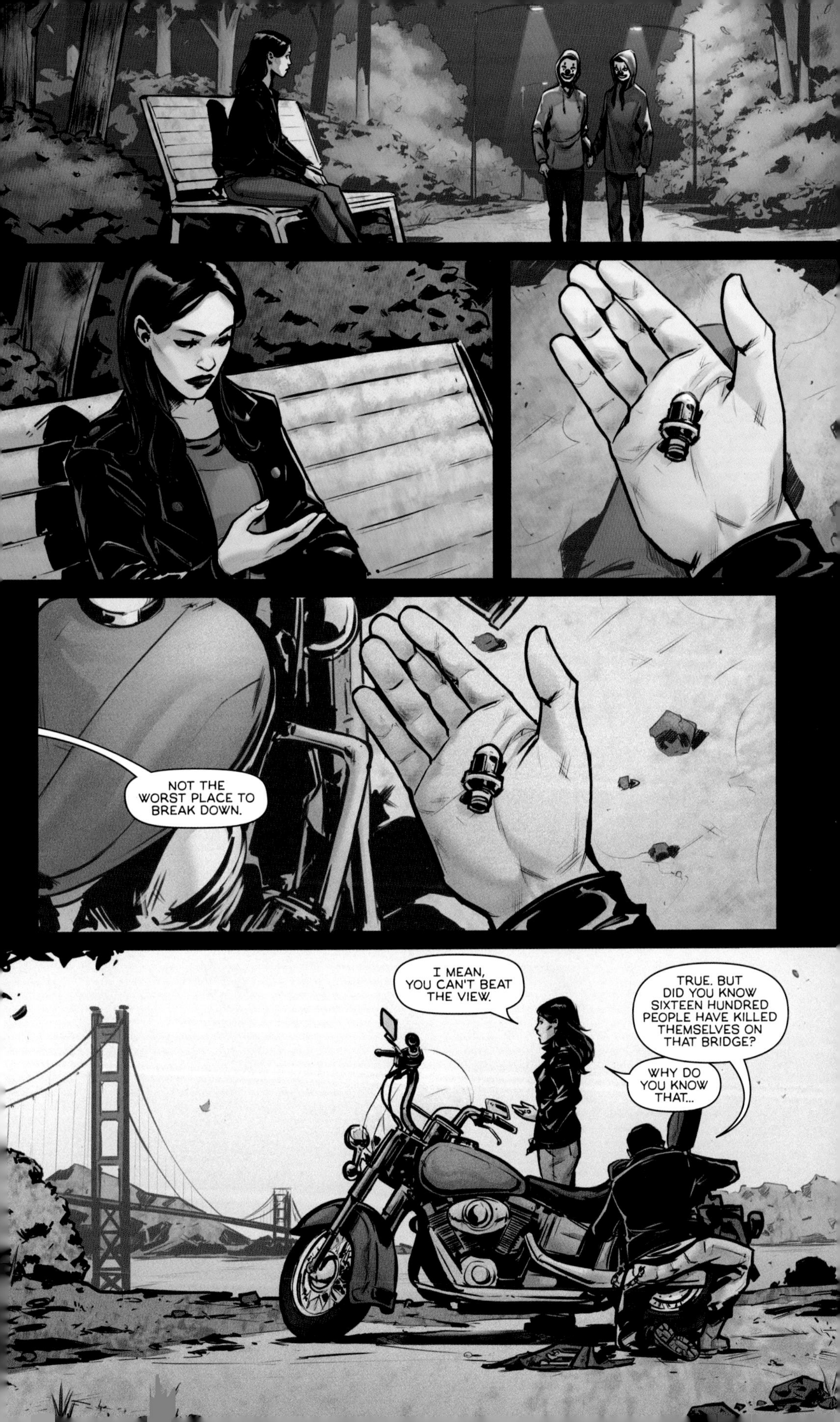
NOT THE WORST PLACE TO BREAK DOWN.
I MEAN, YOU CAN'T BEAT THE VIEW.
TRUE. BUT DID YOU KNOW SIXTEEN HUNDRED PEOPLE HAVE KILLED THEMSELVES ON THAT BRIDGE?
WHY DO YOU KNOW THAT...

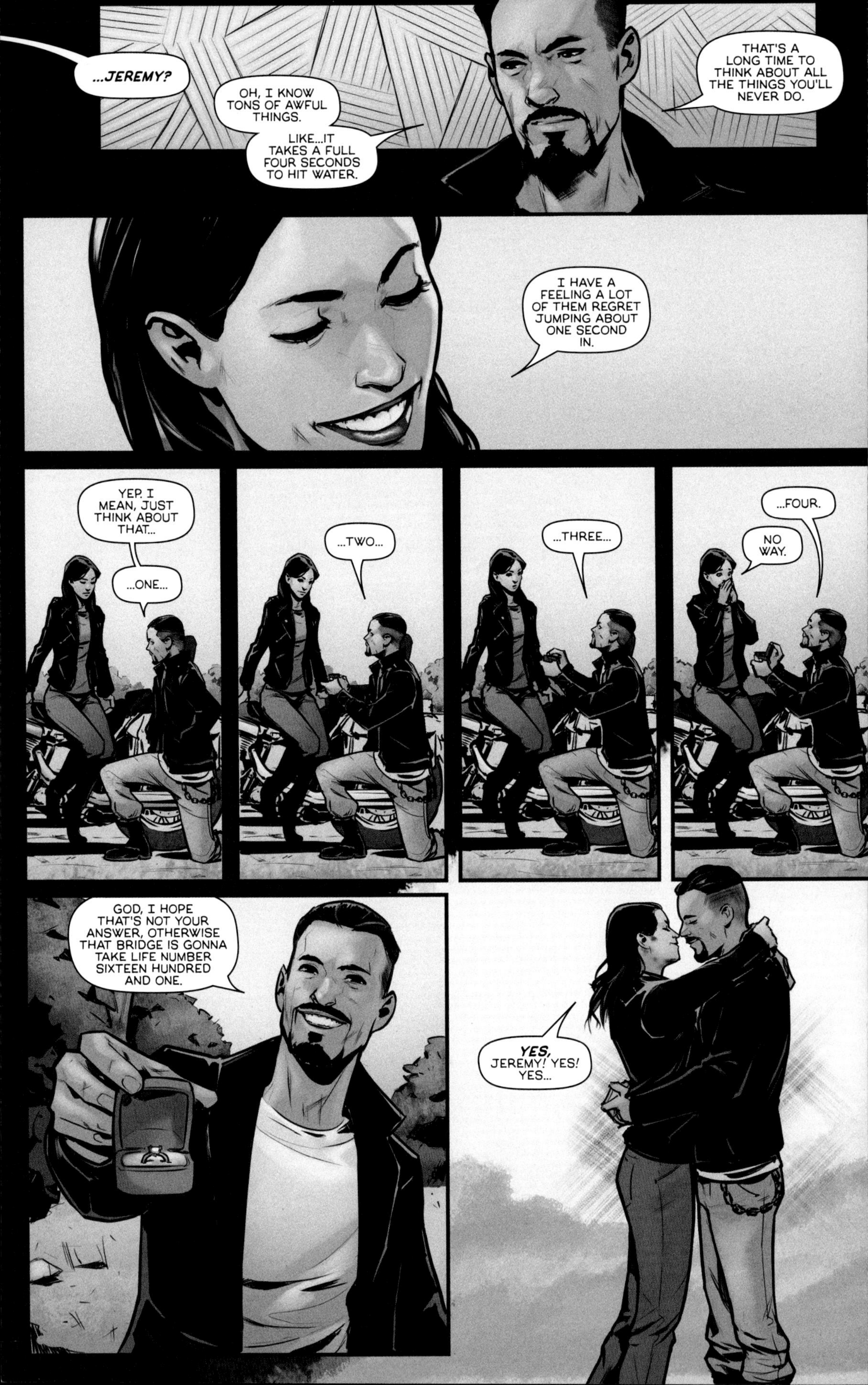
...JEREMY?
OH, I KNOW TONS OF AWFUL THINGS.
LIKE...IT TAKES A FULL FOUR SECONDS TO HIT WATER.
THAT'S A LONG TIME TO THINK ABOUT ALL THE THINGS YOU'LL NEVER DO.
I HAVE A FEELING A LOT OF THEM REGRET JUMPING ABOUT ONE SECOND IN.
YEP. I MEAN, JUST THINK ABOUT THAT...
...ONE...
...TWO...
...THREE...
NO WAY.
...FOUR.
GOD, I HOPE THAT'S NOT YOUR ANSWER, OTHERWISE THAT BRIDGE IS GONNA TAKE LIFE NUMBER SIXTEEN HUNDRED AND ONE.
YES, JEREMY! YES! YES...

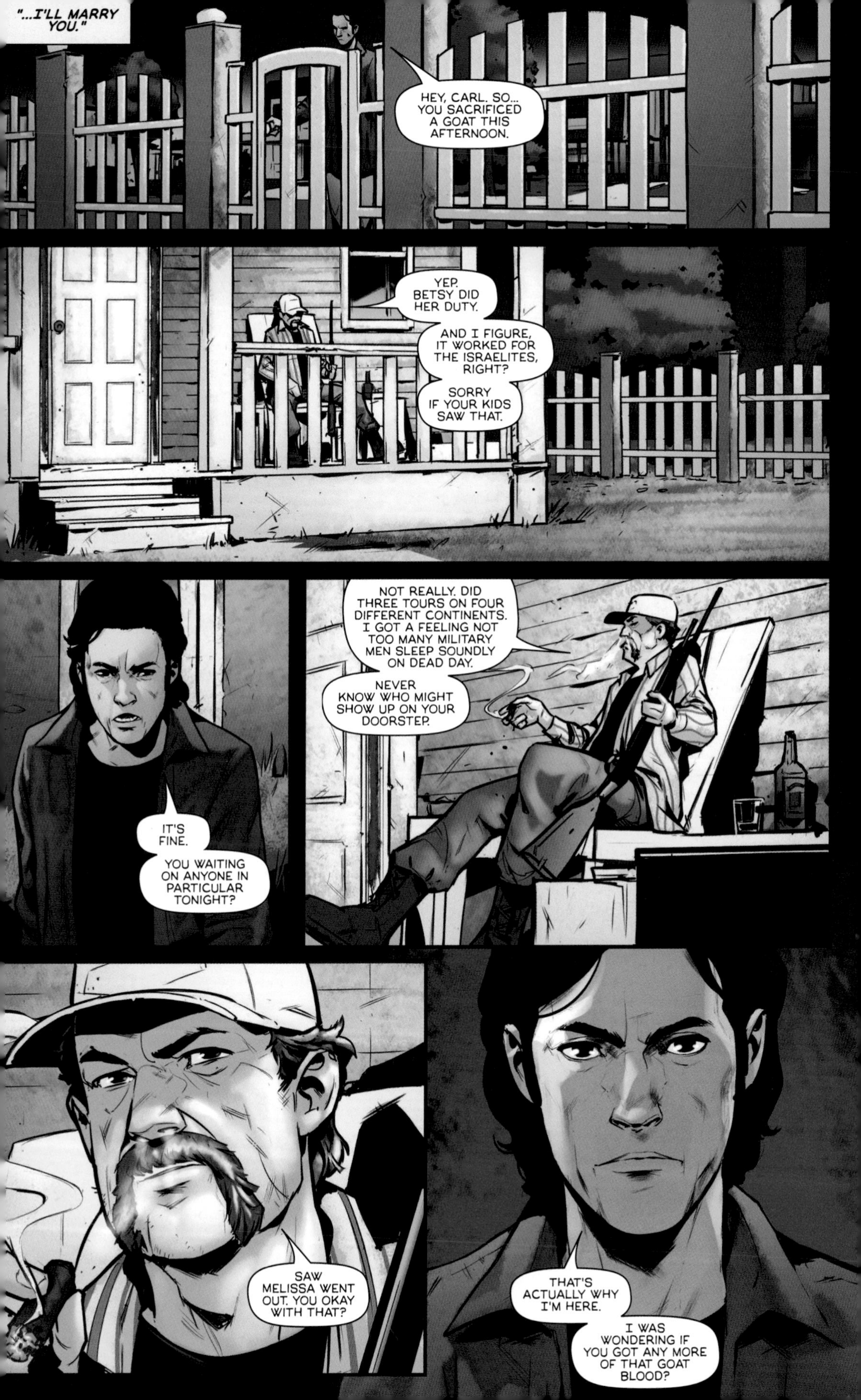
"...I'LL MARRY YOU."
HEY, CARL. SO... YOU SACRIFICED A GOAT THIS AFTERNOON.
YEP. BETSY DID HER DUTY.
AND I FIGURE, IT WORKED FOR THE ISRAELITES, RIGHT?
SORRY IF YOUR KIDS SAW THAT.
IT'S FINE.
YOU WAITING ON ANYONE IN PARTICULAR TONIGHT?
NOT REALLY. DID THREE TOURS ON FOUR DIFFERENT CONTINENTS. I GOT A FEELING NOT TOO MANY MILITARY MEN SLEEP SOUNDLY ON DEAD DAY.
NEVER KNOW WHO MIGHT SHOW UP ON YOUR DOORSTEP.
SAW MELISSA WENT OUT. YOU OKAY WITH THAT?
THAT'S ACTUALLY WHY I'M HERE.
I WAS WONDERING IF YOU GOT ANY MORE OF THAT GOAT BLOOD?

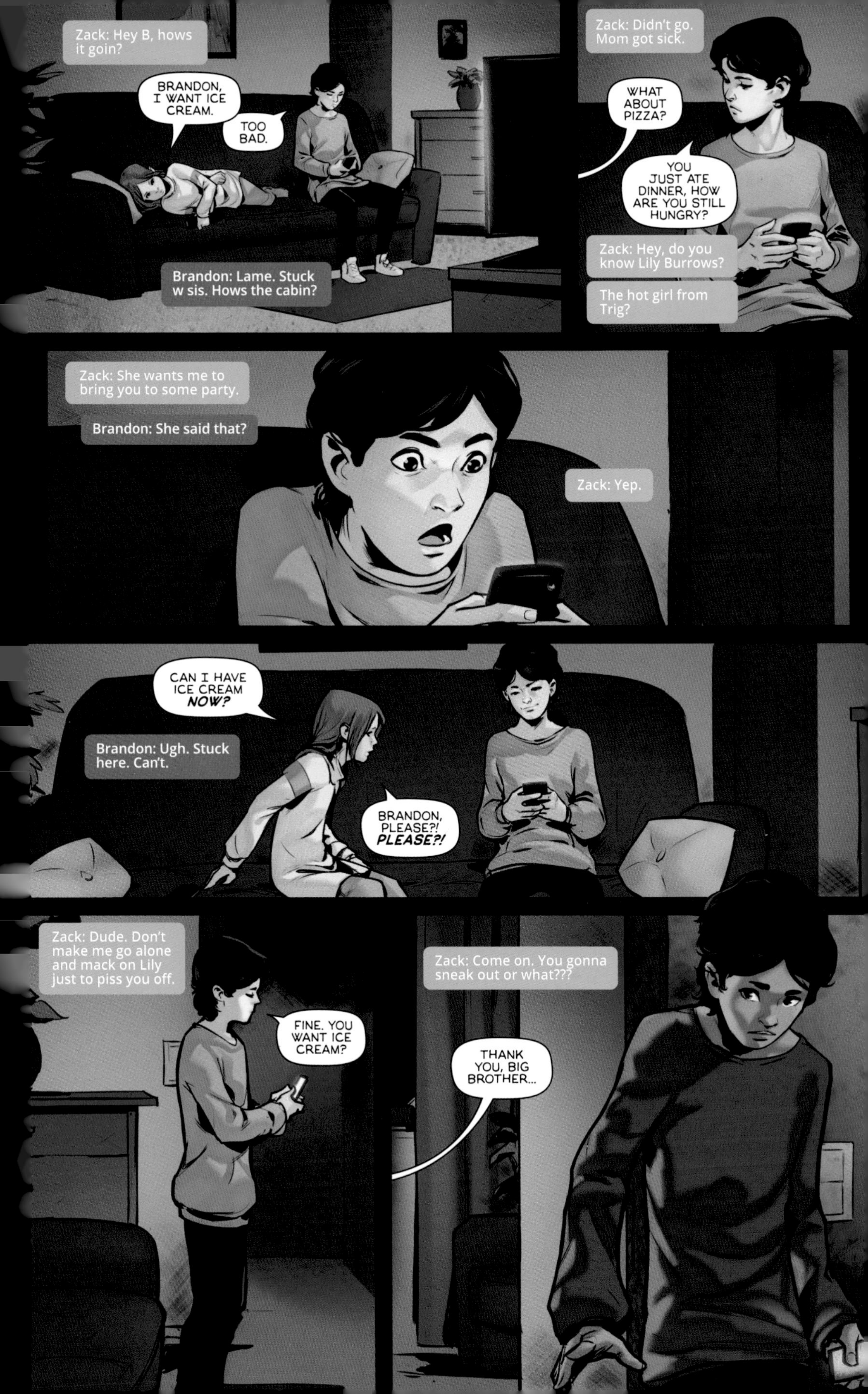
Zack: Hey B, hows it goin?
BRANDON, I WANT ICE CREAM.
TOO BAD.
Brandon: Lame. Stuck w sis. Hows the cabin?
Zack: Didn't go. Mom got sick.
WHAT ABOUT PIZZA?
YOU JUST ATE DINNER, HOW ARE YOU STILL HUNGRY?
Zack: Hey, do you know Lily Burrows?
The hot girl from Trig?
Zack: She wants me to bring you to some party.
Brandon: She said that?
Zack: Yep.
CAN I HAVE ICE CREAM *NOW?*
Brandon: Ugh. Stuck here. Can't.
BRANDON, PLEASE?! ***PLEASE?!***
Zack: Dude. Don't make me go alone and mack on Lily just to piss you off.
FINE. YOU WANT ICE CREAM?
Zack: Come on. You gonna sneak out or what???
THANK YOU, BIG BROTHER...

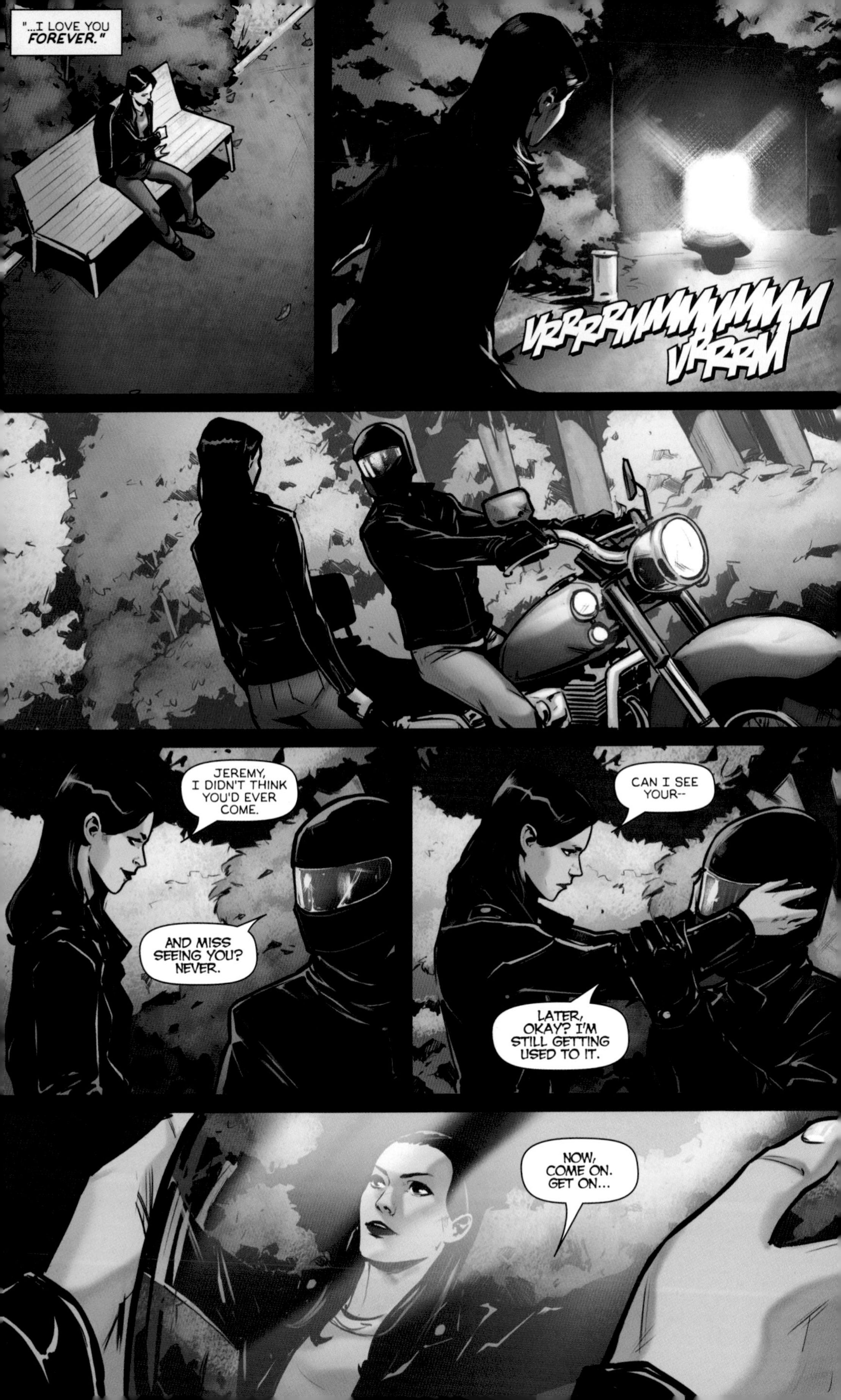
"...I LOVE YOU FOREVER."
VRRRRMMMMMMM
VRRRM
JEREMY, I DIDN'T THINK YOU'D EVER COME.
AND MISS SEEING YOU? NEVER.
CAN I SEE YOUR--
LATER, OKAY? I'M STILL GETTING USED TO IT.
NOW, COME ON. GET ON...

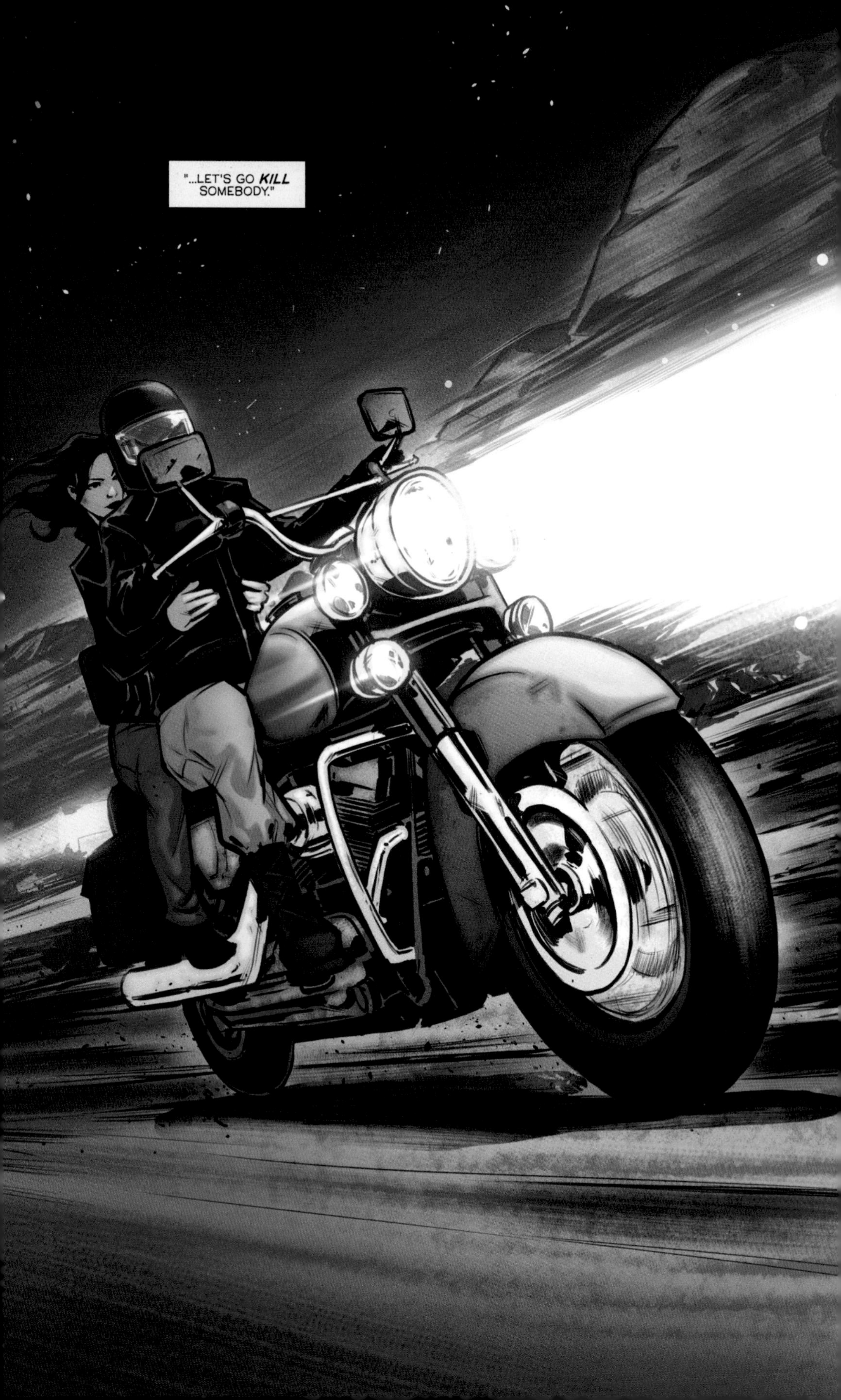
"...LET'S GO KILL SOMEBODY."

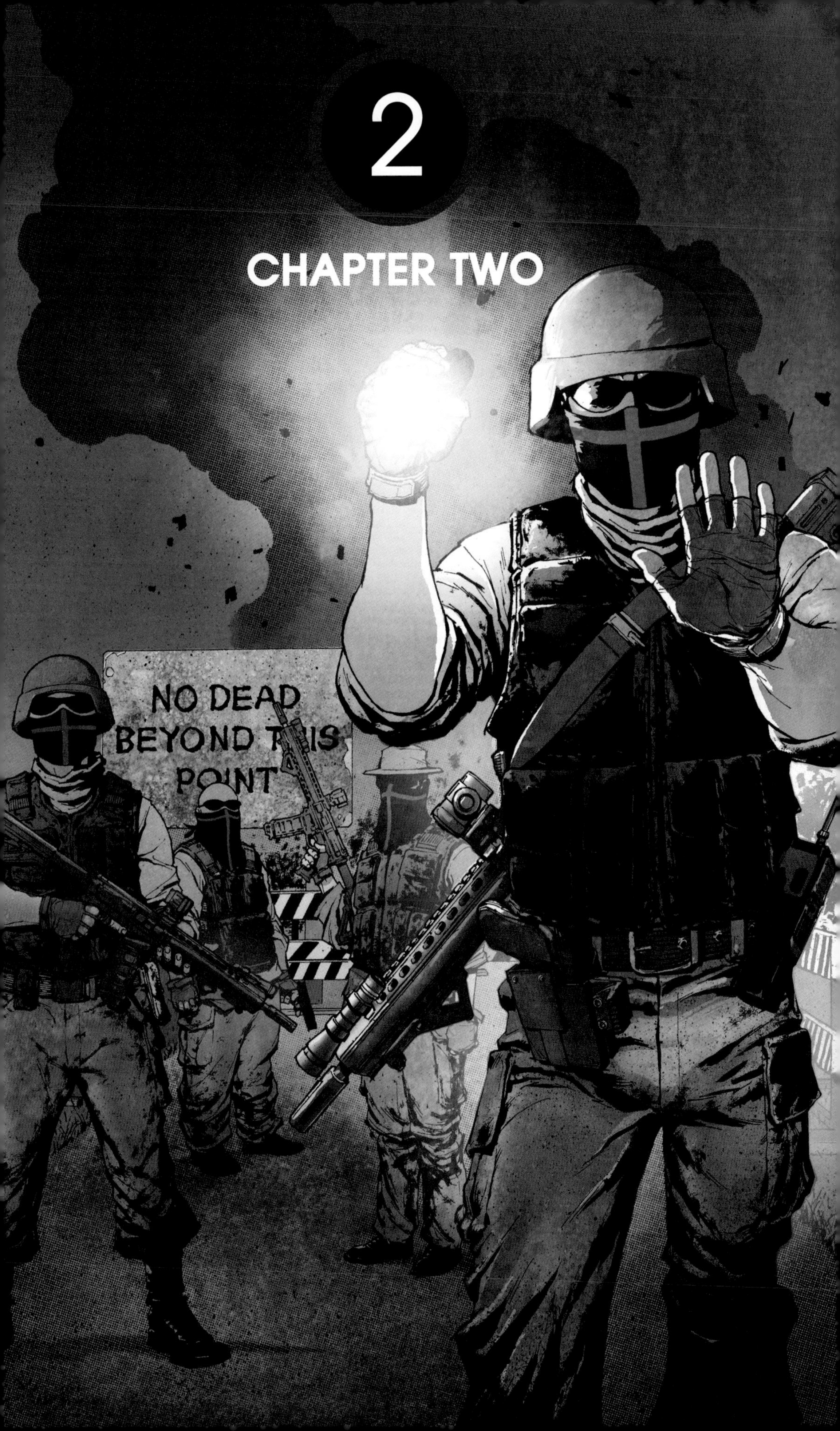
2
CHAPTER TWO
NO DEAD
BEYOND T IS
POINT

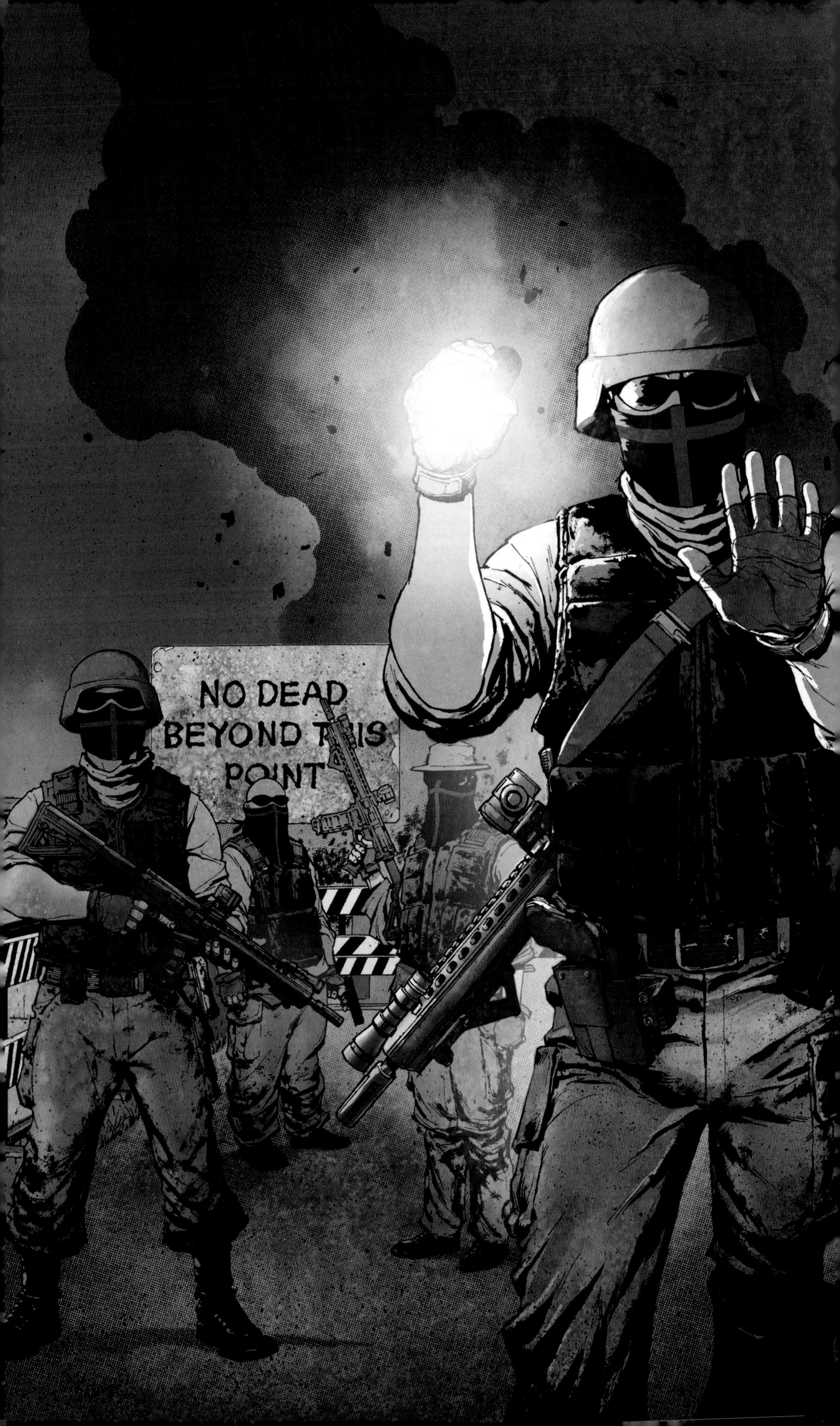
NO DEAD
BEYOND THIS
POINT

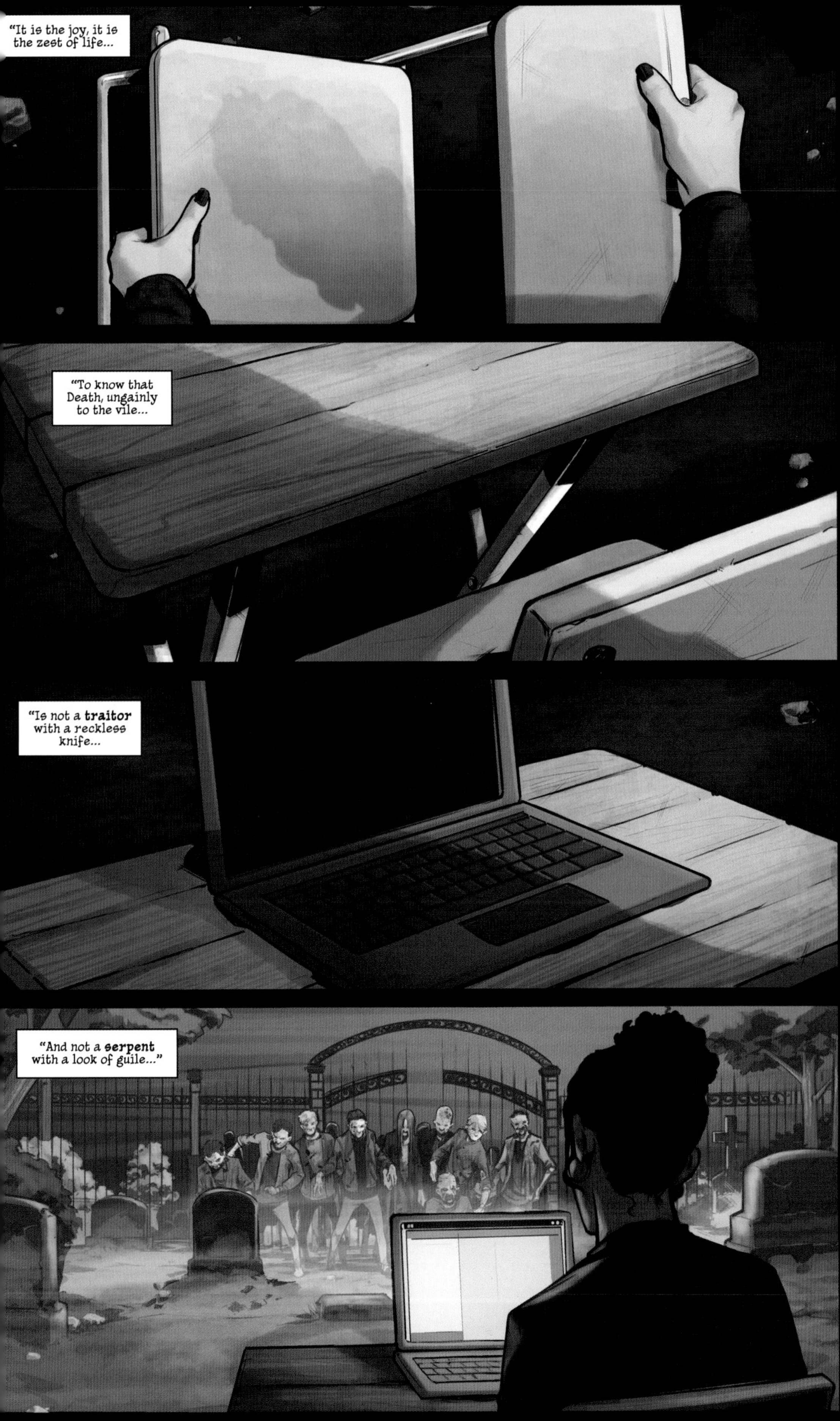
"It is the joy, it is the zest of life...
"To know that Death, ungainly to the vile...
"Is not a **traitor** with a reckless knife...
"And not a **serpent** with a look of guile..."

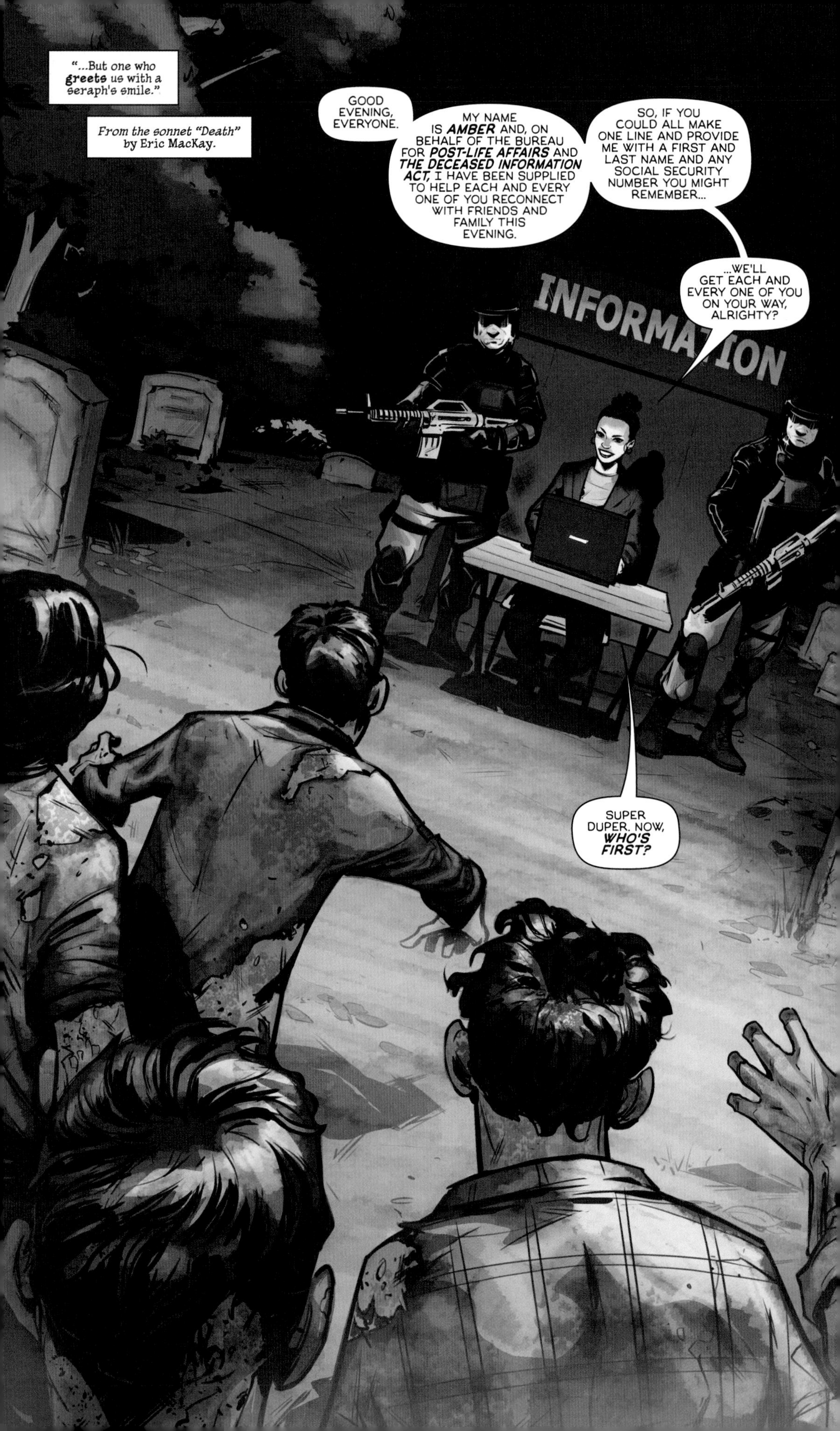
"...But one who **greets** us with a seraph's smile."
From the sonnet "Death" by Eric MacKay.
GOOD EVENING, EVERYONE.
MY NAME IS ***AMBER*** AND, ON BEHALF OF THE BUREAU FOR ***POST-LIFE AFFAIRS*** AND ***THE DECEASED INFORMATION ACT,*** I HAVE BEEN SUPPLIED TO HELP EACH AND EVERY ONE OF YOU RECONNECT WITH FRIENDS AND FAMILY THIS EVENING.
SO, IF YOU COULD ALL MAKE ONE LINE AND PROVIDE ME WITH A FIRST AND LAST NAME AND ANY SOCIAL SECURITY NUMBER YOU MIGHT REMEMBER...
...WE'LL GET EACH AND EVERY ONE OF YOU ON YOUR WAY, ALRIGHTY?
INFORMATION
SUPER DUPER. NOW, ***WHO'S FIRST?***

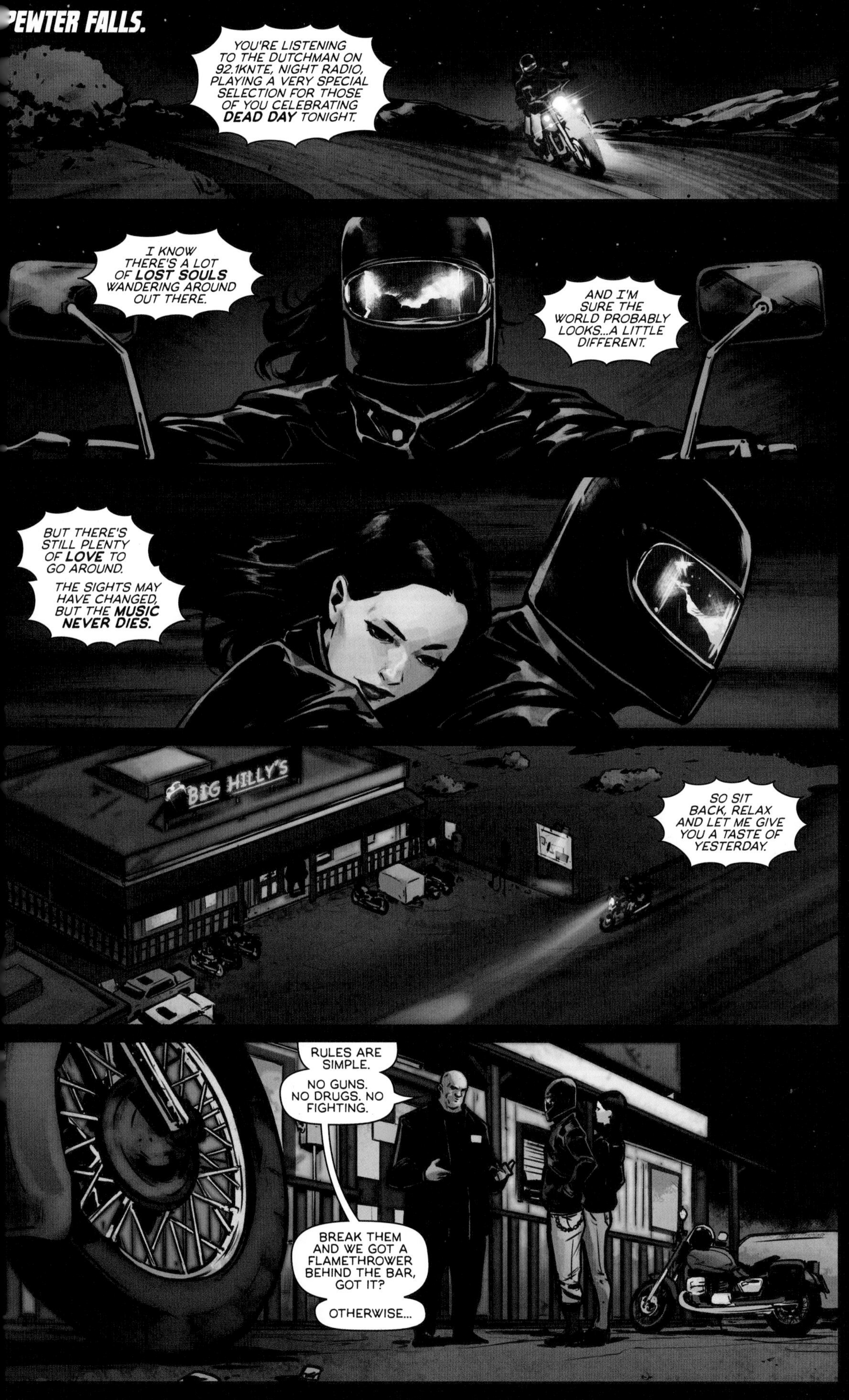
PEWTER FALLS.
YOU'RE LISTENING TO THE DUTCHMAN ON 92.1KNTE, NIGHT RADIO, PLAYING A VERY SPECIAL SELECTION FOR THOSE OF YOU CELEBRATING DEAD DAY TONIGHT.
I KNOW THERE'S A LOT OF LOST SOULS WANDERING AROUND OUT THERE.
AND I'M SURE THE WORLD PROBABLY LOOKS...A LITTLE DIFFERENT.
BUT THERE'S STILL PLENTY OF LOVE TO GO AROUND.
THE SIGHTS MAY HAVE CHANGED, BUT THE MUSIC NEVER DIES.
BIG HILLY'S
SO SIT BACK, RELAX AND LET ME GIVE YOU A TASTE OF YESTERDAY.
RULES ARE SIMPLE.
NO GUNS. NO DRUGS. NO FIGHTING.
BREAK THEM AND WE GOT A FLAMETHROWER BEHIND THE BAR, GOT IT?
OTHERWISE...

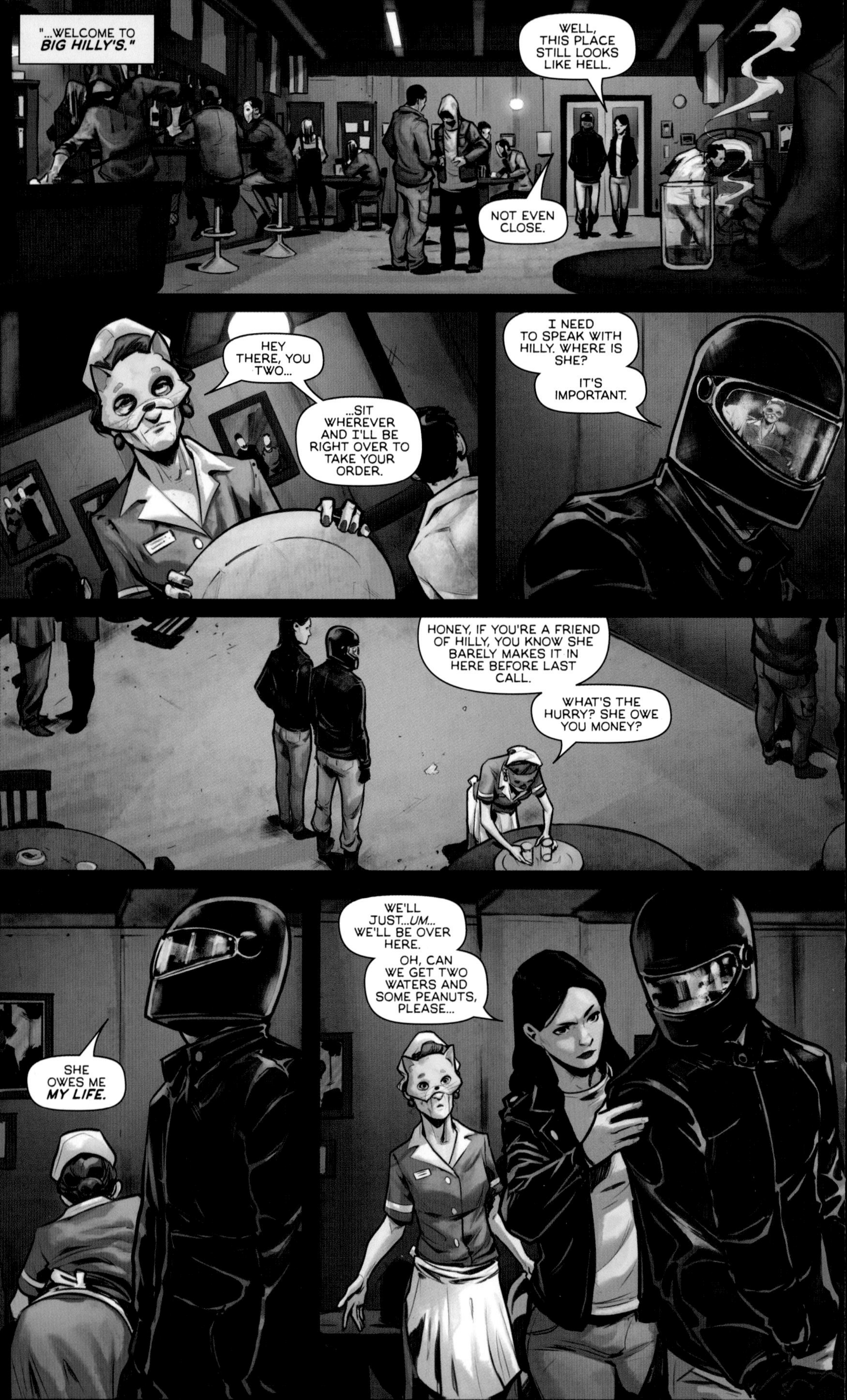
"...WELCOME TO BIG HILLY'S."
WELL, THIS PLACE STILL LOOKS LIKE HELL.
NOT EVEN CLOSE.
HEY THERE, YOU TWO...
...SIT WHEREVER AND I'LL BE RIGHT OVER TO TAKE YOUR ORDER.
I NEED TO SPEAK WITH HILLY. WHERE IS SHE?
IT'S IMPORTANT.
HONEY, IF YOU'RE A FRIEND OF HILLY, YOU KNOW SHE BARELY MAKES IT IN HERE BEFORE LAST CALL.
WHAT'S THE HURRY? SHE OWE YOU MONEY?
SHE OWES ME MY LIFE.
WE'LL JUST...UM... WE'LL BE OVER HERE.
OH, CAN WE GET TWO WATERS AND SOME PEANUTS, PLEASE...

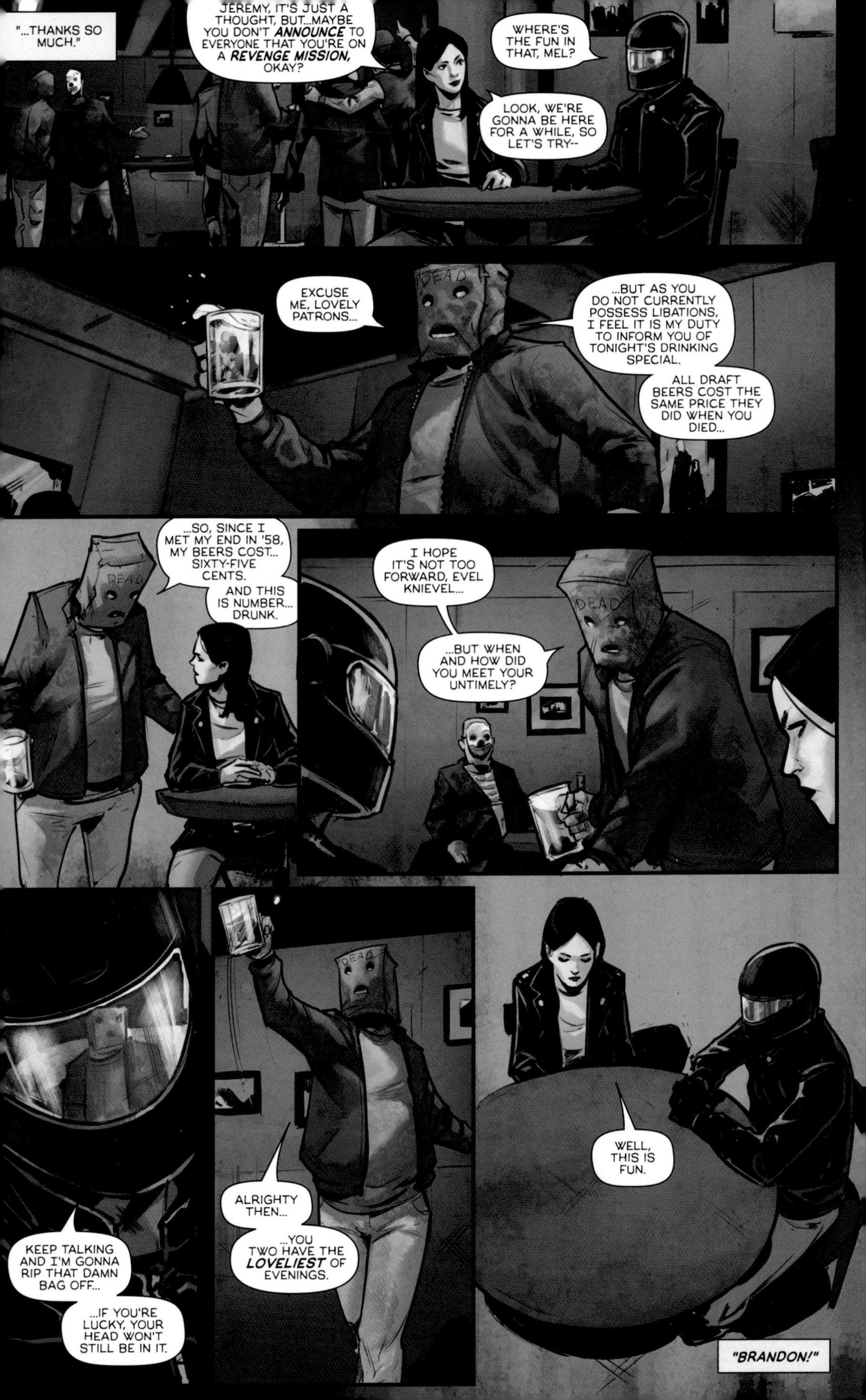
"...THANKS SO MUCH."
JEREMY, IT'S JUST A THOUGHT, BUT...MAYBE YOU DON'T ANNOUNCE TO EVERYONE THAT YOU'RE ON A REVENGE MISSION, OKAY?
WHERE'S THE FUN IN THAT, MEL?
LOOK, WE'RE GONNA BE HERE FOR A WHILE, SO LET'S TRY--
EXCUSE ME, LOVELY PATRONS...
...BUT AS YOU DO NOT CURRENTLY POSSESS LIBATIONS, I FEEL IT IS MY DUTY TO INFORM YOU OF TONIGHT'S DRINKING SPECIAL.
ALL DRAFT BEERS COST THE SAME PRICE THEY DID WHEN YOU DIED...
...SO, SINCE I MET MY END IN '58, MY BEERS COST... SIXTY-FIVE CENTS.
AND THIS IS NUMBER... DRUNK.
I HOPE IT'S NOT TOO FORWARD, EVEL KNIEVEL...
...BUT WHEN AND HOW DID YOU MEET YOUR UNTIMELY?
KEEP TALKING AND I'M GONNA RIP THAT DAMN BAG OFF...
...IF YOU'RE LUCKY, YOUR HEAD WON'T STILL BE IN IT.
ALRIGHTY THEN...
...YOU TWO HAVE THE LOVELIEST OF EVENINGS.
WELL, THIS IS FUN.
"BRANDON!"

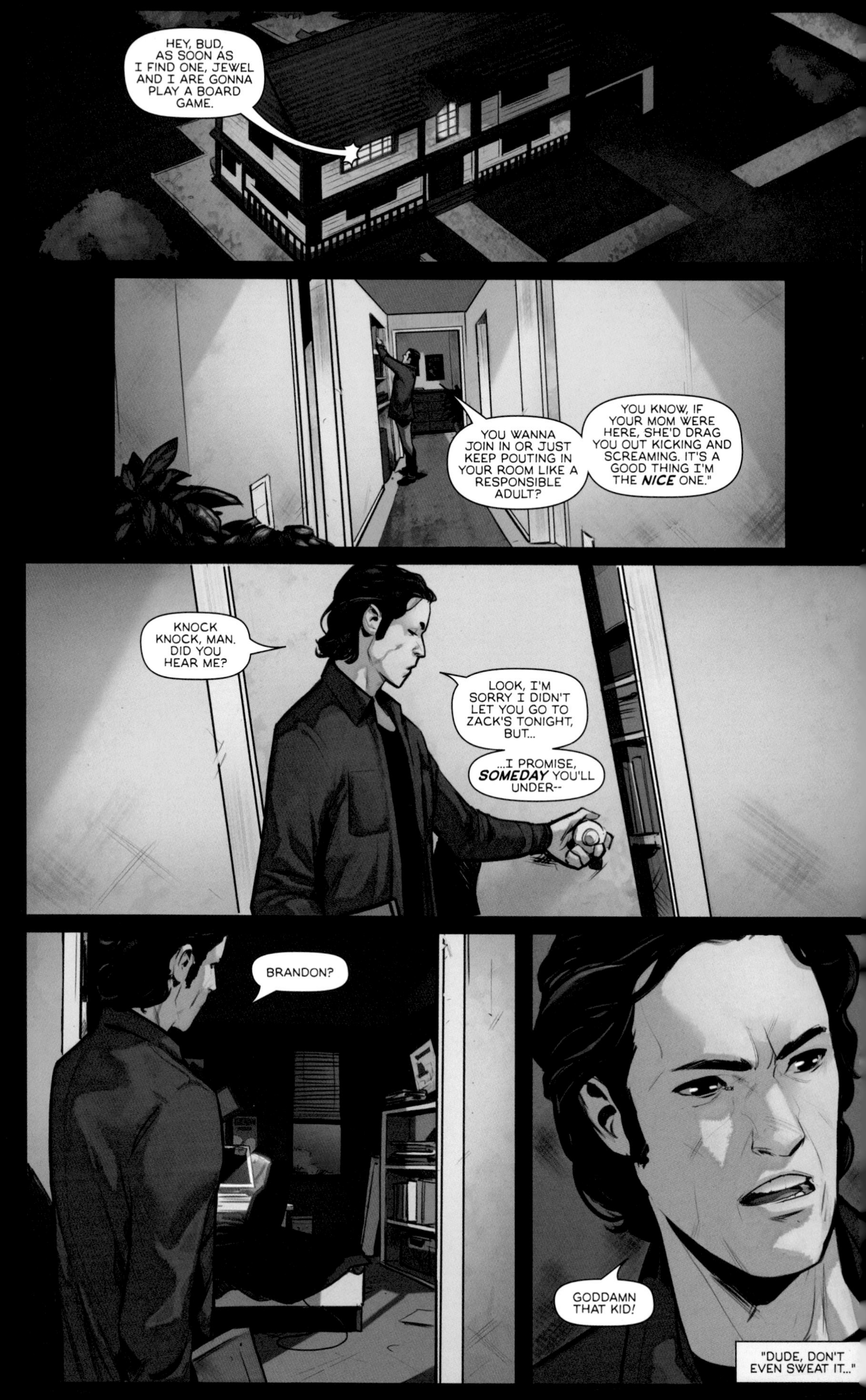
HEY, BUD, AS SOON AS I FIND ONE, JEWEL AND I ARE GONNA PLAY A BOARD GAME.
YOU WANNA JOIN IN OR JUST KEEP POUTING IN YOUR ROOM LIKE A RESPONSIBLE ADULT?
YOU KNOW, IF YOUR MOM WERE HERE, SHE'D DRAG YOU OUT KICKING AND SCREAMING. IT'S A GOOD THING I'M THE NICE ONE."
KNOCK KNOCK, MAN. DID YOU HEAR ME?
LOOK, I'M SORRY I DIDN'T LET YOU GO TO ZACK'S TONIGHT, BUT...
...I PROMISE, SOMEDAY YOU'LL UNDER--
BRANDON?
GODDAMN THAT KID!
"DUDE, DON'T EVEN SWEAT IT..."

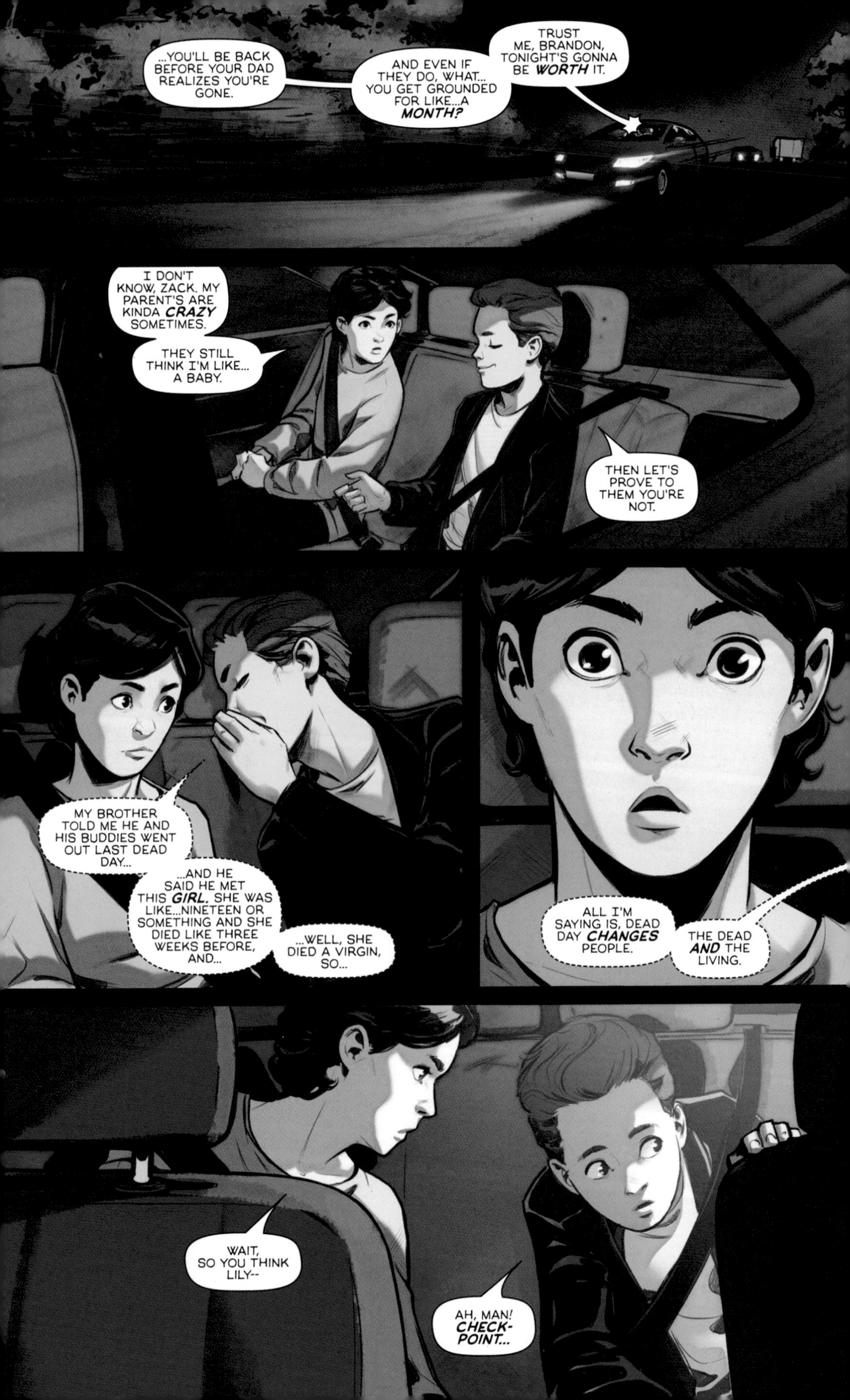
...YOU'LL BE BACK BEFORE YOUR DAD REALIZES YOU'RE GONE.
AND EVEN IF THEY DO, WHAT... YOU GET GROUNDED FOR LIKE...A MONTH?
TRUST ME, BRANDON, TONIGHT'S GONNA BE WORTH IT.
I DON'T KNOW, ZACK. MY PARENT'S ARE KINDA CRAZY SOMETIMES.
THEY STILL THINK I'M LIKE... A BABY.
THEN LET'S PROVE TO THEM YOU'RE NOT.
MY BROTHER TOLD ME HE AND HIS BUDDIES WENT OUT LAST DEAD DAY...
...AND HE SAID HE MET THIS GIRL. SHE WAS LIKE...NINETEEN OR SOMETHING AND SHE DIED LIKE THREE WEEKS BEFORE, AND...
...WELL, SHE DIED A VIRGIN, SO...
ALL I'M SAYING IS, DEAD DAY CHANGES PEOPLE.
THE DEAD AND THE LIVING.
WAIT, SO YOU THINK LILY--
AH, MAN! CHECK-POINT...

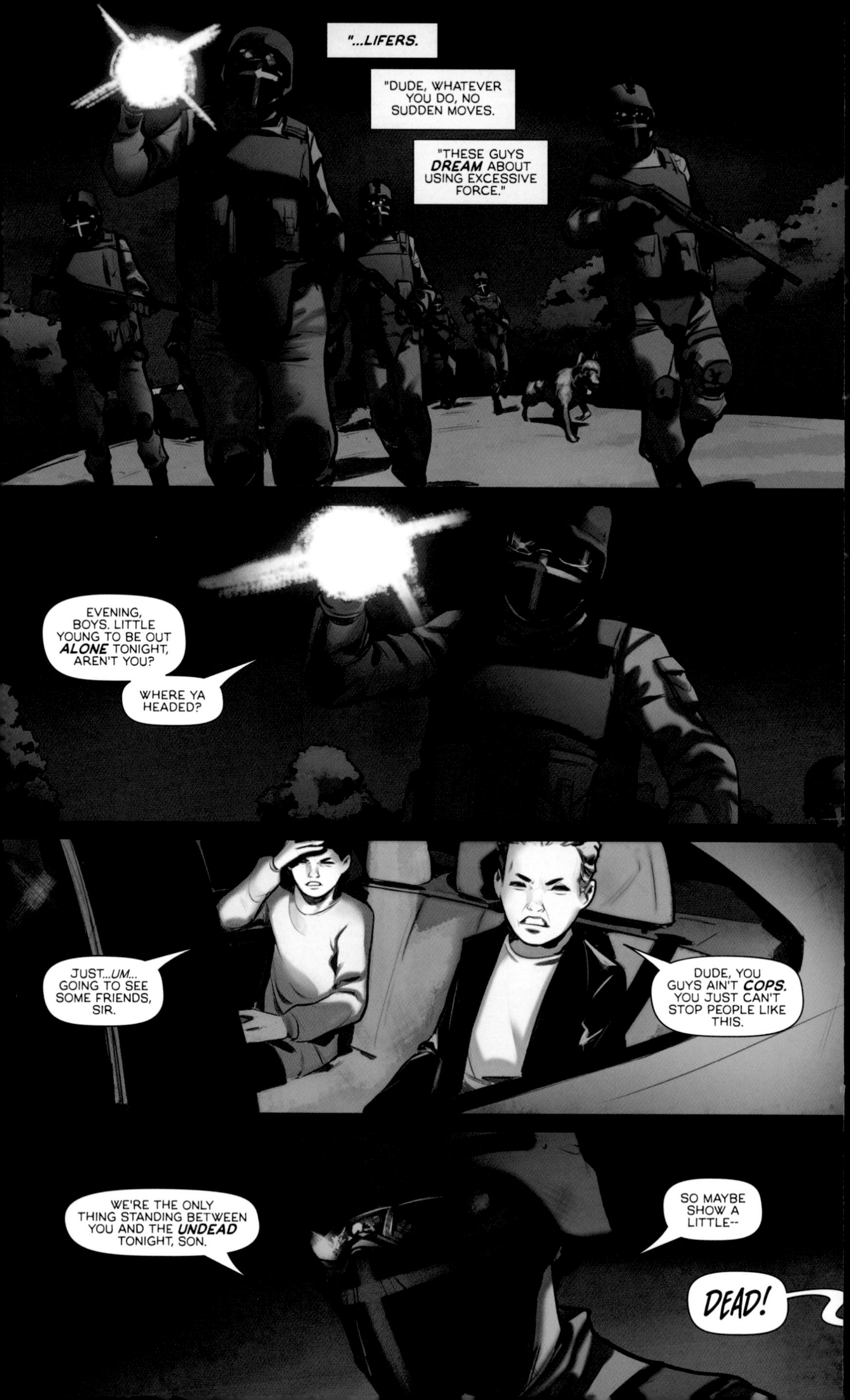
"...LIFERS.
"DUDE, WHATEVER YOU DO, NO SUDDEN MOVES.
"THESE GUYS DREAM ABOUT USING EXCESSIVE FORCE."
EVENING, BOYS. LITTLE YOUNG TO BE OUT ALONE TONIGHT, AREN'T YOU?
WHERE YA HEADED?
JUST...UM... GOING TO SEE SOME FRIENDS, SIR.
DUDE, YOU GUYS AIN'T COPS. YOU JUST CAN'T STOP PEOPLE LIKE THIS.
WE'RE THE ONLY THING STANDING BETWEEN YOU AND THE UNDEAD TONIGHT, SON.
SO MAYBE SHOW A LITTLE--
DEAD!

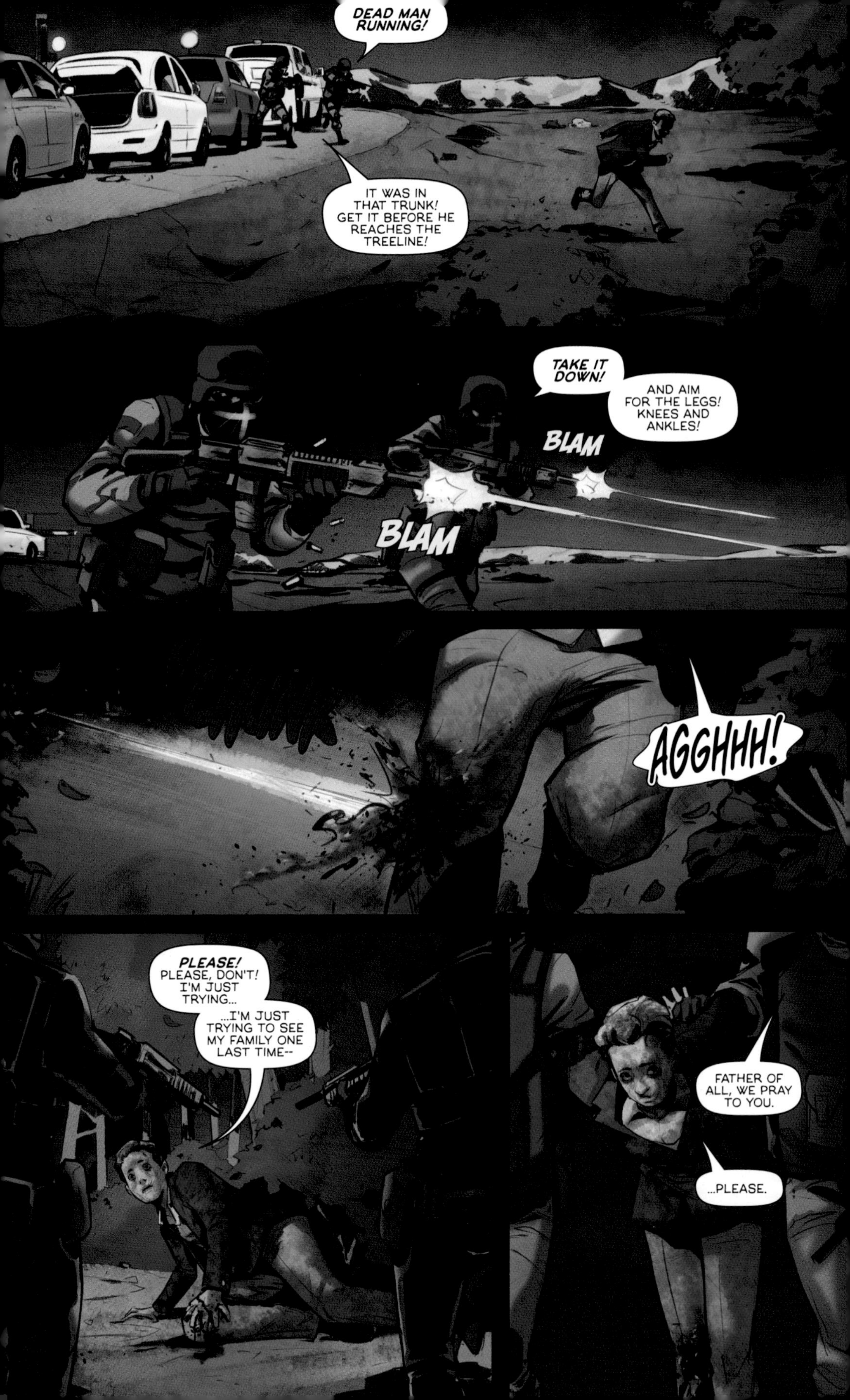
DEAD MAN RUNNING!
IT WAS IN THAT TRUNK! GET IT BEFORE HE REACHES THE TREELINE!
TAKE IT DOWN!
AND AIM FOR THE LEGS! KNEES AND ANKLES!
BLAM
BLAM
AGGHHH!
PLEASE! PLEASE, DON'T! I'M JUST TRYING...
...I'M JUST TRYING TO SEE MY FAMILY ONE LAST TIME--
FATHER OF ALL, WE PRAY TO YOU.
...PLEASE.

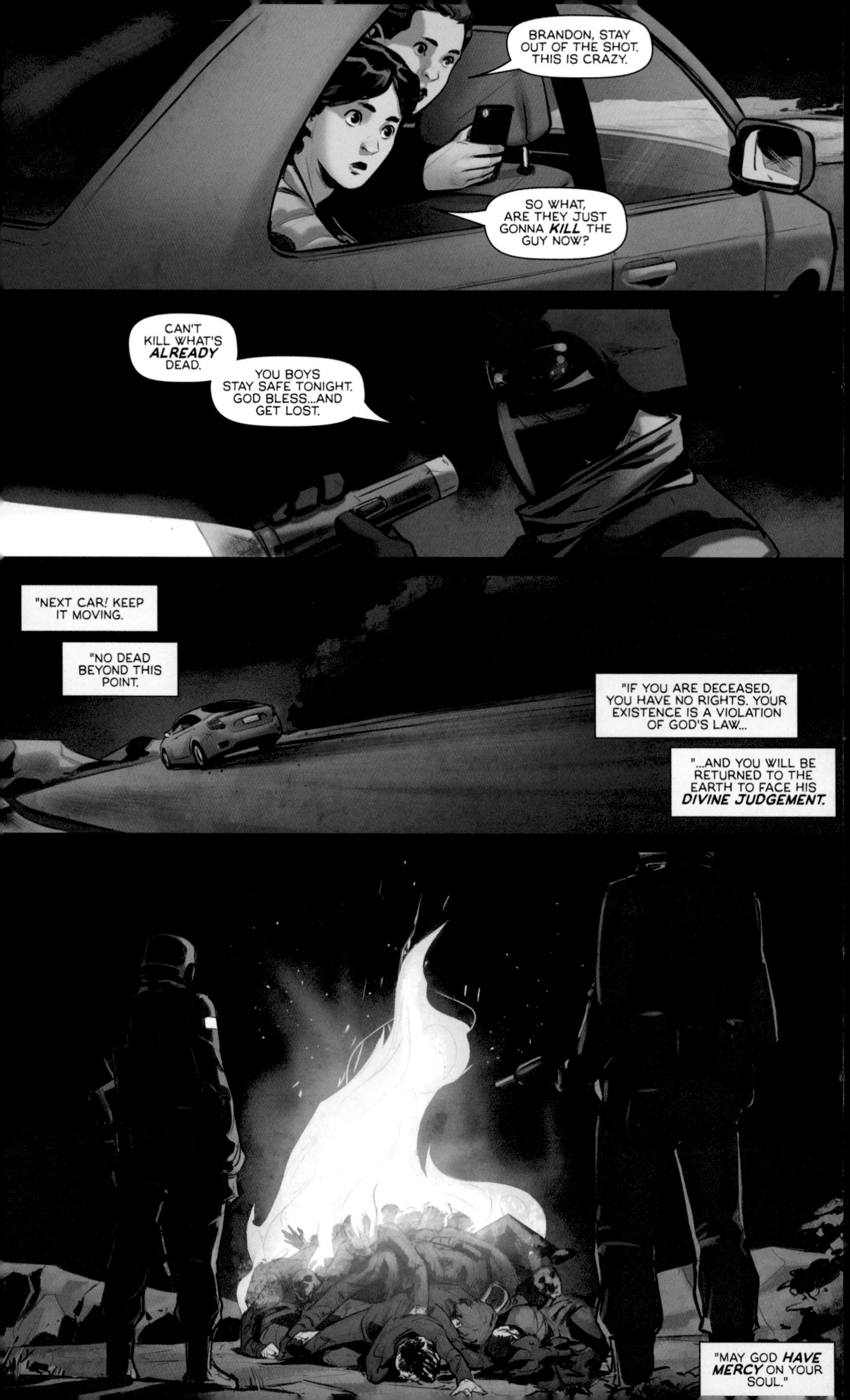
BRANDON, STAY OUT OF THE SHOT. THIS IS CRAZY.
SO WHAT, ARE THEY JUST GONNA KILL THE GUY NOW?
CAN'T KILL WHAT'S ALREADY DEAD.
YOU BOYS STAY SAFE TONIGHT. GOD BLESS...AND GET LOST.
"NEXT CAR! KEEP IT MOVING.
"NO DEAD BEYOND THIS POINT.
"IF YOU ARE DECEASED, YOU HAVE NO RIGHTS. YOUR EXISTENCE IS A VIOLATION OF GOD'S LAW...
"...AND YOU WILL BE RETURNED TO THE EARTH TO FACE HIS DIVINE JUDGEMENT.
"MAY GOD HAVE MERCY ON YOUR SOUL."

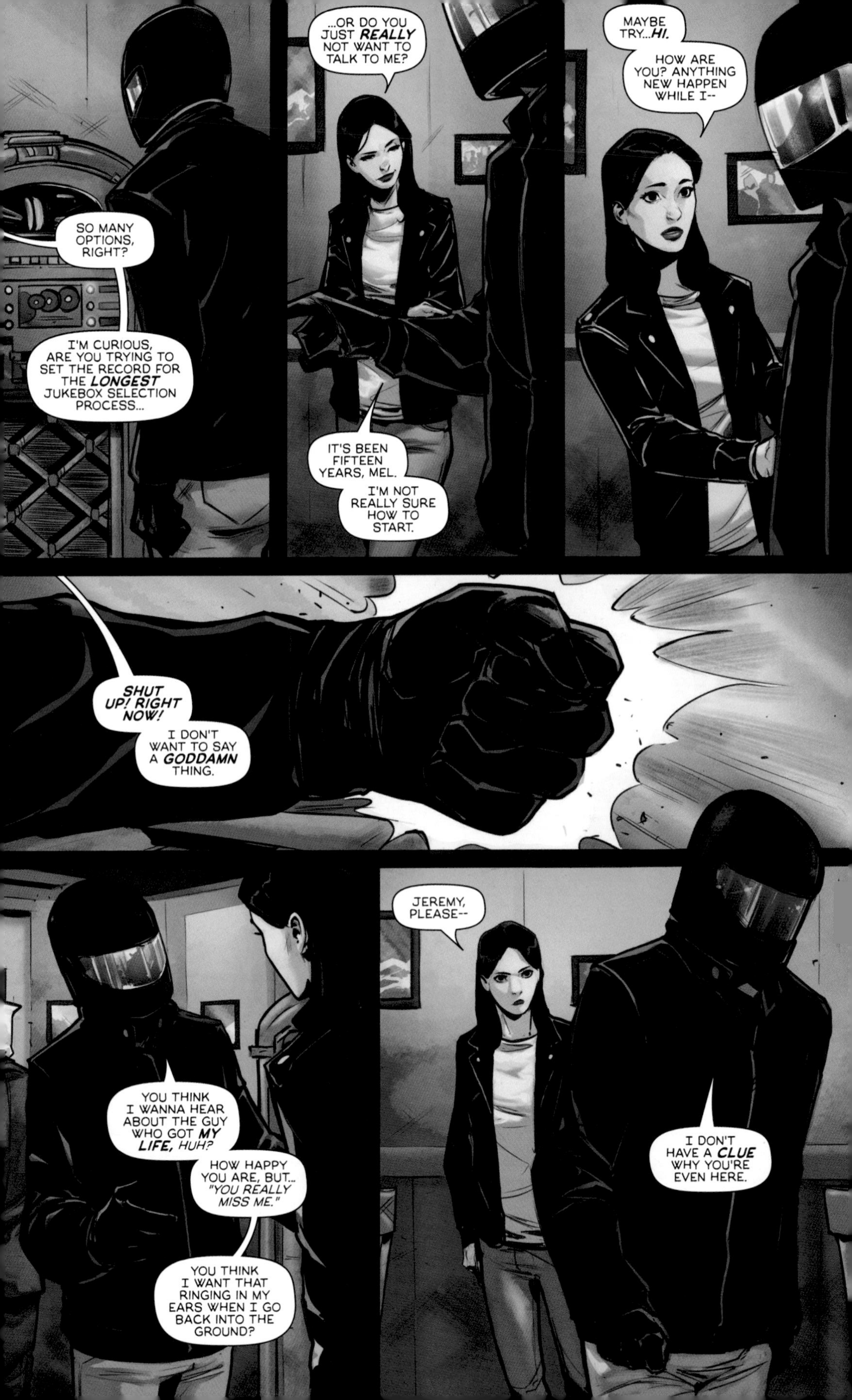
SO MANY OPTIONS, RIGHT?
I'M CURIOUS, ARE YOU TRYING TO SET THE RECORD FOR THE LONGEST JUKEBOX SELECTION PROCESS...
...OR DO YOU JUST REALLY NOT WANT TO TALK TO ME?
IT'S BEEN FIFTEEN YEARS, MEL.
I'M NOT REALLY SURE HOW TO START.
MAYBE TRY...HI.
HOW ARE YOU? ANYTHING NEW HAPPEN WHILE I--
SHUT UP! RIGHT NOW!
I DON'T WANT TO SAY A GODDAMN THING.
YOU THINK I WANNA HEAR ABOUT THE GUY WHO GOT MY LIFE, HUH?
HOW HAPPY YOU ARE, BUT... "YOU REALLY MISS ME."
YOU THINK I WANT THAT RINGING IN MY EARS WHEN I GO BACK INTO THE GROUND?
JEREMY, PLEASE--
I DON'T HAVE A CLUE WHY YOU'RE EVEN HERE.

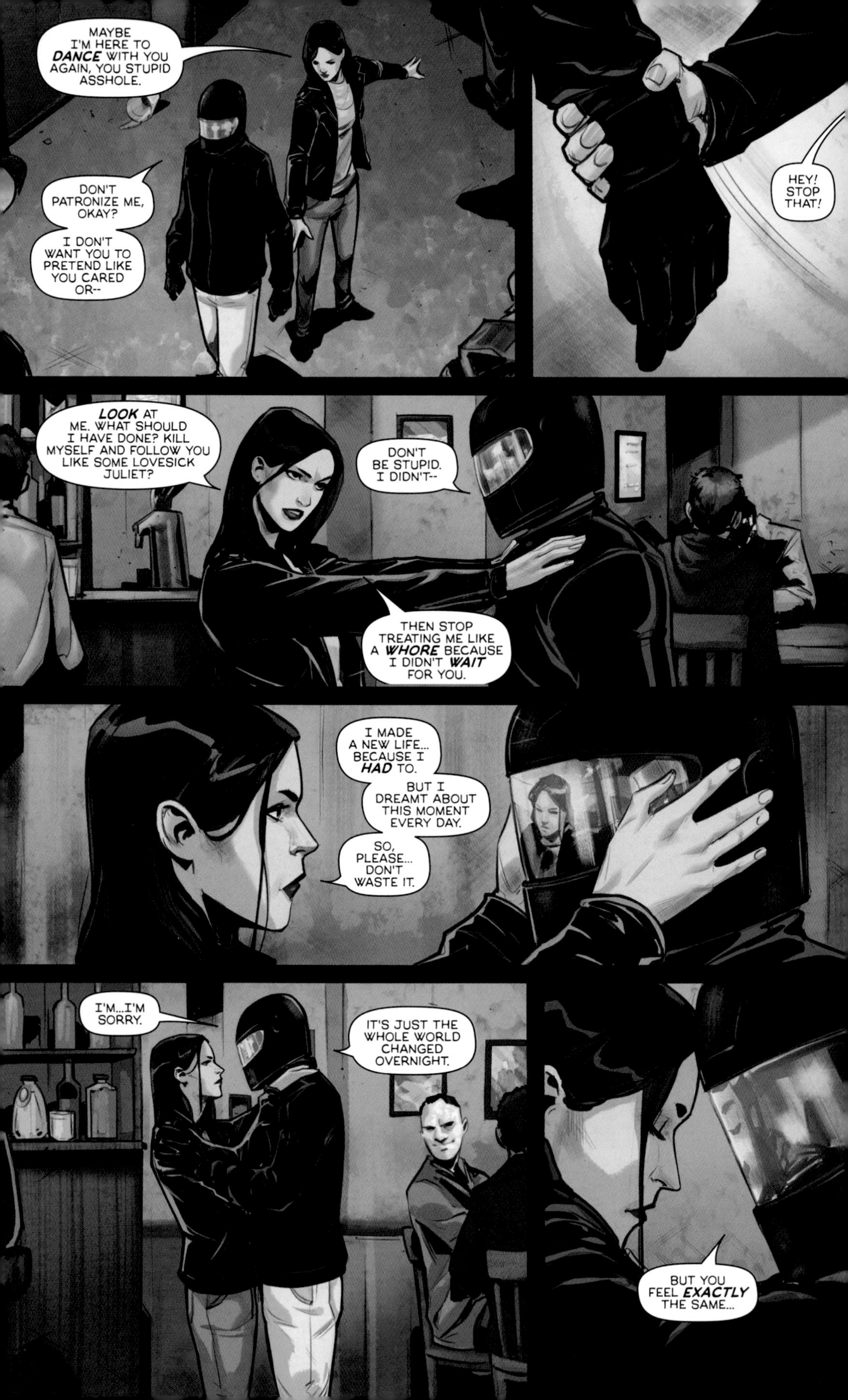
MAYBE I'M HERE TO DANCE WITH YOU AGAIN, YOU STUPID ASSHOLE.
DON'T PATRONIZE ME, OKAY?
I DON'T WANT YOU TO PRETEND LIKE YOU CARED OR--
HEY! STOP THAT!
LOOK AT ME. WHAT SHOULD I HAVE DONE? KILL MYSELF AND FOLLOW YOU LIKE SOME LOVESICK JULIET?
DON'T BE STUPID. I DIDN'T--
THEN STOP TREATING ME LIKE A WHORE BECAUSE I DIDN'T WAIT FOR YOU.
I MADE A NEW LIFE... BECAUSE I HAD TO.
BUT I DREAMT ABOUT THIS MOMENT EVERY DAY.
SO, PLEASE... DON'T WASTE IT.
I'M...I'M SORRY.
IT'S JUST THE WHOLE WORLD CHANGED OVERNIGHT.
BUT YOU FEEL EXACTLY THE SAME...

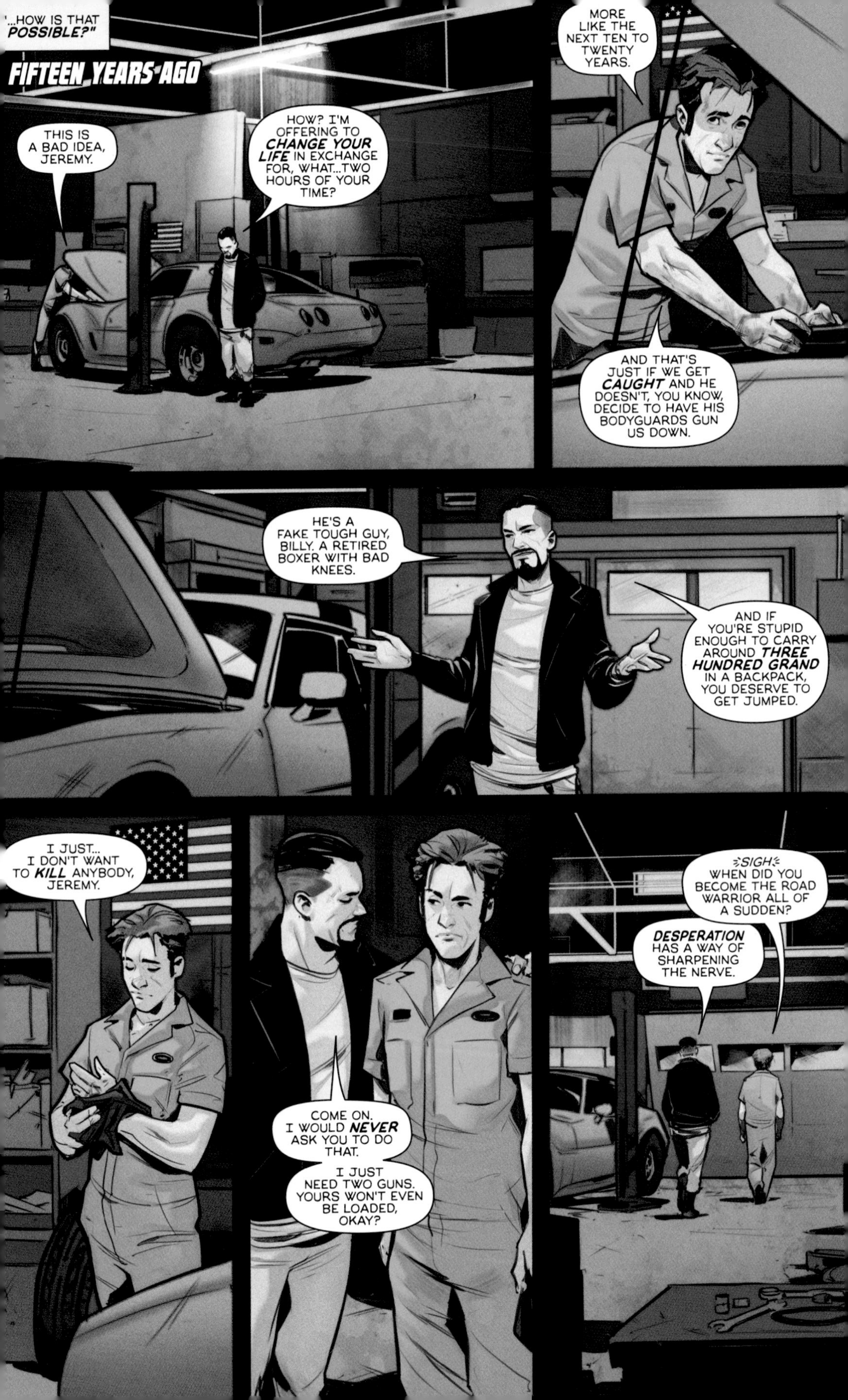
"...HOW IS THAT POSSIBLE?"
FIFTEEN YEARS AGO
THIS IS A BAD IDEA, JEREMY.
HOW? I'M OFFERING TO CHANGE YOUR LIFE IN EXCHANGE FOR, WHAT...TWO HOURS OF YOUR TIME?
MORE LIKE THE NEXT TEN TO TWENTY YEARS.
AND THAT'S JUST IF WE GET CAUGHT AND HE DOESN'T, YOU KNOW, DECIDE TO HAVE HIS BODYGUARDS GUN US DOWN.
HE'S A FAKE TOUGH GUY, BILLY. A RETIRED BOXER WITH BAD KNEES.
AND IF YOU'RE STUPID ENOUGH TO CARRY AROUND THREE HUNDRED GRAND IN A BACKPACK, YOU DESERVE TO GET JUMPED.
I JUST... I DON'T WANT TO KILL ANYBODY, JEREMY.
COME ON. I WOULD NEVER ASK YOU TO DO THAT.
I JUST NEED TWO GUNS. YOURS WON'T EVEN BE LOADED, OKAY?
SIGH WHEN DID YOU BECOME THE ROAD WARRIOR ALL OF A SUDDEN?
DESPERATION HAS A WAY OF SHARPENING THE NERVE.

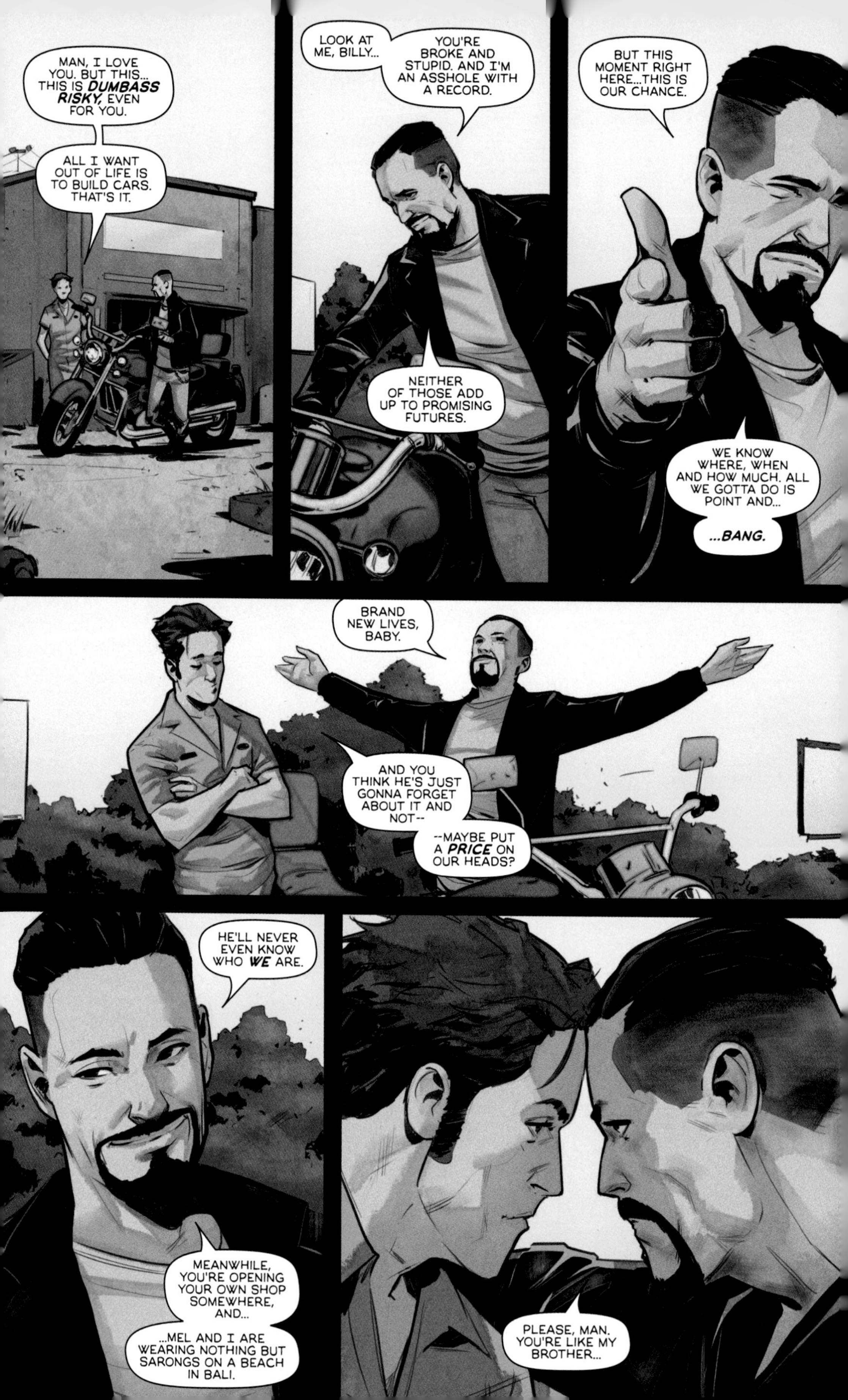
MAN, I LOVE YOU. BUT THIS... THIS IS *DUMBASS RISKY,* EVEN FOR YOU.
ALL I WANT OUT OF LIFE IS TO BUILD CARS. THAT'S IT.
LOOK AT ME, BILLY...
YOU'RE BROKE AND STUPID. AND I'M AN ASSHOLE WITH A RECORD.
NEITHER OF THOSE ADD UP TO PROMISING FUTURES.
BUT THIS MOMENT RIGHT HERE...THIS IS OUR CHANCE.
WE KNOW WHERE, WHEN AND HOW MUCH. ALL WE GOTTA DO IS POINT AND...
...BANG.
BRAND NEW LIVES, BABY.
AND YOU THINK HE'S JUST GONNA FORGET ABOUT IT AND NOT--
--MAYBE PUT A *PRICE* ON OUR HEADS?
HE'LL NEVER EVEN KNOW WHO *WE* ARE.
MEANWHILE, YOU'RE OPENING YOUR OWN SHOP SOMEWHERE, AND...
...MEL AND I ARE WEARING NOTHING BUT SARONGS ON A BEACH IN BALI.
PLEASE, MAN. YOU'RE LIKE MY BROTHER...

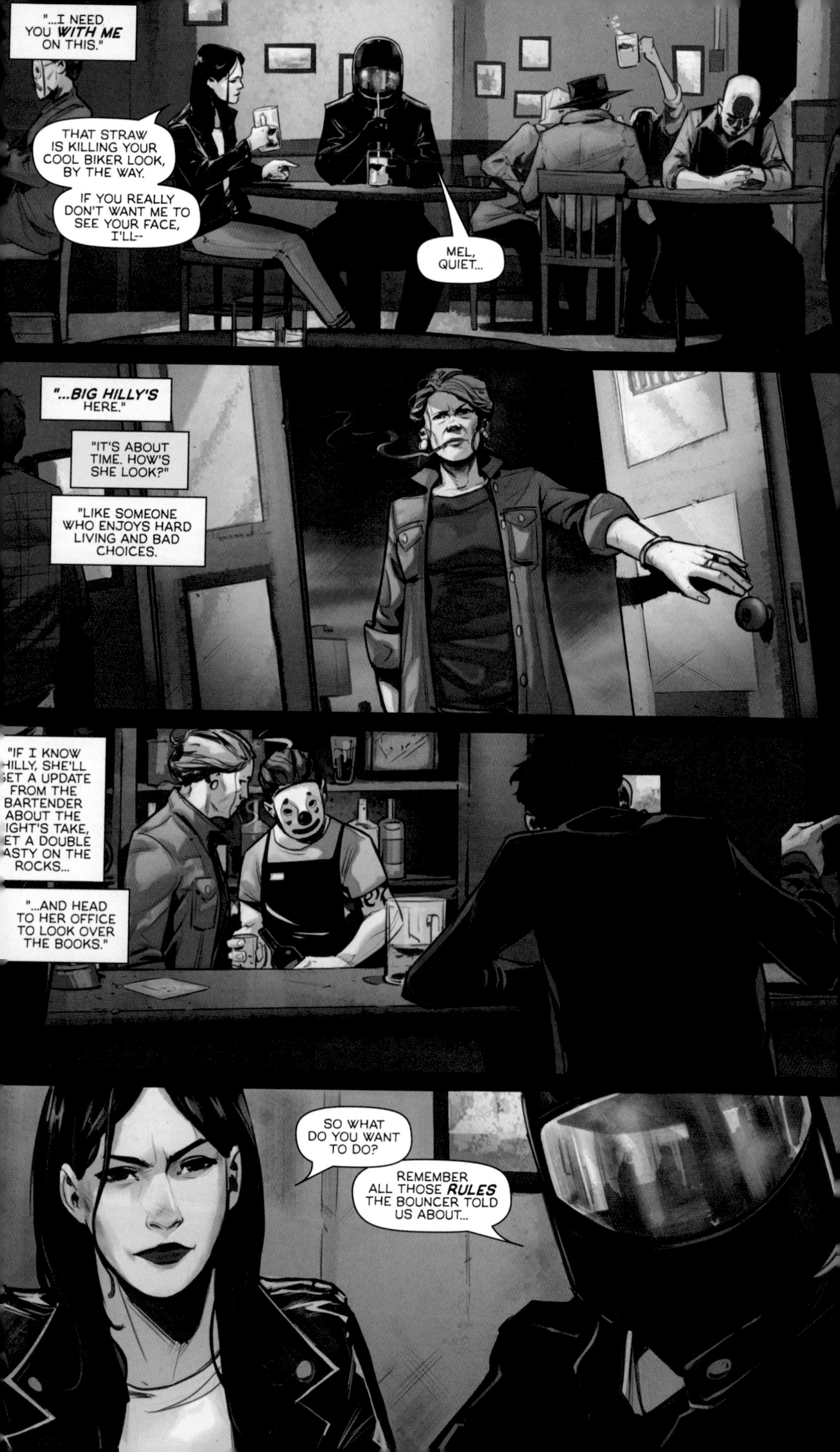

"...I NEED YOU WITH ME ON THIS."
THAT STRAW IS KILLING YOUR COOL BIKER LOOK, BY THE WAY.
IF YOU REALLY DON'T WANT ME TO SEE YOUR FACE, I'LL--
MEL, QUIET...
"...BIG HILLY'S HERE."
"IT'S ABOUT TIME. HOW'S SHE LOOK?"
"LIKE SOMEONE WHO ENJOYS HARD LIVING AND BAD CHOICES.
"IF I KNOW HILLY, SHE'LL GET A UPDATE FROM THE BARTENDER ABOUT THE NIGHT'S TAKE, GET A DOUBLE NASTY ON THE ROCKS...
"...AND HEAD TO HER OFFICE TO LOOK OVER THE BOOKS."
SO WHAT DO YOU WANT TO DO?
REMEMBER ALL THOSE RULES THE BOUNCER TOLD US ABOUT...

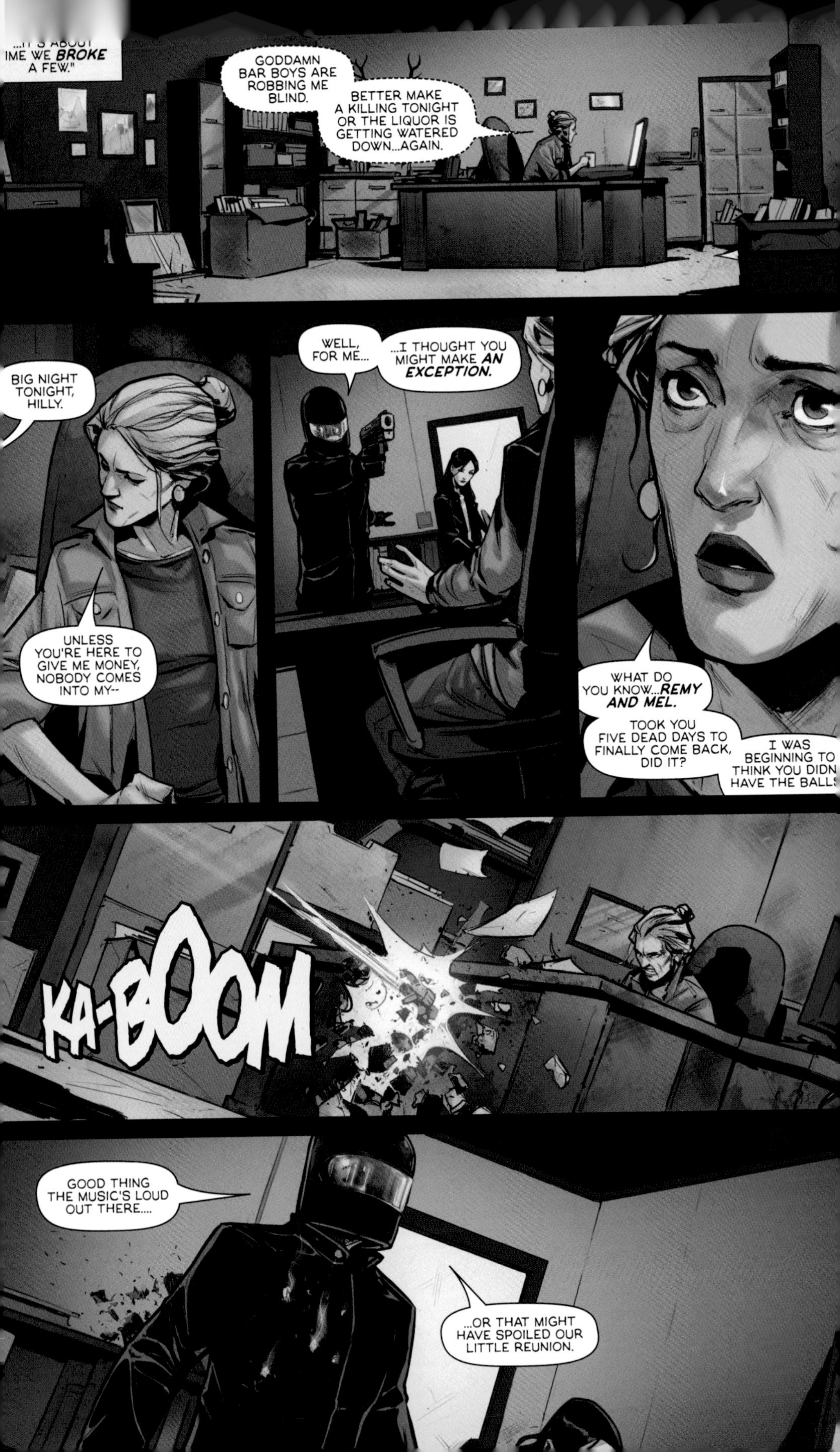

...IT'S ABOUT TIME WE BROKE A FEW."
GODDAMN BAR BOYS ARE ROBBING ME BLIND.
BETTER MAKE A KILLING TONIGHT OR THE LIQUOR IS GETTING WATERED DOWN...AGAIN.
BIG NIGHT TONIGHT, HILLY.
UNLESS YOU'RE HERE TO GIVE ME MONEY, NOBODY COMES INTO MY--
WELL, FOR ME...
...I THOUGHT YOU MIGHT MAKE AN EXCEPTION.
WHAT DO YOU KNOW...REMY AND MEL.
TOOK YOU FIVE DEAD DAYS TO FINALLY COME BACK, DID IT?
I WAS BEGINNING TO THINK YOU DIDN HAVE THE BALLS
KA-BOOM
GOOD THING THE MUSIC'S LOUD OUT THERE....
...OR THAT MIGHT HAVE SPOILED OUR LITTLE REUNION.

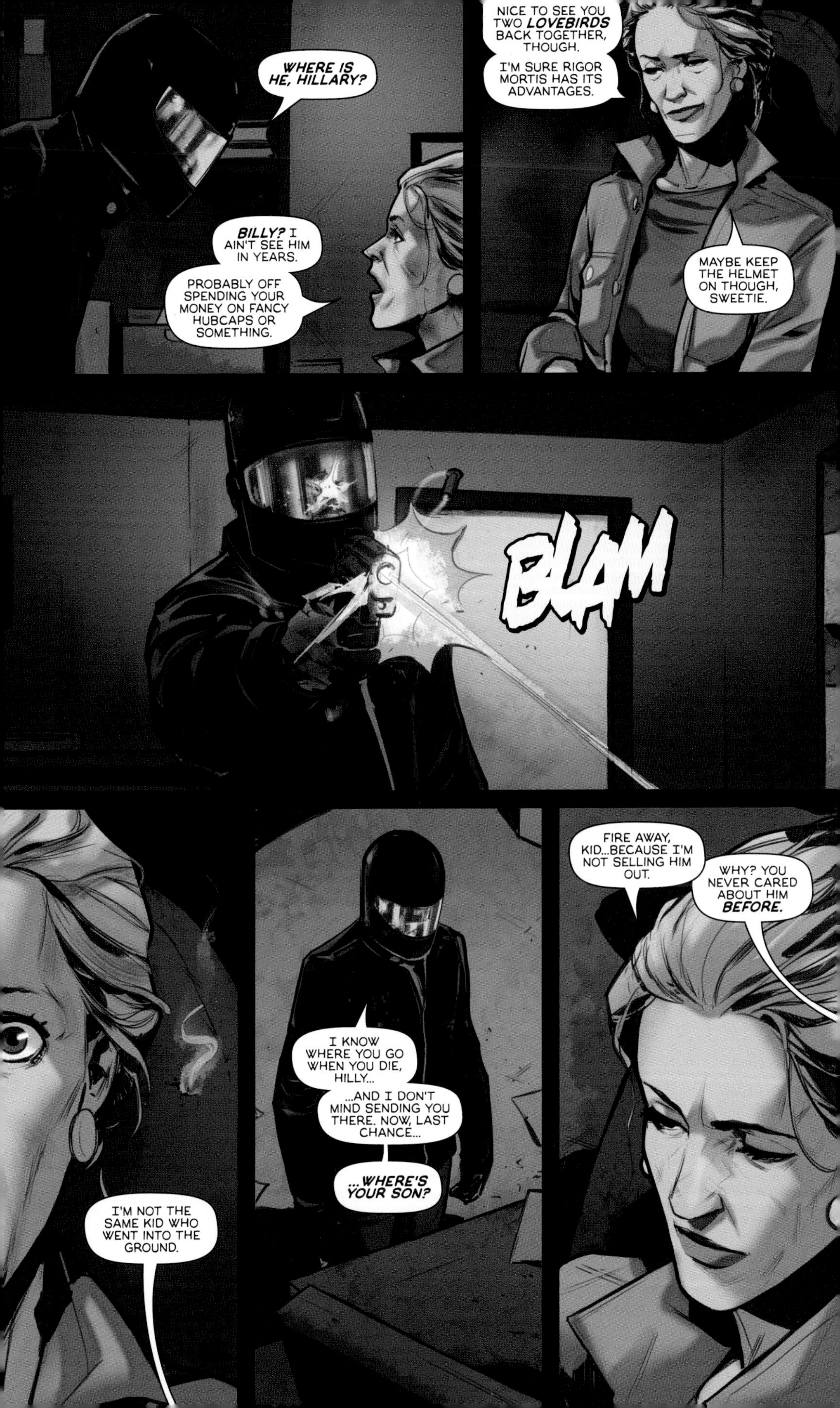
WHERE IS HE, HILLARY?
BILLY? I AIN'T SEE HIM IN YEARS.
PROBABLY OFF SPENDING YOUR MONEY ON FANCY HUBCAPS OR SOMETHING.
NICE TO SEE YOU TWO LOVEBIRDS BACK TOGETHER, THOUGH.
I'M SURE RIGOR MORTIS HAS ITS ADVANTAGES.
MAYBE KEEP THE HELMET ON THOUGH, SWEETIE.
BLAM
I'M NOT THE SAME KID WHO WENT INTO THE GROUND.
I KNOW WHERE YOU GO WHEN YOU DIE, HILLY...
...AND I DON'T MIND SENDING YOU THERE. NOW, LAST CHANCE...
...WHERE'S YOUR SON?
FIRE AWAY, KID...BECAUSE I'M NOT SELLING HIM OUT.
WHY? YOU NEVER CARED ABOUT HIM BEFORE.

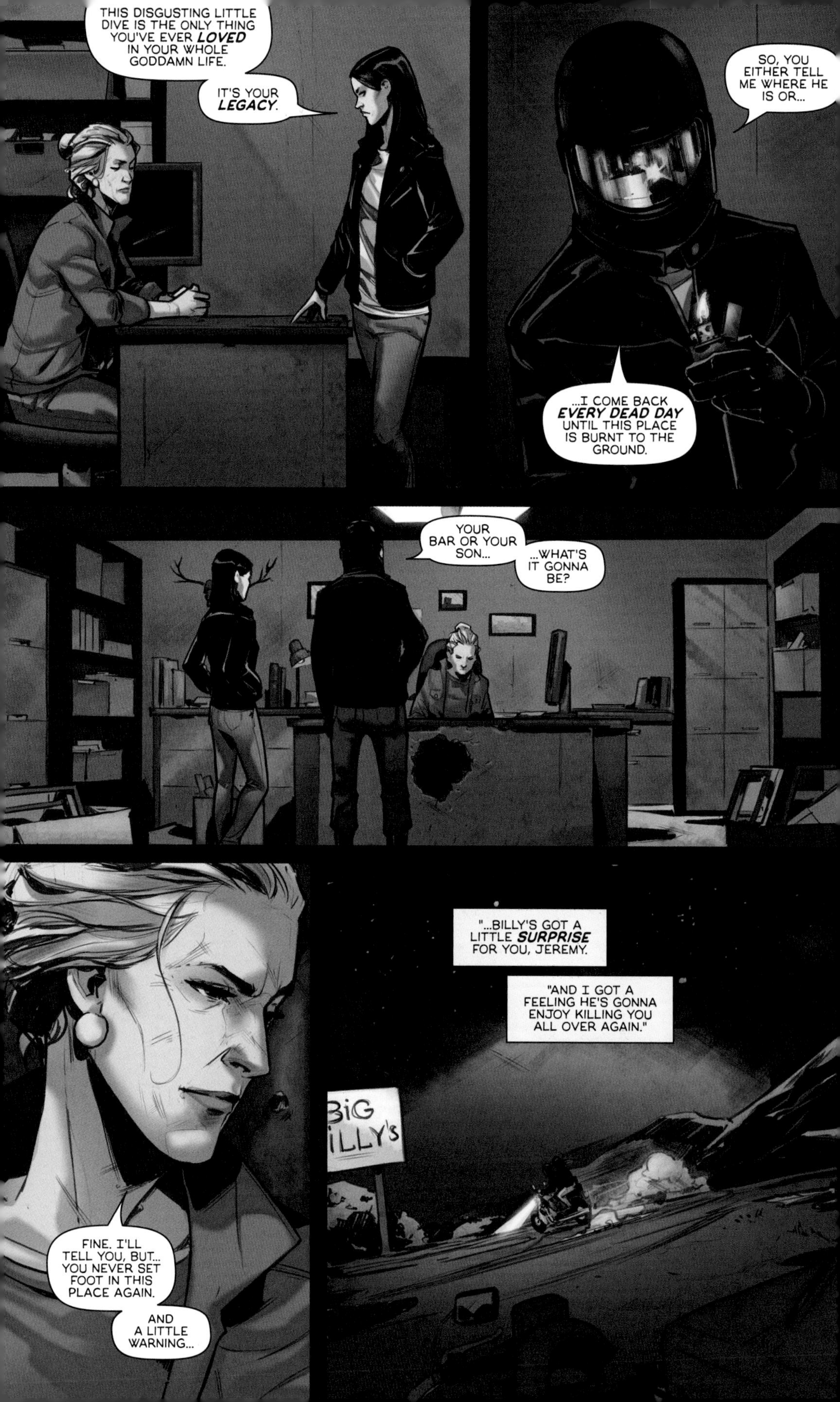
THIS DISGUSTING LITTLE DIVE IS THE ONLY THING YOU'VE EVER **LOVED** IN YOUR WHOLE GODDAMN LIFE.
IT'S YOUR **LEGACY**.
SO, YOU EITHER TELL ME WHERE HE IS OR...
...I COME BACK **EVERY DEAD DAY** UNTIL THIS PLACE IS BURNT TO THE GROUND.
YOUR BAR OR YOUR SON...
...WHAT'S IT GONNA BE?
FINE. I'LL TELL YOU, BUT... YOU NEVER SET FOOT IN THIS PLACE AGAIN.
AND A LITTLE WARNING...
"...BILLY'S GOT A LITTLE **SURPRISE** FOR YOU, JEREMY.
"AND I GOT A FEELING HE'S GONNA ENJOY KILLING YOU ALL OVER AGAIN."
BIG ILLY'S

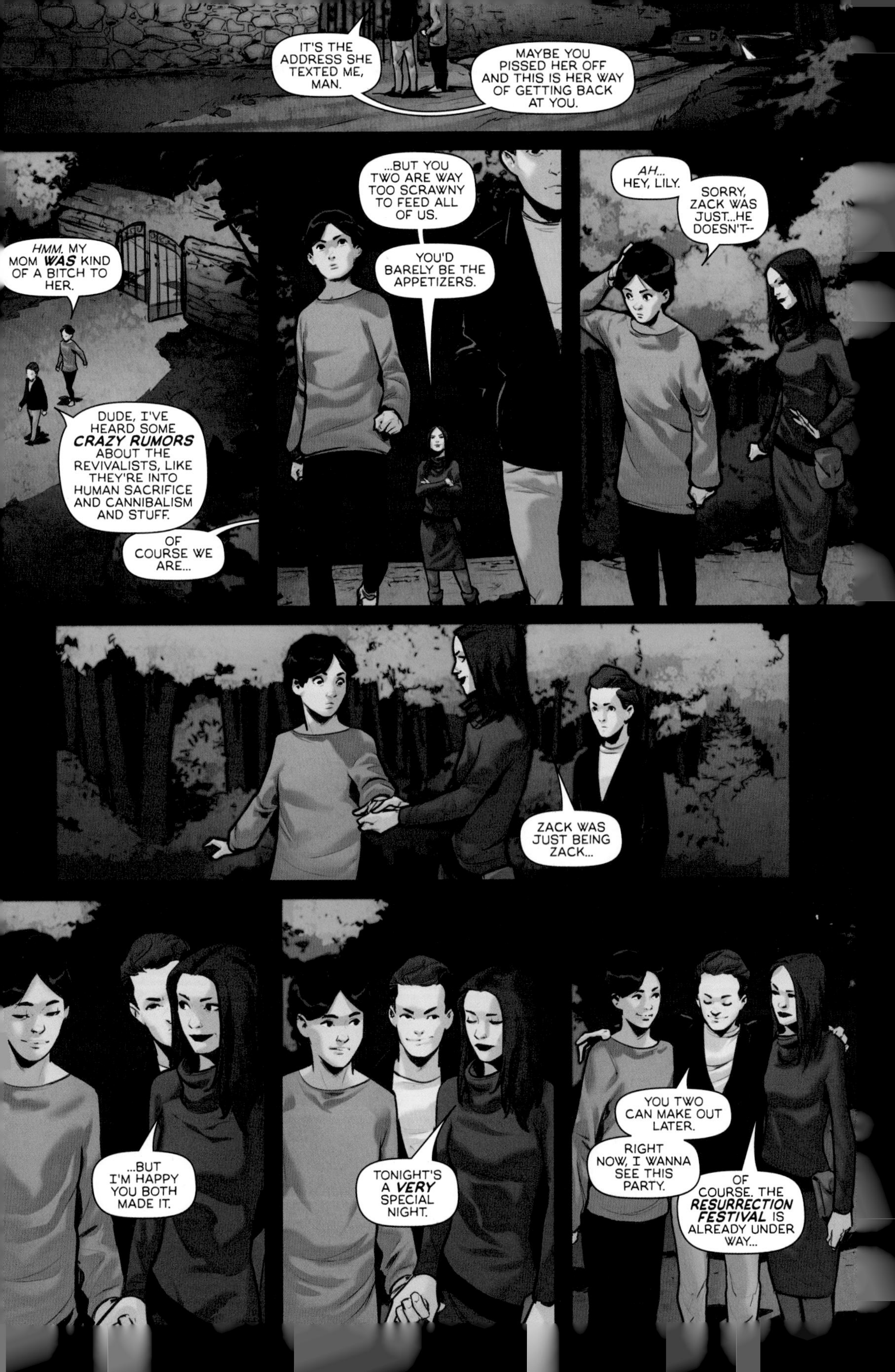
IT'S THE ADDRESS SHE TEXTED ME, MAN.
MAYBE YOU PISSED HER OFF AND THIS IS HER WAY OF GETTING BACK AT YOU.
HMM. MY MOM WAS KIND OF A BITCH TO HER.
DUDE, I'VE HEARD SOME CRAZY RUMORS ABOUT THE REVIVALISTS, LIKE THEY'RE INTO HUMAN SACRIFICE AND CANNIBALISM AND STUFF.
OF COURSE WE ARE...
...BUT YOU TWO ARE WAY TOO SCRAWNY TO FEED ALL OF US.
YOU'D BARELY BE THE APPETIZERS.
AH... HEY, LILY.
SORRY, ZACK WAS JUST...HE DOESN'T--
ZACK WAS JUST BEING ZACK...
...BUT I'M HAPPY YOU BOTH MADE IT.
TONIGHT'S A VERY SPECIAL NIGHT.
YOU TWO CAN MAKE OUT LATER.
RIGHT NOW, I WANNA SEE THIS PARTY.
OF COURSE. THE RESURRECTION FESTIVAL IS ALREADY UNDER WAY...

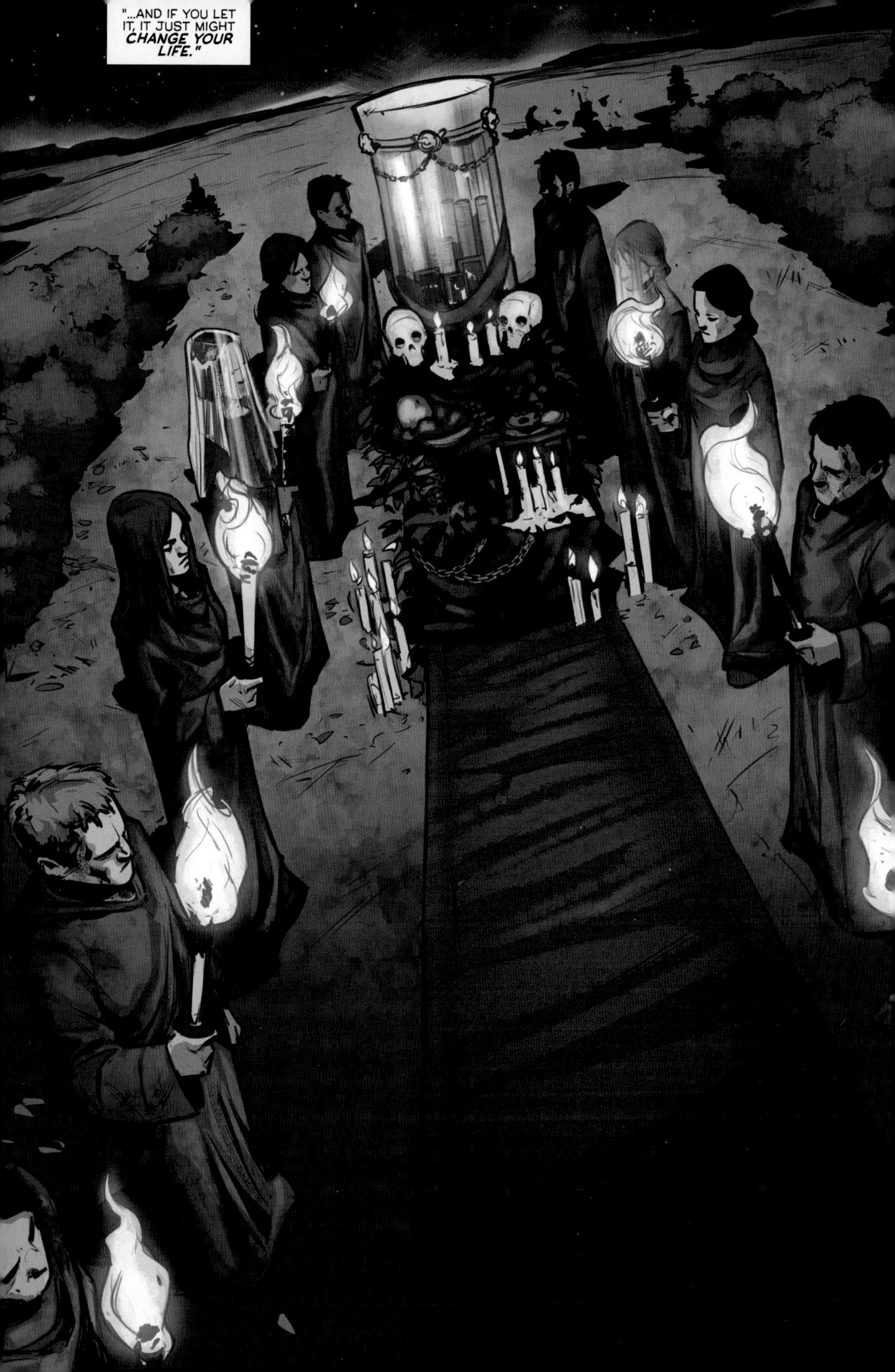
"...AND IF YOU LET IT, IT JUST MIGHT CHANGE YOUR LIFE."

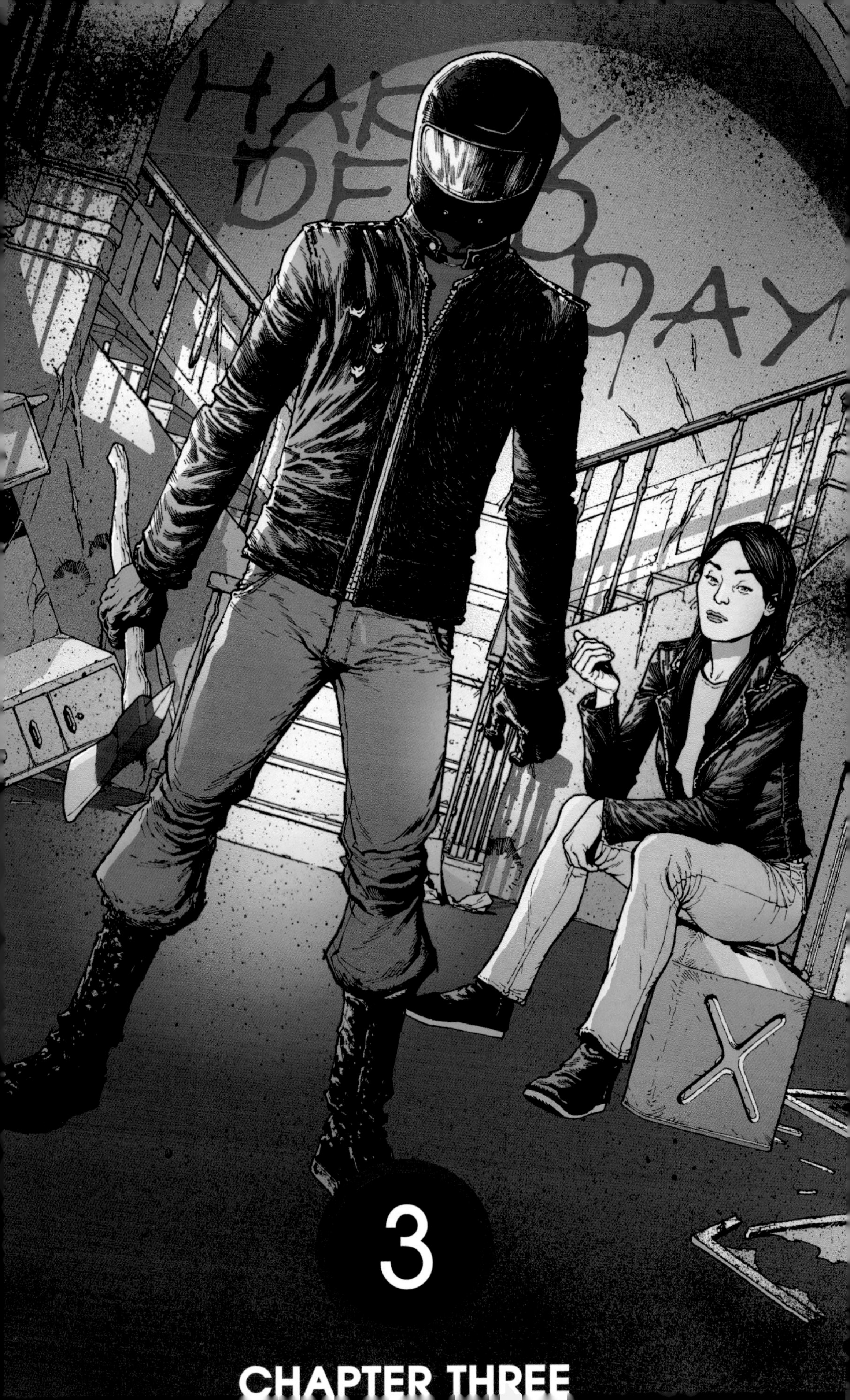

3

CHAPTER THREE

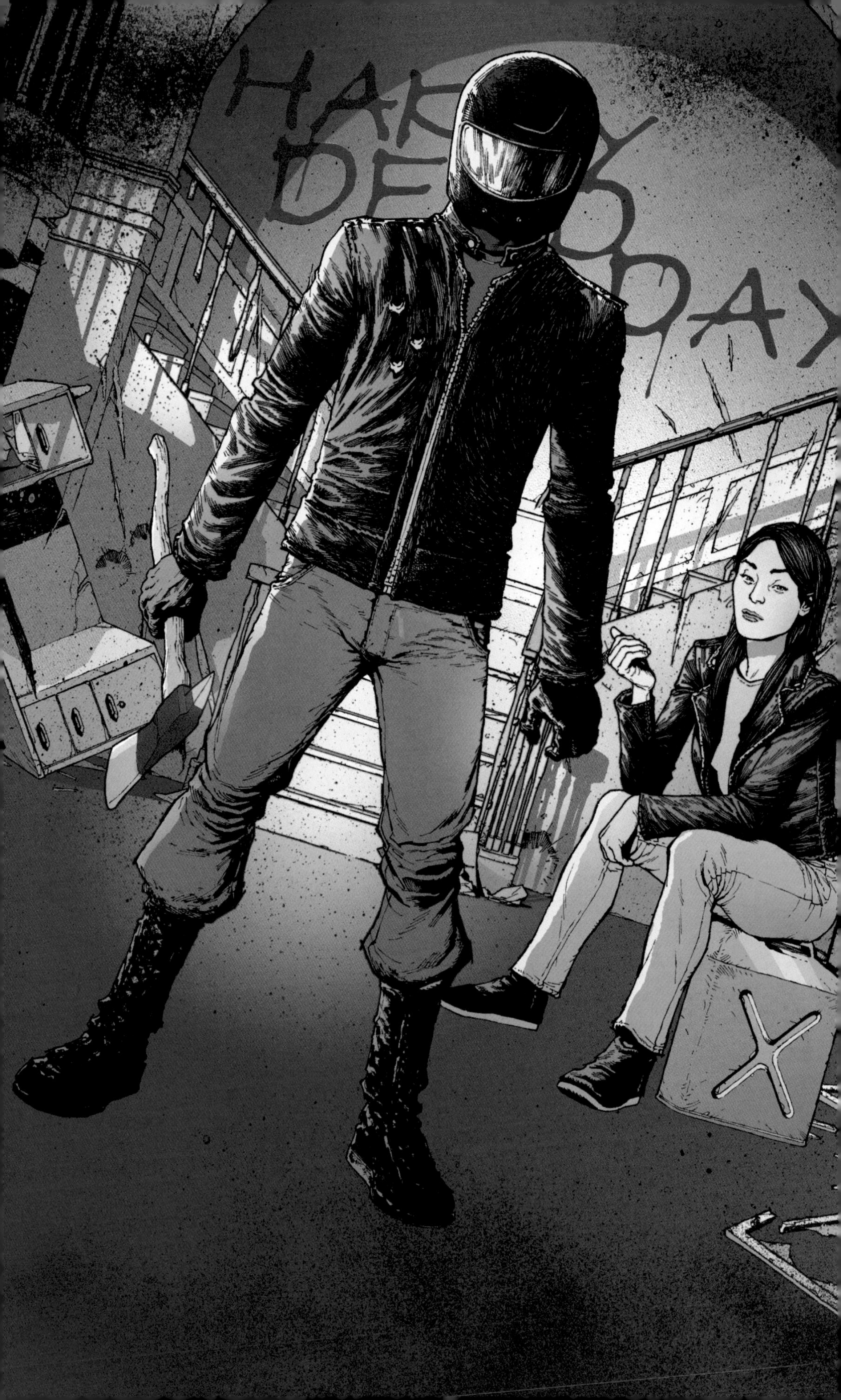

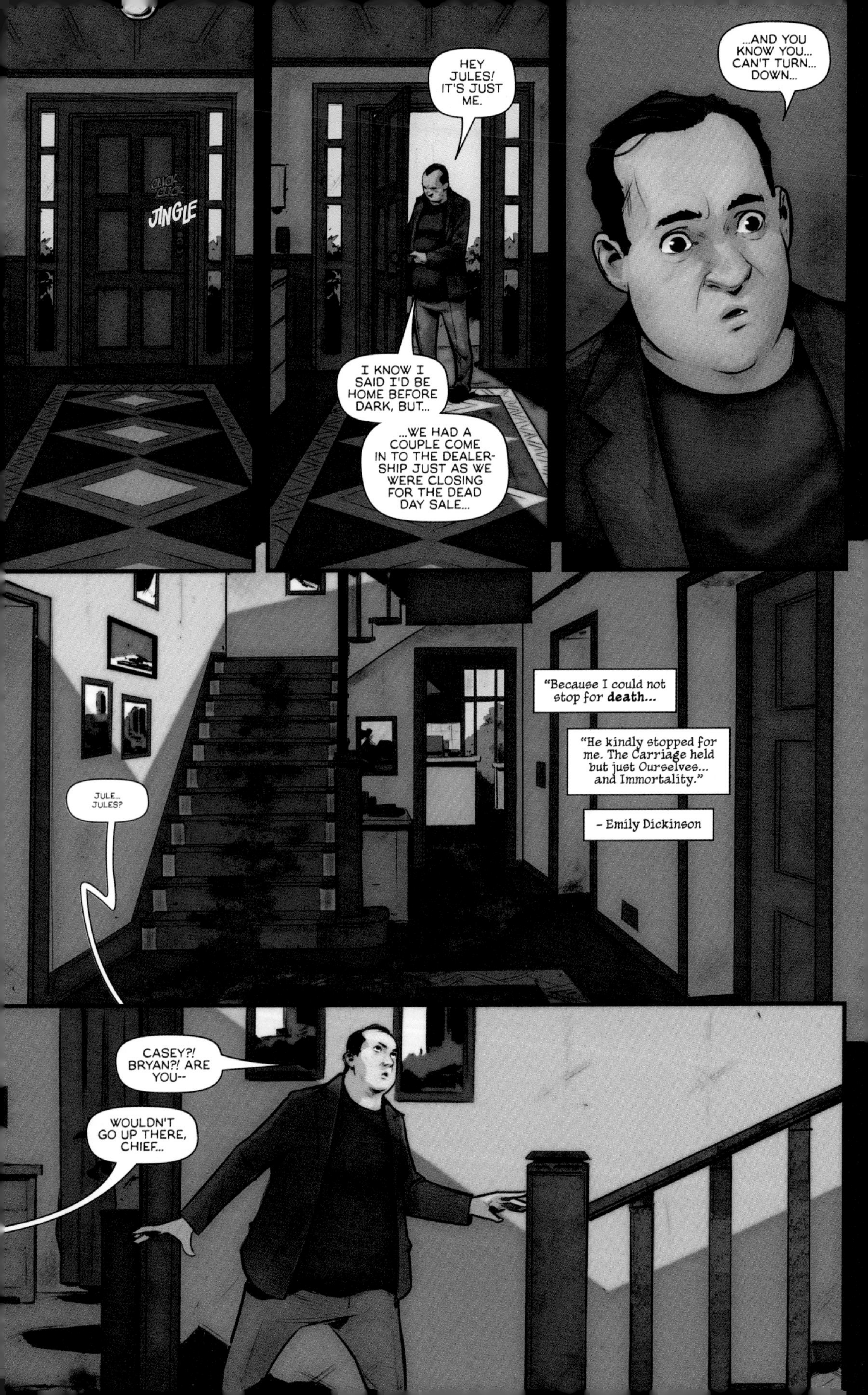
CLICK CLICK
JINGLE
HEY JULES! IT'S JUST ME.
I KNOW I SAID I'D BE HOME BEFORE DARK, BUT...
...WE HAD A COUPLE COME IN TO THE DEALER-SHIP JUST AS WE WERE CLOSING FOR THE DEAD DAY SALE...
...AND YOU KNOW YOU... CAN'T TURN... DOWN...
"Because I could not stop for **death...**
"He kindly stopped for me. The Carriage held but just Ourselves... and Immortality."
– Emily Dickinson
JULE... JULES?
CASEY?! BRYAN?! ARE YOU--
WOULDN'T GO UP THERE, CHIEF...

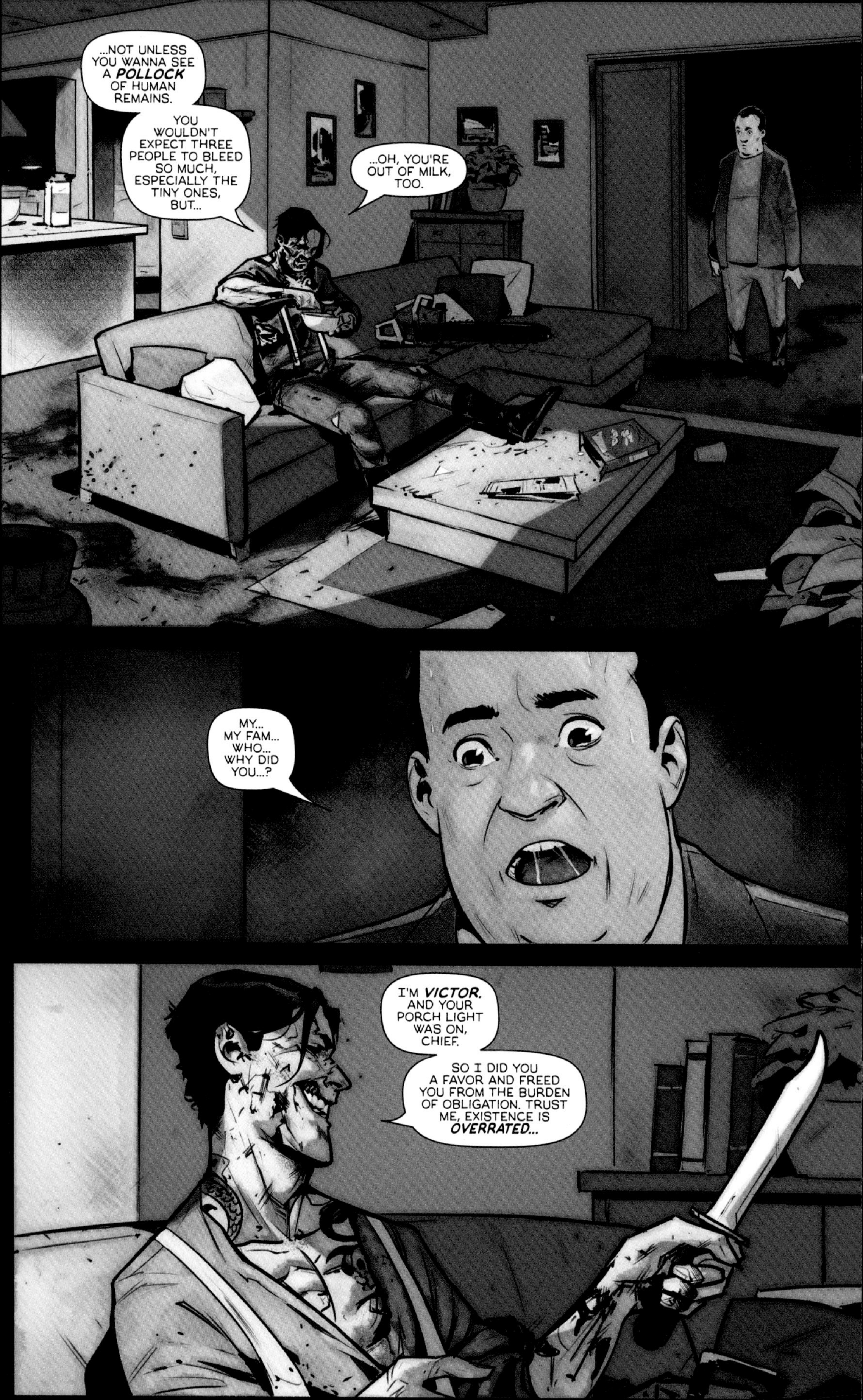
...NOT UNLESS YOU WANNA SEE A POLLOCK OF HUMAN REMAINS.
YOU WOULDN'T EXPECT THREE PEOPLE TO BLEED SO MUCH, ESPECIALLY THE TINY ONES, BUT...
...OH, YOU'RE OUT OF MILK, TOO.
MY... MY FAM... WHO... WHY DID YOU...?
I'M VICTOR. AND YOUR PORCH LIGHT WAS ON, CHIEF.
SO I DID YOU A FAVOR AND FREED YOU FROM THE BURDEN OF OBLIGATION. TRUST ME, EXISTENCE IS OVERRATED...

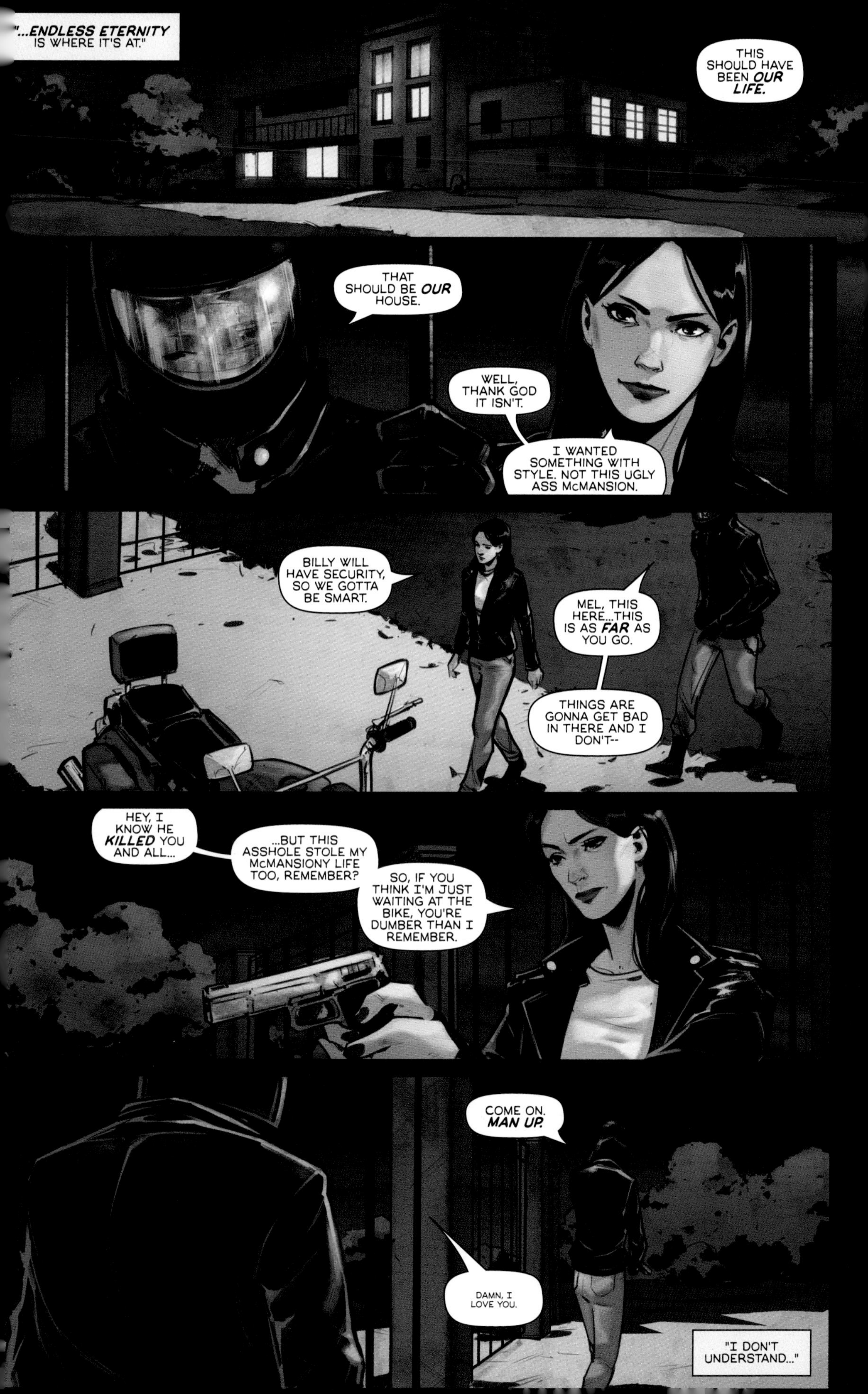
"...ENDLESS ETERNITY IS WHERE IT'S AT."
THIS SHOULD HAVE BEEN OUR LIFE.
THAT SHOULD BE OUR HOUSE.
WELL, THANK GOD IT ISN'T.
I WANTED SOMETHING WITH STYLE. NOT THIS UGLY ASS McMANSION.
BILLY WILL HAVE SECURITY, SO WE GOTTA BE SMART.
MEL, THIS HERE...THIS IS AS FAR AS YOU GO.
THINGS ARE GONNA GET BAD IN THERE AND I DON'T--
HEY, I KNOW HE KILLED YOU AND ALL...
...BUT THIS ASSHOLE STOLE MY McMANSIONY LIFE TOO, REMEMBER?
SO, IF YOU THINK I'M JUST WAITING AT THE BIKE, YOU'RE DUMBER THAN I REMEMBER.
COME ON. MAN UP.
DAMN, I LOVE YOU.
"I DON'T UNDERSTAND..."

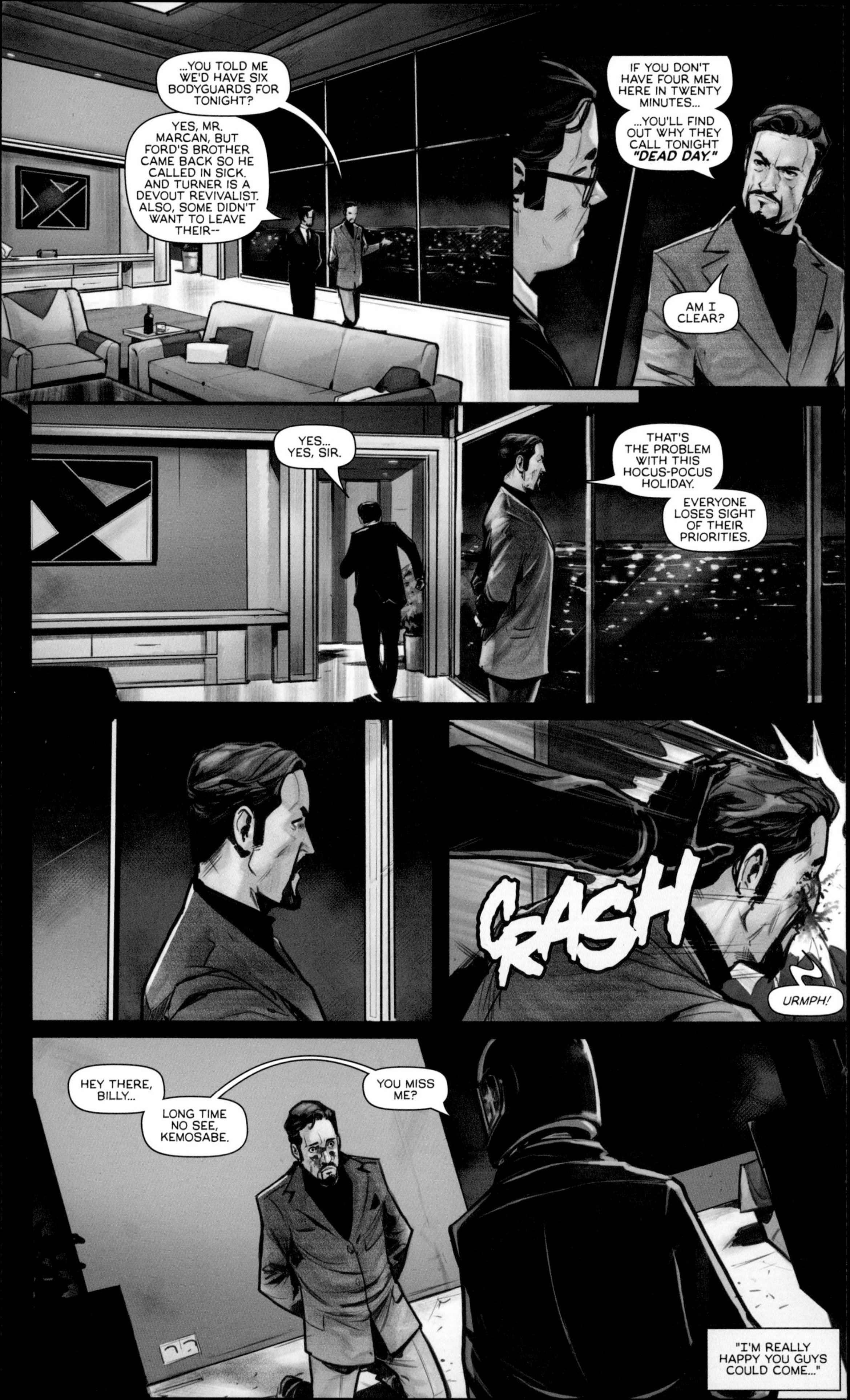

...YOU TOLD ME WE'D HAVE SIX BODYGUARDS FOR TONIGHT?
YES, MR. MARCAN, BUT FORD'S BROTHER CAME BACK SO HE CALLED IN SICK. AND TURNER IS A DEVOUT REVIVALIST. ALSO, SOME DIDN'T WANT TO LEAVE THEIR--
IF YOU DON'T HAVE FOUR MEN HERE IN TWENTY MINUTES...
...YOU'LL FIND OUT WHY THEY CALL TONIGHT "DEAD DAY."
AM I CLEAR?
YES... YES, SIR.
THAT'S THE PROBLEM WITH THIS HOCUS-POCUS HOLIDAY.
EVERYONE LOSES SIGHT OF THEIR PRIORITIES.
CRASH
URMPH!
HEY THERE, BILLY...
LONG TIME NO SEE, KEMOSABE.
YOU MISS ME?
"I'M REALLY HAPPY YOU GUYS COULD COME..."

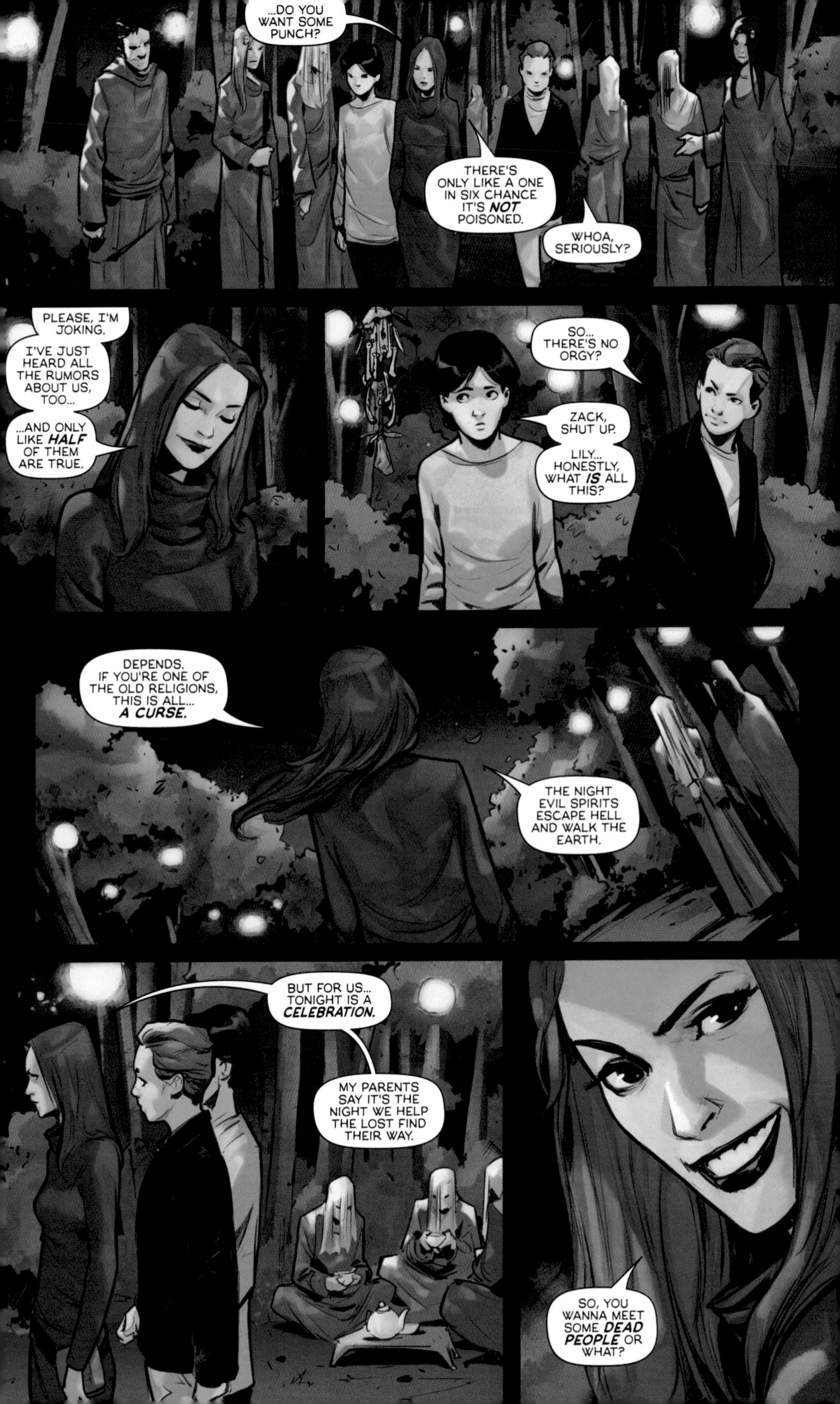
...DO YOU WANT SOME PUNCH?
THERE'S ONLY LIKE A ONE IN SIX CHANCE IT'S NOT POISONED.
WHOA, SERIOUSLY?
PLEASE, I'M JOKING.
I'VE JUST HEARD ALL THE RUMORS ABOUT US, TOO...
...AND ONLY LIKE HALF OF THEM ARE TRUE.
SO... THERE'S NO ORGY?
ZACK, SHUT UP.
LILY... HONESTLY, WHAT IS ALL THIS?
DEPENDS. IF YOU'RE ONE OF THE OLD RELIGIONS, THIS IS ALL... A CURSE.
THE NIGHT EVIL SPIRITS ESCAPE HELL AND WALK THE EARTH.
BUT FOR US... TONIGHT IS A CELEBRATION.
MY PARENTS SAY IT'S THE NIGHT WE HELP THE LOST FIND THEIR WAY.
SO, YOU WANNA MEET SOME DEAD PEOPLE OR WHAT?

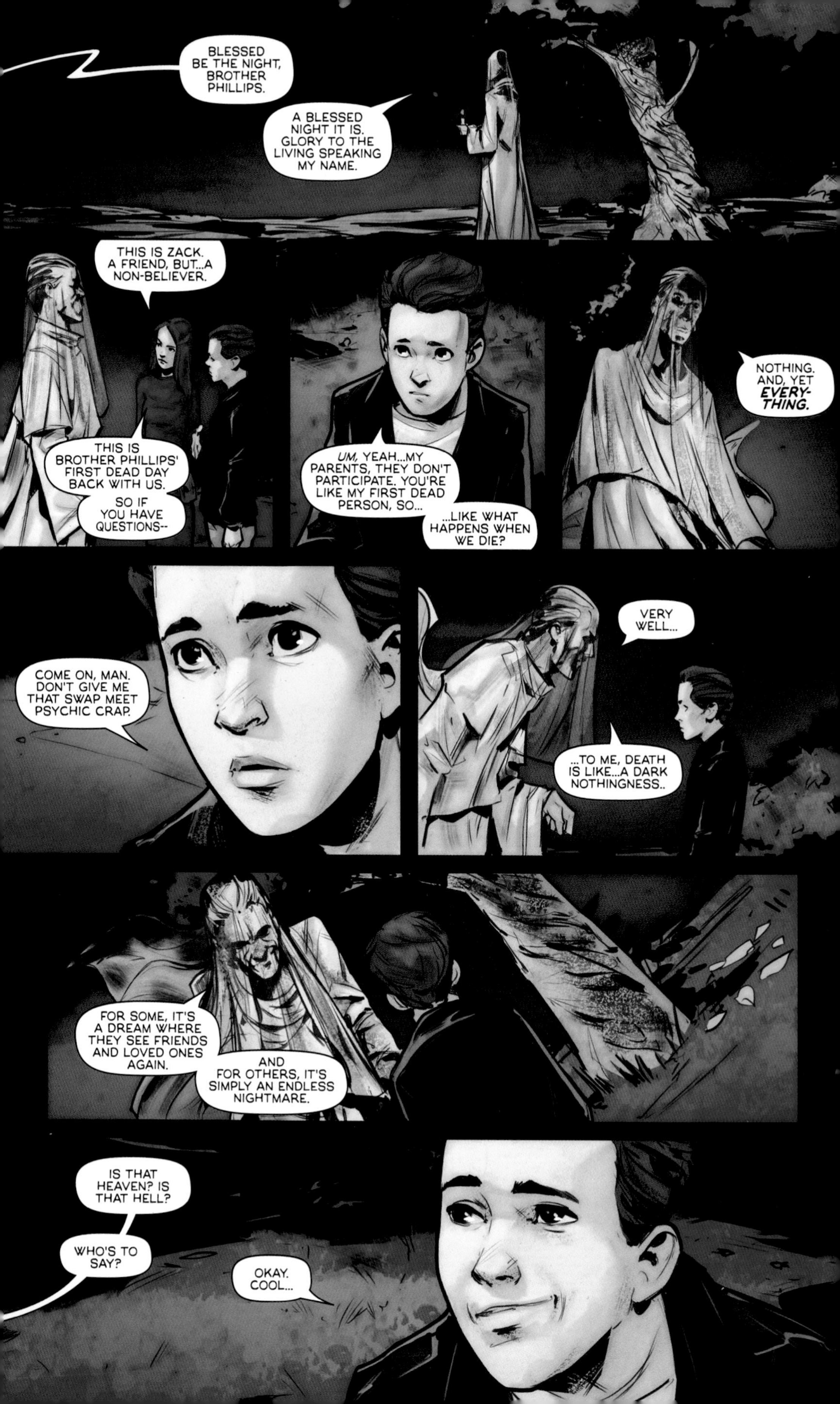
BLESSED BE THE NIGHT, BROTHER PHILLIPS.
A BLESSED NIGHT IT IS. GLORY TO THE LIVING SPEAKING MY NAME.
THIS IS ZACK. A FRIEND, BUT...A NON-BELIEVER.
THIS IS BROTHER PHILLIPS' FIRST DEAD DAY BACK WITH US.
SO IF YOU HAVE QUESTIONS--
UM, YEAH...MY PARENTS, THEY DON'T PARTICIPATE. YOU'RE LIKE MY FIRST DEAD PERSON, SO...
...LIKE WHAT HAPPENS WHEN WE DIE?
NOTHING. AND, YET EVERY-THING.
COME ON, MAN. DON'T GIVE ME THAT SWAP MEET PSYCHIC CRAP.
VERY WELL...
...TO ME, DEATH IS LIKE...A DARK NOTHINGNESS..
FOR SOME, IT'S A DREAM WHERE THEY SEE FRIENDS AND LOVED ONES AGAIN.
AND FOR OTHERS, IT'S SIMPLY AN ENDLESS NIGHTMARE.
IS THAT HEAVEN? IS THAT HELL?
WHO'S TO SAY?
OKAY. COOL...

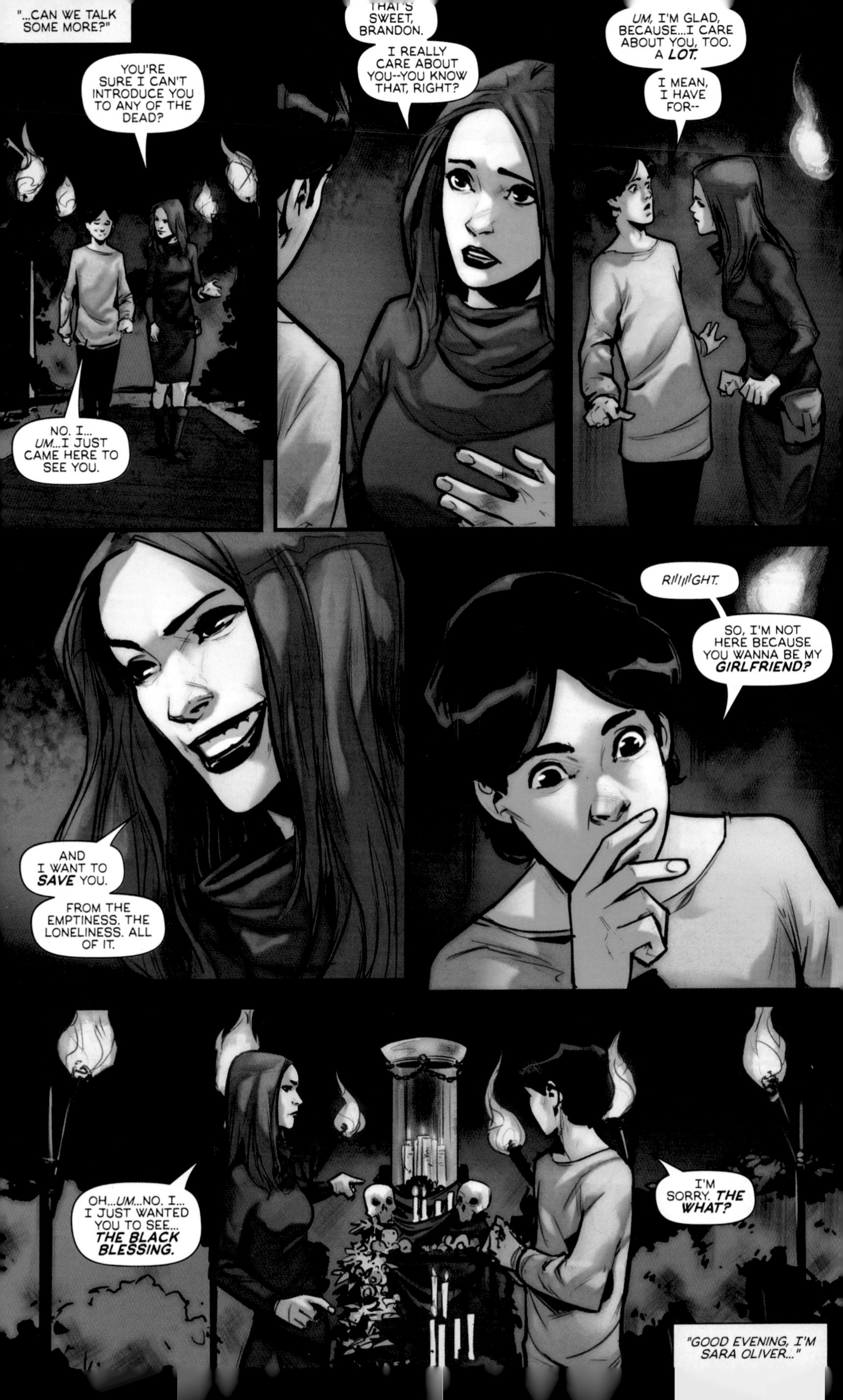
"...CAN WE TALK SOME MORE?"
YOU'RE SURE I CAN'T INTRODUCE YOU TO ANY OF THE DEAD?
NO. I... UM...I JUST CAME HERE TO SEE YOU.
THAT'S SWEET, BRANDON.
I REALLY CARE ABOUT YOU--YOU KNOW THAT, RIGHT?
UM, I'M GLAD, BECAUSE...I CARE ABOUT YOU, TOO. A LOT.
I MEAN, I HAVE FOR--
AND I WANT TO SAVE YOU.
FROM THE EMPTINESS. THE LONELINESS. ALL OF IT.
RIIIIIGHT.
SO, I'M NOT HERE BECAUSE YOU WANNA BE MY GIRLFRIEND?
OH...UM...NO. I... I JUST WANTED YOU TO SEE... THE BLACK BLESSING.
I'M SORRY. THE WHAT?
"GOOD EVENING, I'M SARA OLIVER..."

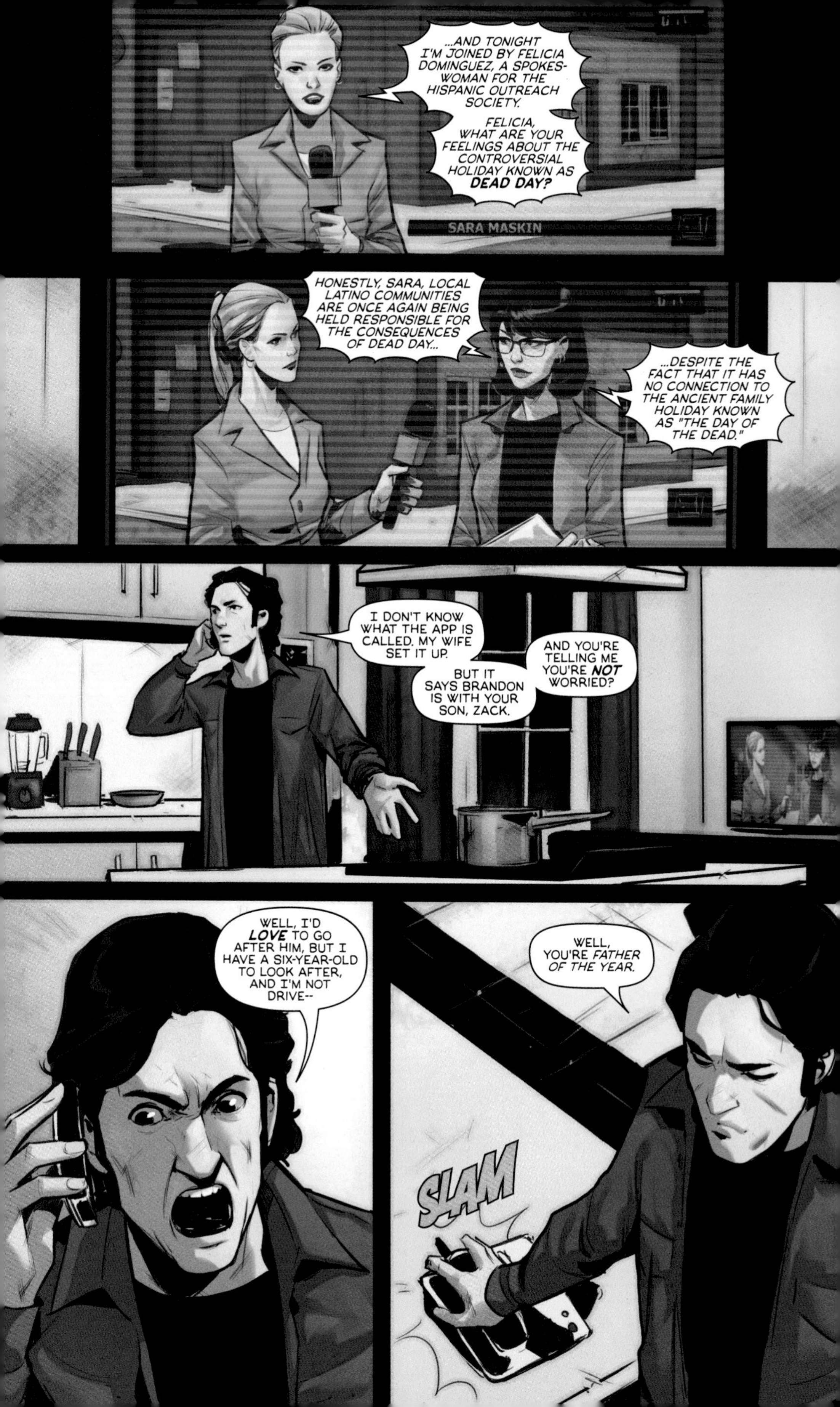
...AND TONIGHT I'M JOINED BY FELICIA DOMINGUEZ, A SPOKES-WOMAN FOR THE HISPANIC OUTREACH SOCIETY.
FELICIA, WHAT ARE YOUR FEELINGS ABOUT THE CONTROVERSIAL HOLIDAY KNOWN AS **DEAD DAY?**
SARA MASKIN
HONESTLY, SARA, LOCAL LATINO COMMUNITIES ARE ONCE AGAIN BEING HELD RESPONSIBLE FOR THE CONSEQUENCES OF DEAD DAY...
...DESPITE THE FACT THAT IT HAS NO CONNECTION TO THE ANCIENT FAMILY HOLIDAY KNOWN AS "THE DAY OF THE DEAD."
I DON'T KNOW WHAT THE APP IS CALLED. MY WIFE SET IT UP.
BUT IT SAYS BRANDON IS WITH YOUR SON, ZACK.
AND YOU'RE TELLING ME YOU'RE **NOT** WORRIED?
WELL, I'D **LOVE** TO GO AFTER HIM, BUT I HAVE A SIX-YEAR-OLD TO LOOK AFTER, AND I'M NOT DRIVE--
WELL, YOU'RE *FATHER OF THE YEAR.*
SLAM

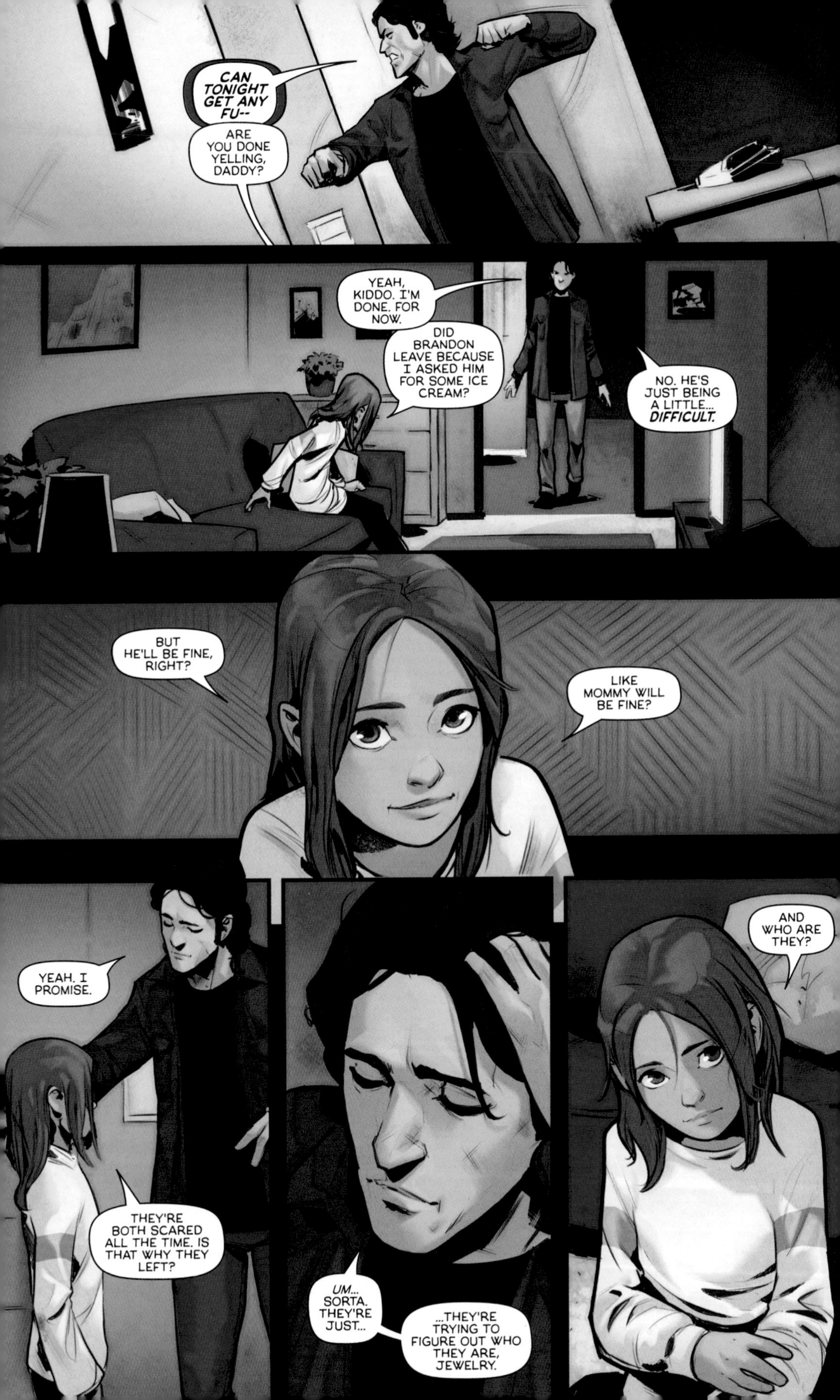

CAN TONIGHT GET ANY FU--
ARE YOU DONE YELLING, DADDY?
YEAH, KIDDO. I'M DONE. FOR NOW.
DID BRANDON LEAVE BECAUSE I ASKED HIM FOR SOME ICE CREAM?
NO. HE'S JUST BEING A LITTLE... ***DIFFICULT.***
BUT HE'LL BE FINE, RIGHT?
LIKE MOMMY WILL BE FINE?
YEAH. I PROMISE.
THEY'RE BOTH SCARED ALL THE TIME. IS THAT WHY THEY LEFT?
UM... SORTA. THEY'RE JUST...
...THEY'RE TRYING TO FIGURE OUT WHO THEY ARE, JEWELRY.
AND WHO ARE THEY?

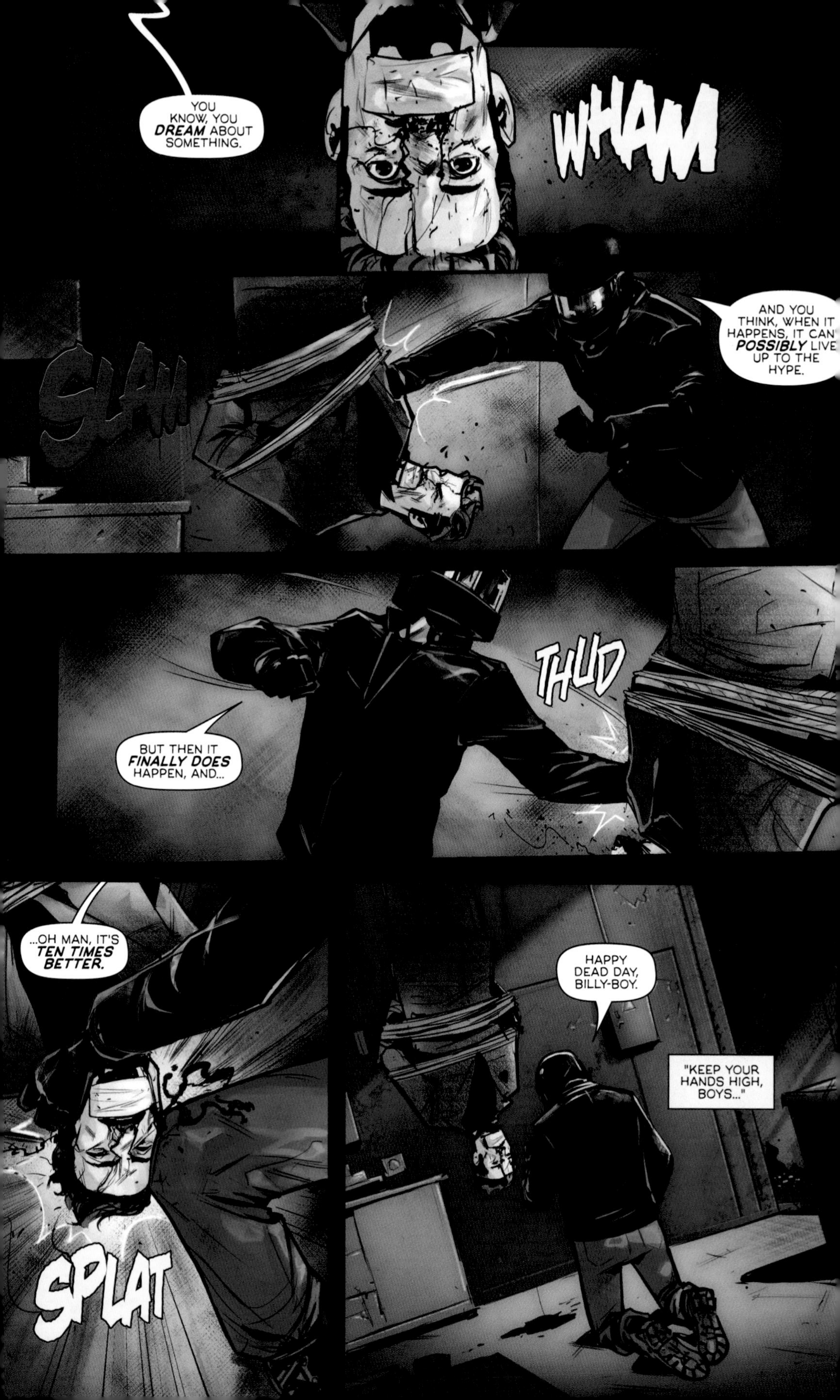

YOU KNOW, YOU *DREAM* ABOUT SOMETHING.
WHAM
AND YOU THINK, WHEN IT HAPPENS, IT CAN *POSSIBLY* LIVE UP TO THE HYPE.
SLAM
THUD
BUT THEN IT *FINALLY DOES* HAPPEN, AND...
...OH MAN, IT'S *TEN TIMES BETTER.*
SPLAT
HAPPY DEAD DAY, BILLY-BOY.
"KEEP YOUR HANDS HIGH, BOYS..."

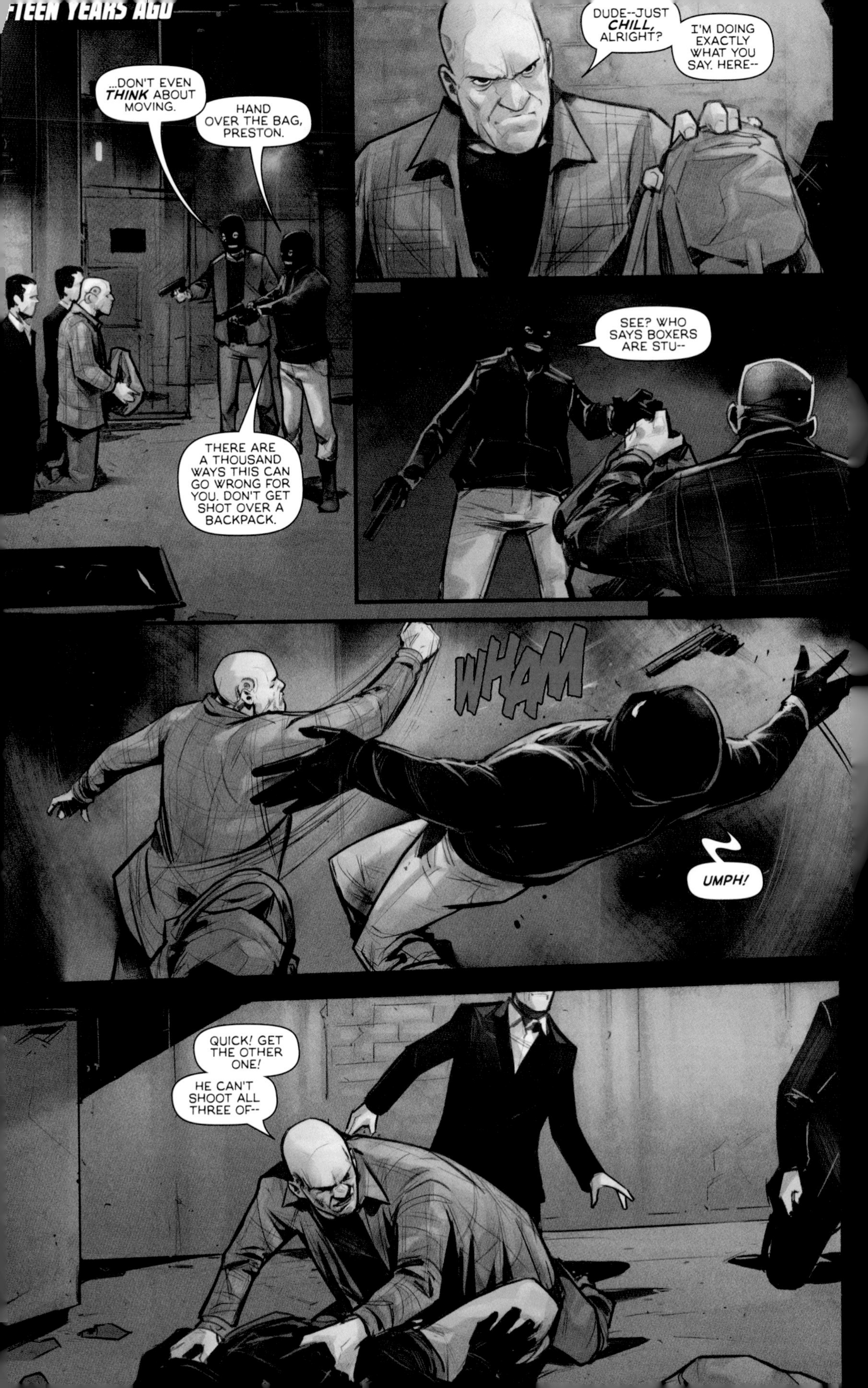

FTEEN YEARS AGO
...DON'T EVEN THINK ABOUT MOVING.
HAND OVER THE BAG, PRESTON.
THERE ARE A THOUSAND WAYS THIS CAN GO WRONG FOR YOU. DON'T GET SHOT OVER A BACKPACK.
DUDE--JUST CHILL, ALRIGHT?
I'M DOING EXACTLY WHAT YOU SAY. HERE--
SEE? WHO SAYS BOXERS ARE STU--
WHAM
UMPH!
QUICK! GET THE OTHER ONE!
HE CAN'T SHOOT ALL THREE OF--

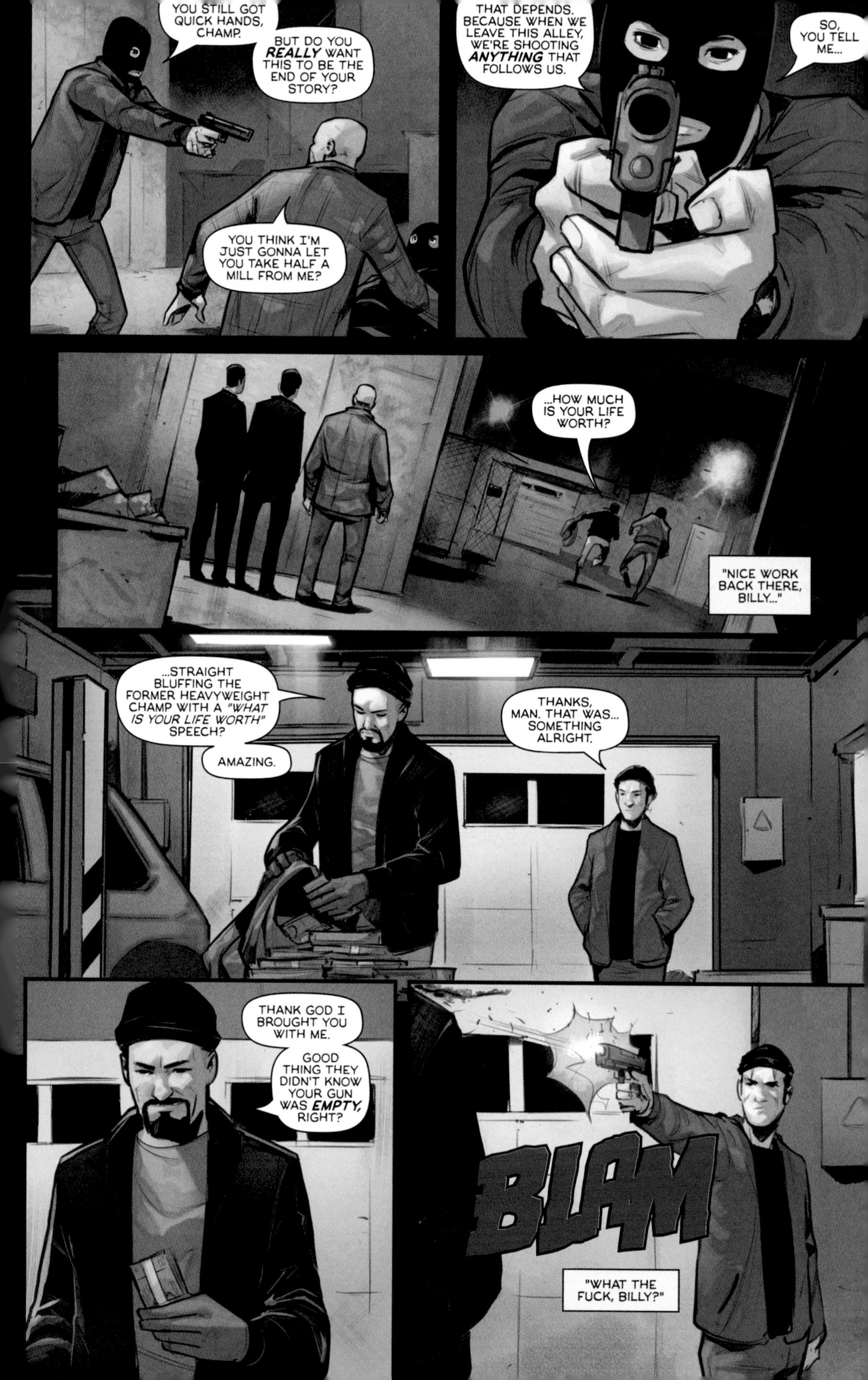
YOU STILL GOT QUICK HANDS, CHAMP.
BUT DO YOU REALLY WANT THIS TO BE THE END OF YOUR STORY?
YOU THINK I'M JUST GONNA LET YOU TAKE HALF A MILL FROM ME?
THAT DEPENDS. BECAUSE WHEN WE LEAVE THIS ALLEY, WE'RE SHOOTING ANYTHING THAT FOLLOWS US.
SO, YOU TELL ME...
...HOW MUCH IS YOUR LIFE WORTH?
"NICE WORK BACK THERE, BILLY..."
...STRAIGHT BLUFFING THE FORMER HEAVYWEIGHT CHAMP WITH A "WHAT IS YOUR LIFE WORTH" SPEECH?
AMAZING.
THANKS, MAN. THAT WAS... SOMETHING ALRIGHT.
THANK GOD I BROUGHT YOU WITH ME.
GOOD THING THEY DIDN'T KNOW YOUR GUN WAS EMPTY, RIGHT?
BLAM
"WHAT THE FUCK, BILLY?"

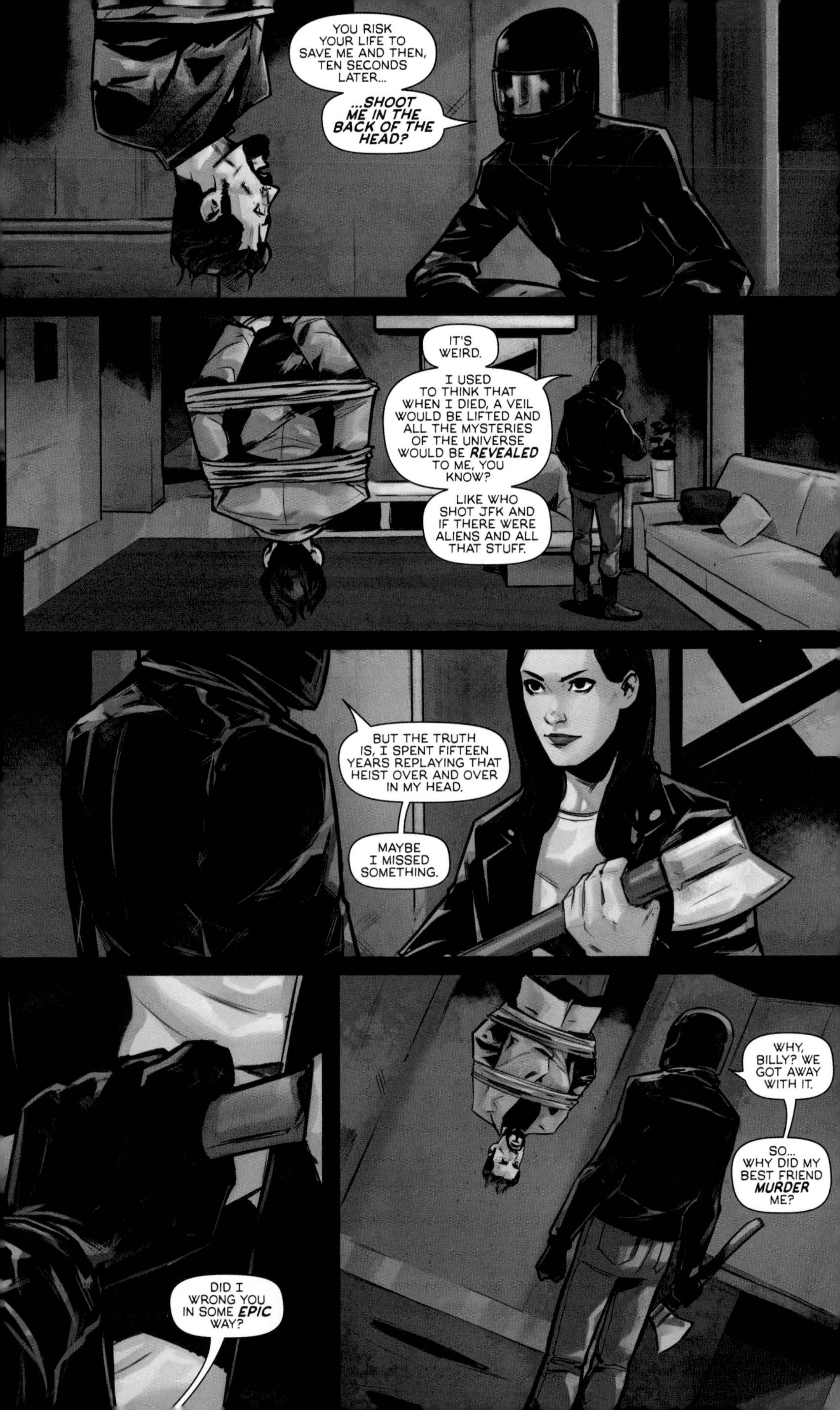

YOU RISK YOUR LIFE TO SAVE ME AND THEN, TEN SECONDS LATER...
...SHOOT ME IN THE BACK OF THE HEAD?
IT'S WEIRD.
I USED TO THINK THAT WHEN I DIED, A VEIL WOULD BE LIFTED AND ALL THE MYSTERIES OF THE UNIVERSE WOULD BE REVEALED TO ME, YOU KNOW?
LIKE WHO SHOT JFK AND IF THERE WERE ALIENS AND ALL THAT STUFF.
BUT THE TRUTH IS, I SPENT FIFTEEN YEARS REPLAYING THAT HEIST OVER AND OVER IN MY HEAD.
MAYBE I MISSED SOMETHING.
DID I WRONG YOU IN SOME EPIC WAY?
WHY, BILLY? WE GOT AWAY WITH IT.
SO... WHY DID MY BEST FRIEND MURDER ME?

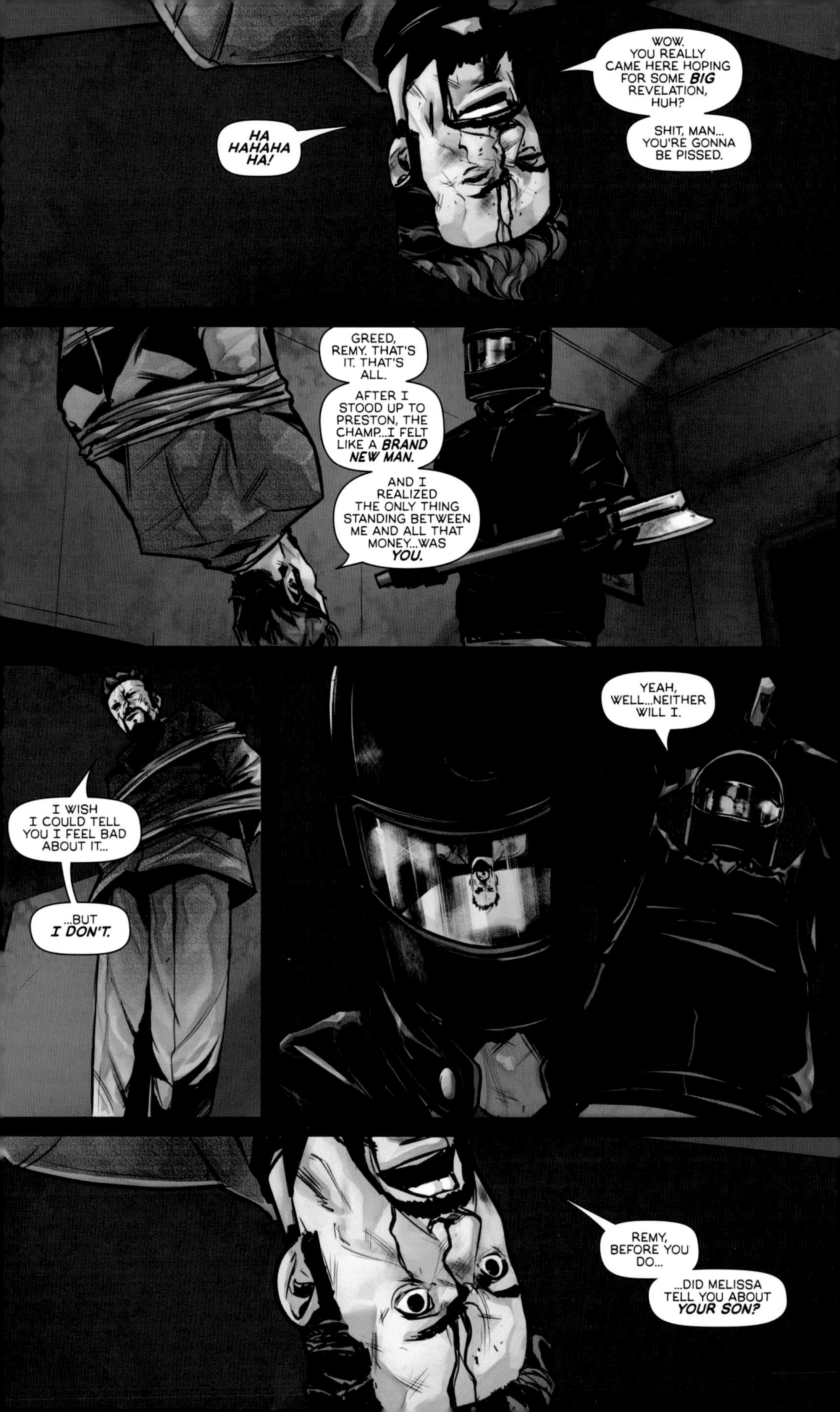
HA HAHAHA HA!
WOW. YOU REALLY CAME HERE HOPING FOR SOME BIG REVELATION, HUH?
SHIT, MAN... YOU'RE GONNA BE PISSED.
GREED, REMY. THAT'S IT. THAT'S ALL.
AFTER I STOOD UP TO PRESTON, THE CHAMP...I FELT LIKE A BRAND NEW MAN.
AND I REALIZED THE ONLY THING STANDING BETWEEN ME AND ALL THAT MONEY...WAS YOU.
I WISH I COULD TELL YOU I FEEL BAD ABOUT IT...
...BUT I DON'T.
YEAH, WELL...NEITHER WILL I.
REMY, BEFORE YOU DO...
...DID MELISSA TELL YOU ABOUT YOUR SON?

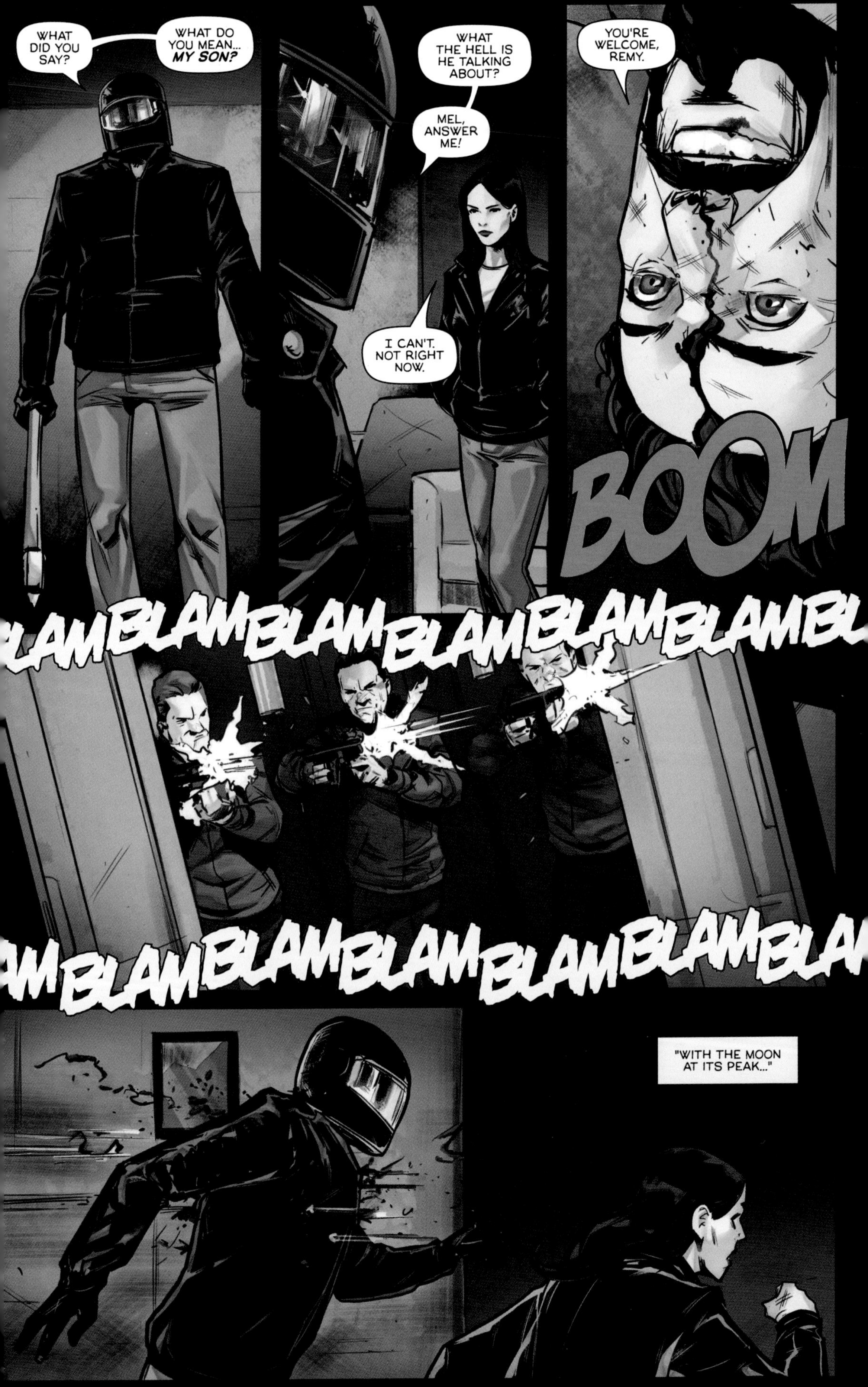
WHAT DID YOU SAY?
WHAT DO YOU MEAN... *MY SON?*
WHAT THE HELL IS HE TALKING ABOUT?
MEL, ANSWER ME!
I CAN'T. NOT RIGHT NOW.
YOU'RE WELCOME, REMY.
BOOM
BLAM BLAM BLAM BLAM BLAM
BLAM BLAM BLAM BLAM BLAM
"WITH THE MOON AT ITS PEAK..."

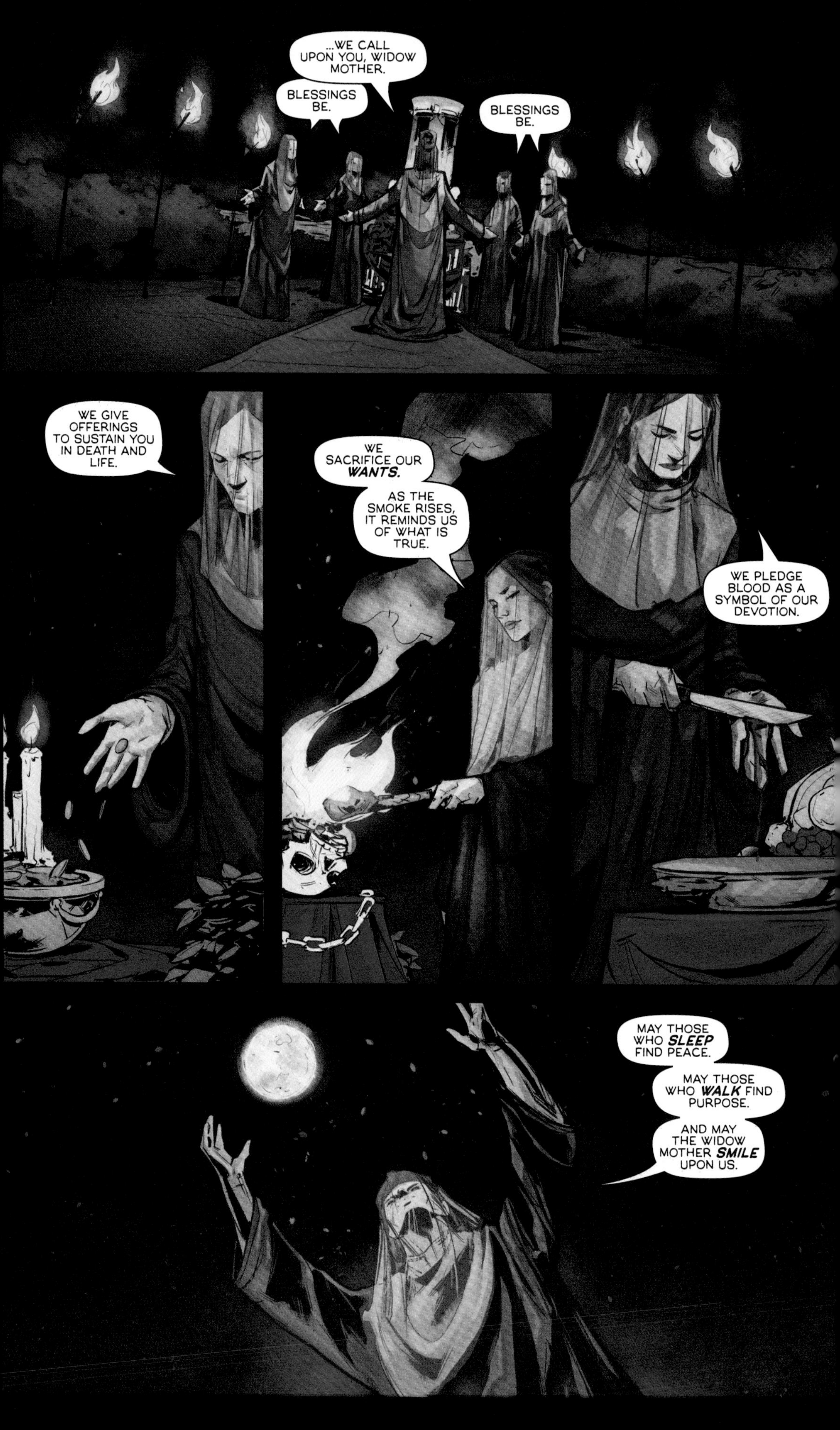
...WE CALL UPON YOU, WIDOW MOTHER.
BLESSINGS BE.
BLESSINGS BE.
WE GIVE OFFERINGS TO SUSTAIN YOU IN DEATH AND LIFE.
WE SACRIFICE OUR WANTS.
AS THE SMOKE RISES, IT REMINDS US OF WHAT IS TRUE.
WE PLEDGE BLOOD AS A SYMBOL OF OUR DEVOTION.
MAY THOSE WHO SLEEP FIND PEACE.
MAY THOSE WHO WALK FIND PURPOSE.
AND MAY THE WIDOW MOTHER SMILE UPON US.

I THINK ZACK AND I NEED TO GET GOING.
BRANDON, I KNOW IT CAN SEEM A LITTLE CRAZY, BUT--
A LITTLE? LILY, I'M LITERALLY WAITING FOR YOU TO SACRIFICE A VIRGIN...
...WHICH I JUST REALIZED COULD BE ME.
YOU DON'T ACTUALLY BELIEVE IN ALL THIS STUFF, DO YOU?
I DO, YES.
MY PARENTS DIDN'T USED TO BELIEVE. WE NEVER WENT TO CHURCH. THERE WAS NO GOD. NO DEVIL.
THEN MY BROTHER CAME BACK THAT FIRST DEAD DAY.
AND FOR A NIGHT, WE WERE A FAMILY AGAIN.
WOW. I...I...
I DON'T EXPECT YOU TO UNDER-STAND.
I DON'T KNOW...

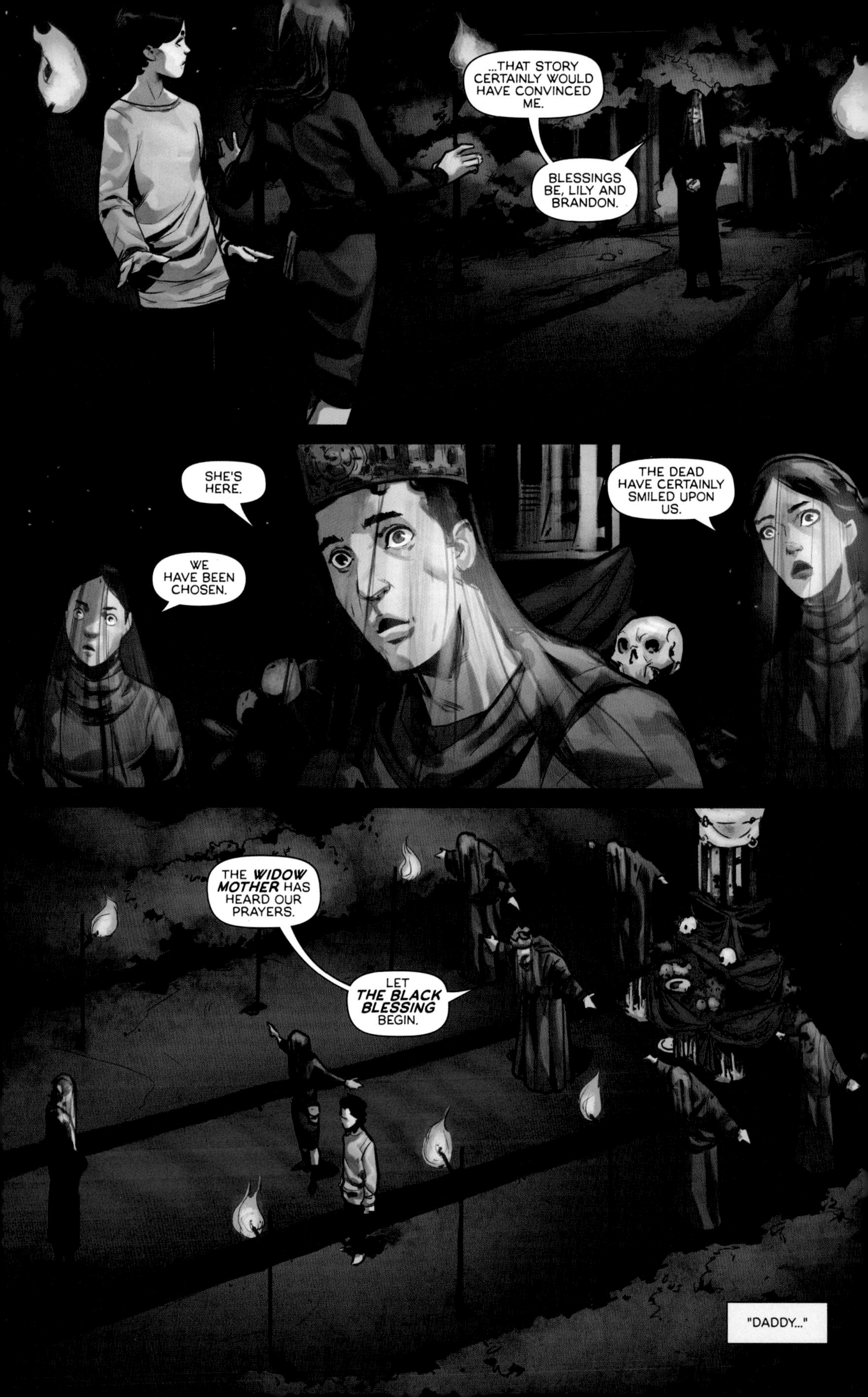
...THAT STORY CERTAINLY WOULD HAVE CONVINCED ME.
BLESSINGS BE, LILY AND BRANDON.
SHE'S HERE.
WE HAVE BEEN CHOSEN.
THE DEAD HAVE CERTAINLY SMILED UPON US.
THE *WIDOW MOTHER* HAS HEARD OUR PRAYERS.
LET *THE BLACK BLESSING* BEGIN.
"DADDY..."

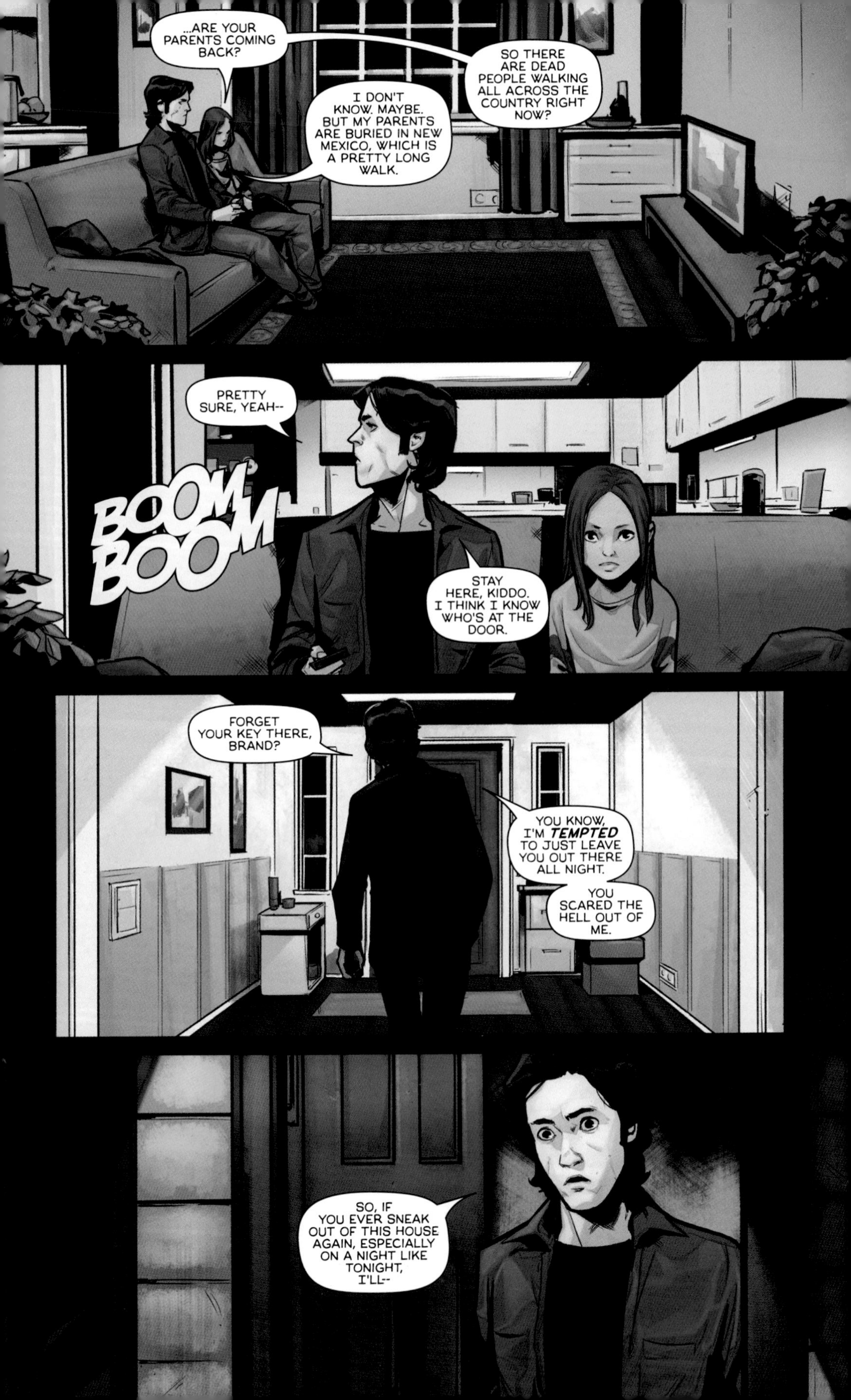
...ARE YOUR PARENTS COMING BACK?
I DON'T KNOW. MAYBE. BUT MY PARENTS ARE BURIED IN NEW MEXICO, WHICH IS A PRETTY LONG WALK.
SO THERE ARE DEAD PEOPLE WALKING ALL ACROSS THE COUNTRY RIGHT NOW?
PRETTY SURE, YEAH--
BOOM BOOM
STAY HERE, KIDDO. I THINK I KNOW WHO'S AT THE DOOR.
FORGET YOUR KEY THERE, BRAND?
YOU KNOW, I'M *TEMPTED* TO JUST LEAVE YOU OUT THERE ALL NIGHT.
YOU SCARED THE HELL OUT OF ME.
SO, IF YOU EVER SNEAK OUT OF THIS HOUSE AGAIN, ESPECIALLY ON A NIGHT LIKE TONIGHT, I'LL--

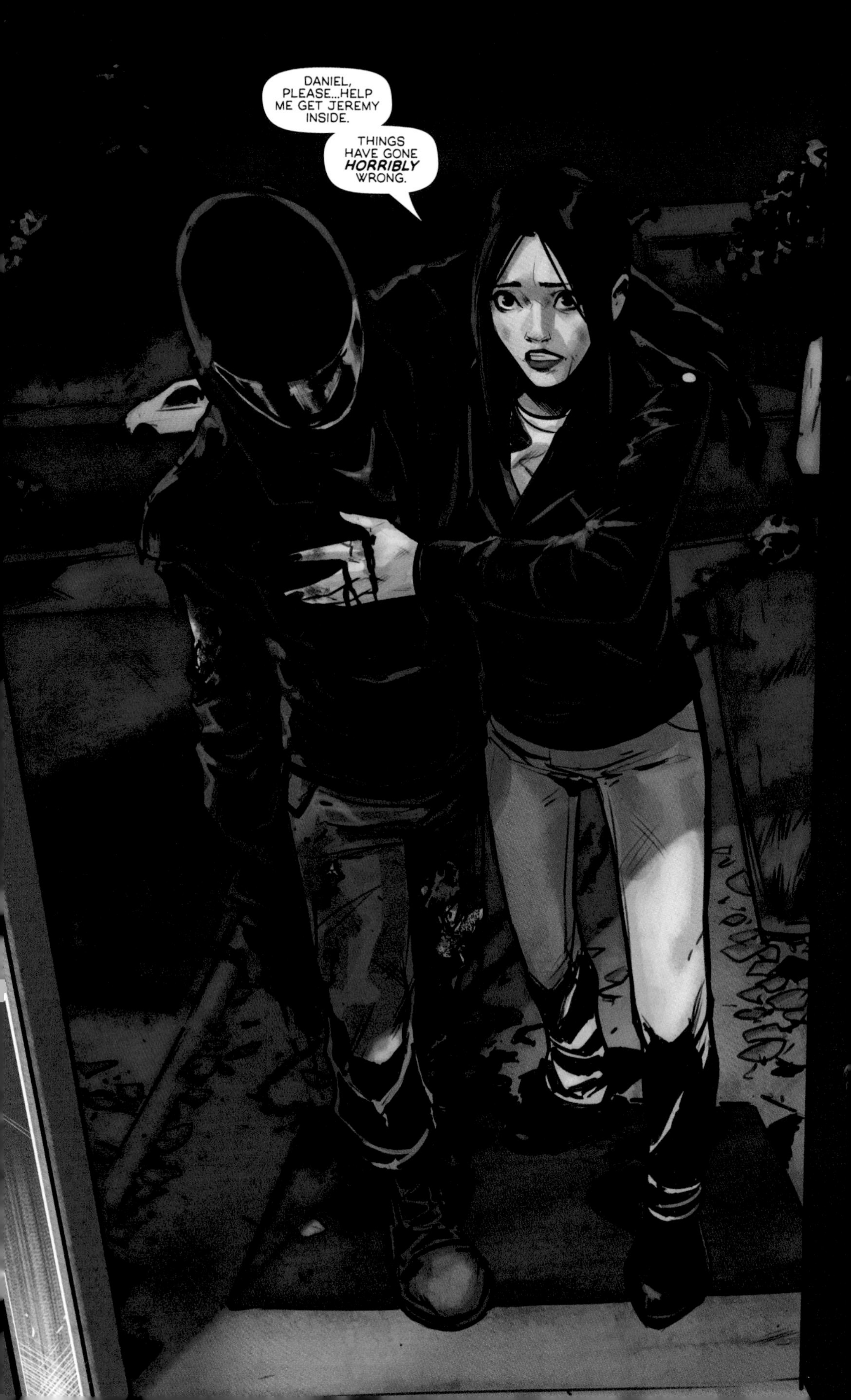
DANIEL, PLEASE...HELP ME GET JEREMY INSIDE.
THINGS HAVE GONE *HORRIBLY* WRONG.

4

CHAPTER FOUR

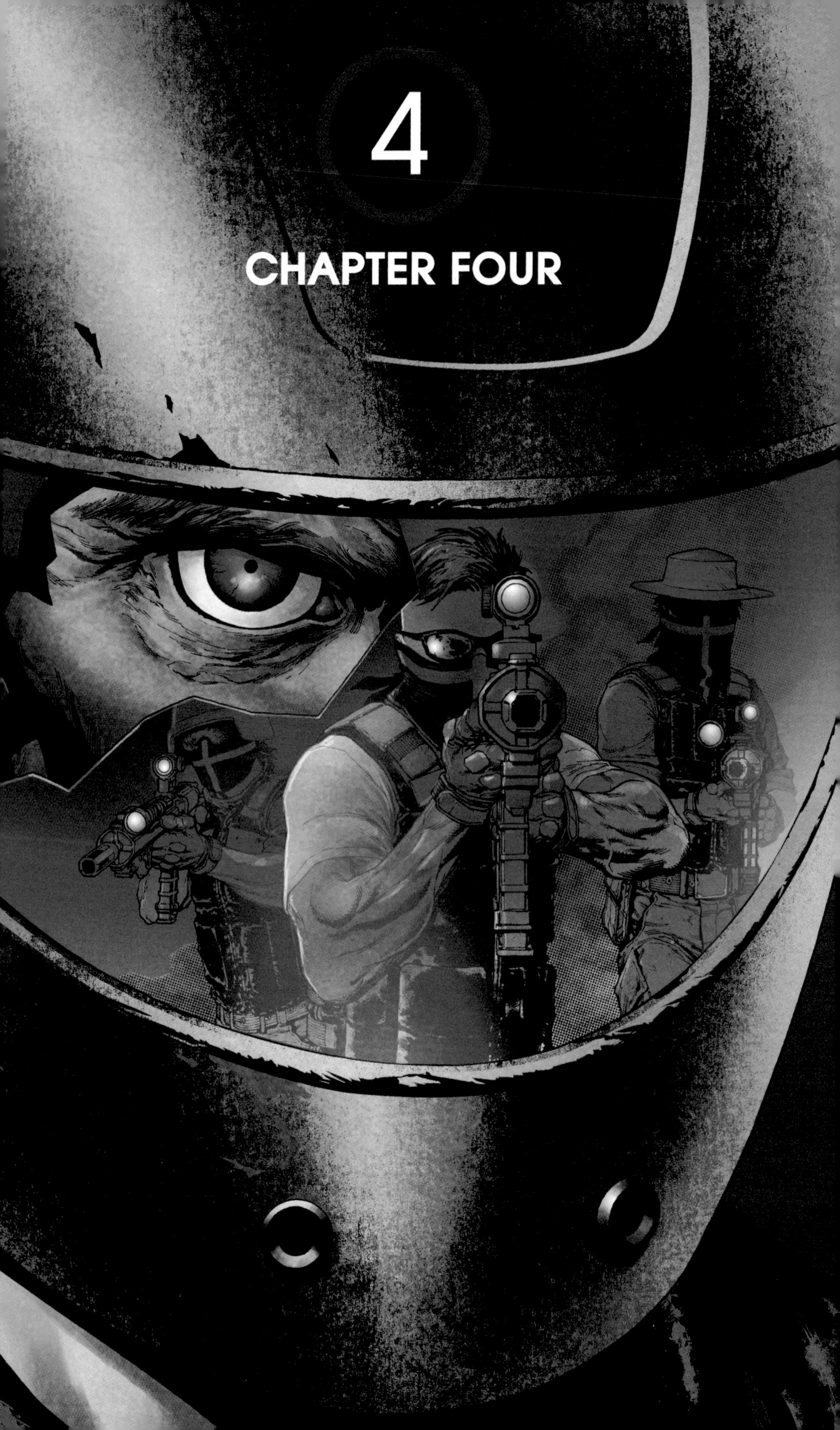

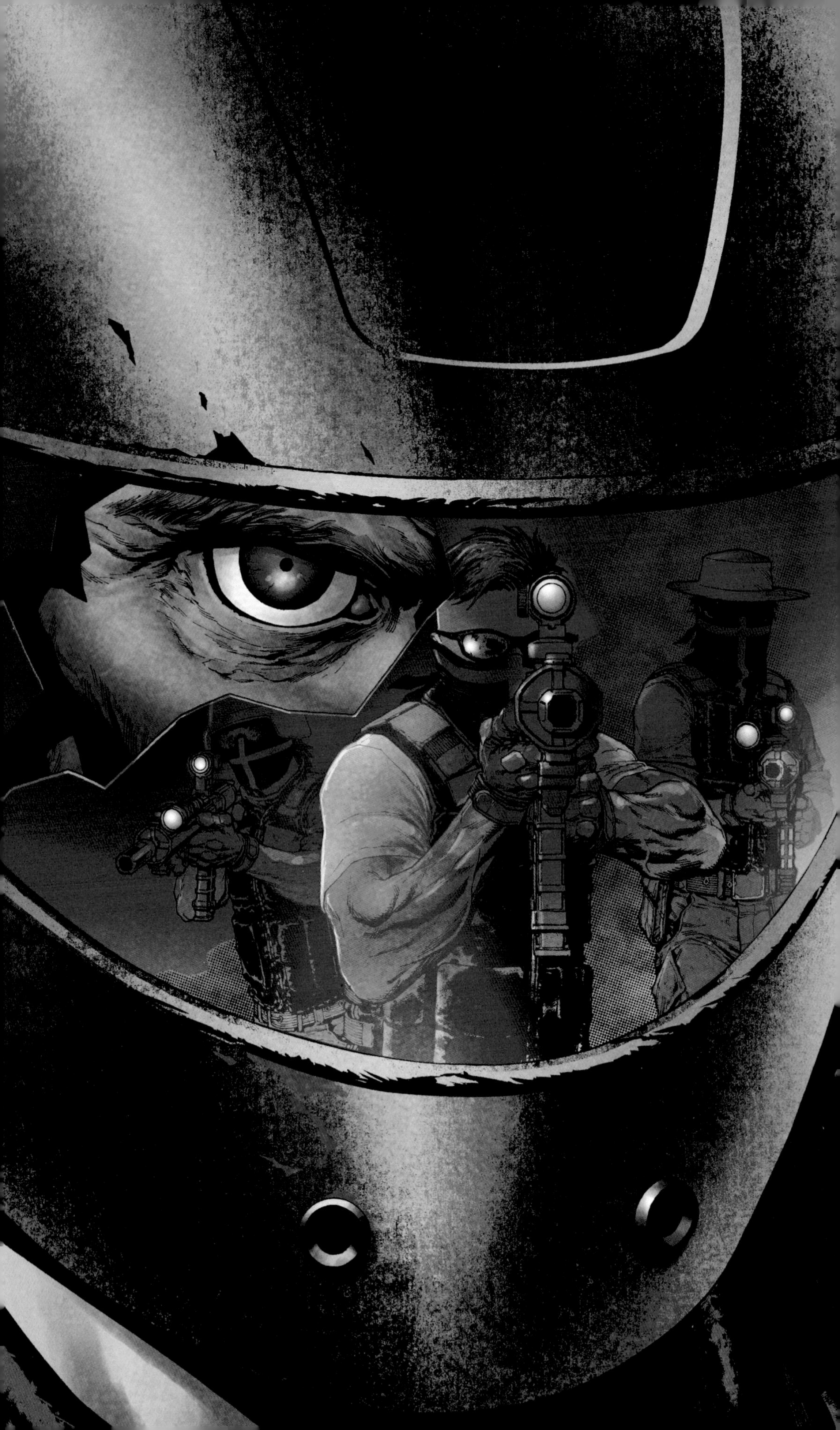

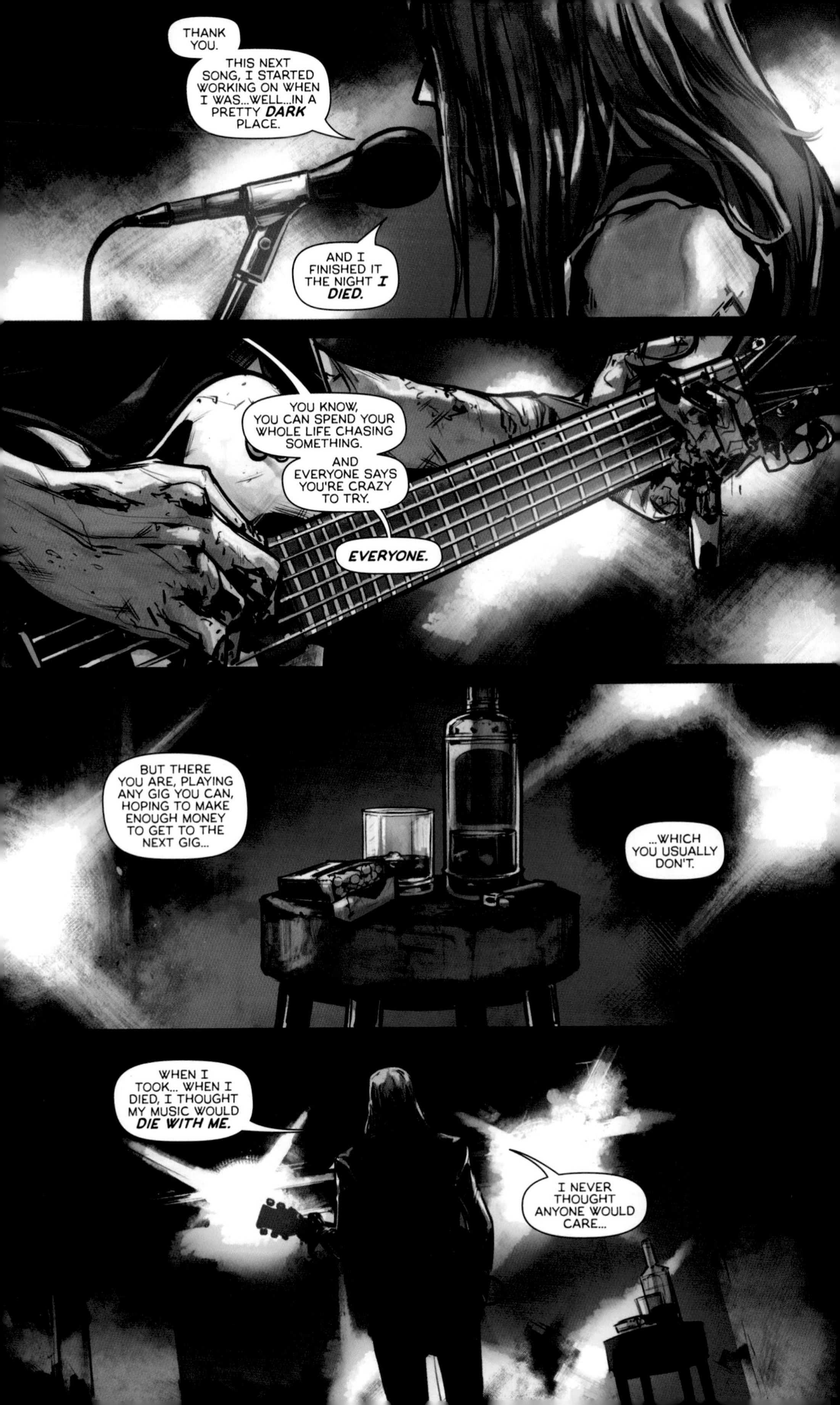
THANK YOU.
THIS NEXT SONG, I STARTED WORKING ON WHEN I WAS...WELL...IN A PRETTY DARK PLACE.
AND I FINISHED IT THE NIGHT I DIED.
YOU KNOW, YOU CAN SPEND YOUR WHOLE LIFE CHASING SOMETHING.
AND EVERYONE SAYS YOU'RE CRAZY TO TRY.
EVERYONE.
BUT THERE YOU ARE, PLAYING ANY GIG YOU CAN, HOPING TO MAKE ENOUGH MONEY TO GET TO THE NEXT GIG...
...WHICH YOU USUALLY DON'T.
WHEN I TOOK... WHEN I DIED, I THOUGHT MY MUSIC WOULD DIE WITH ME.
I NEVER THOUGHT ANYONE WOULD CARE...

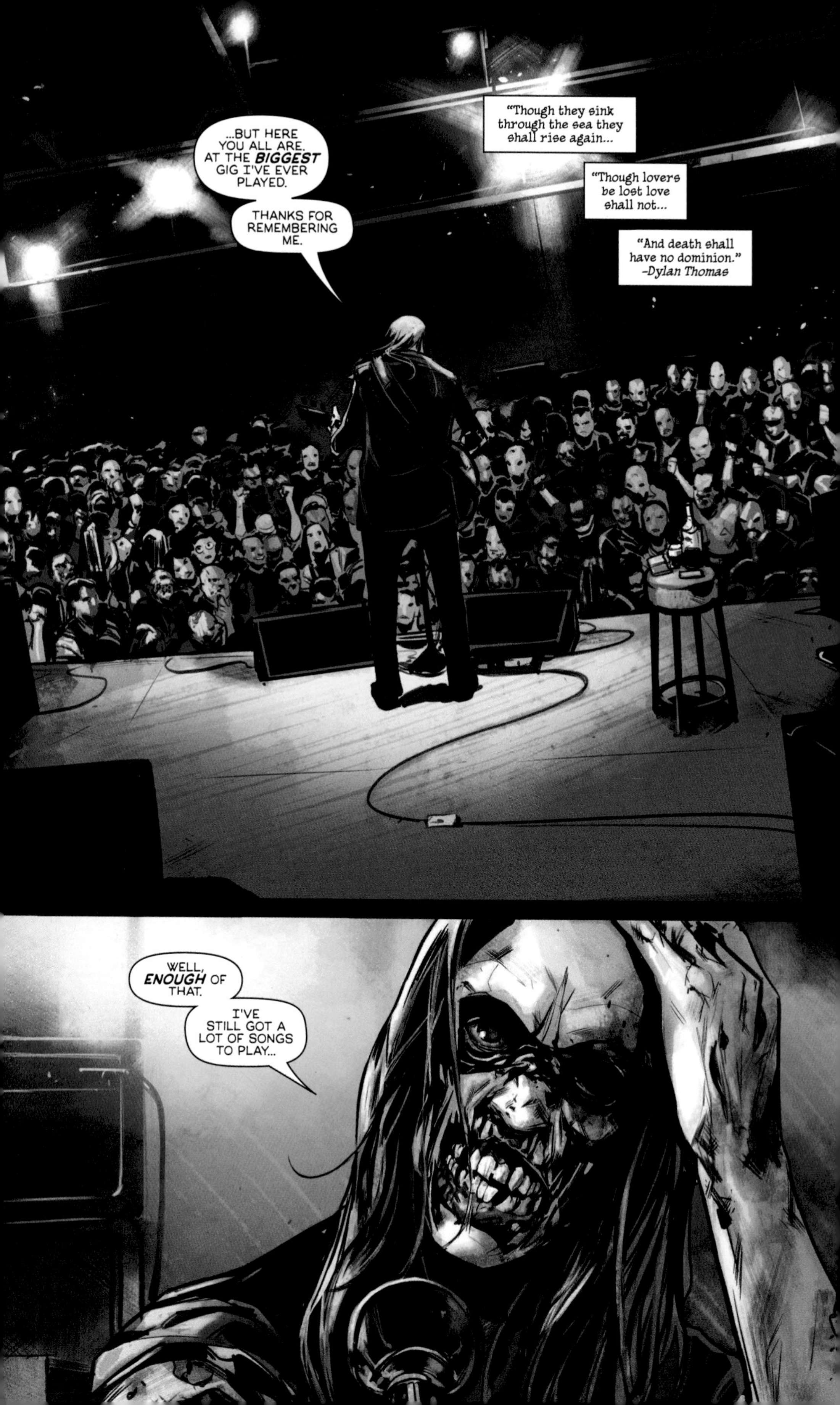

...BUT HERE YOU ALL ARE. AT THE ***BIGGEST*** GIG I'VE EVER PLAYED.
THANKS FOR REMEMBERING ME.
"Though they sink through the sea they shall rise again...
"Though lovers be lost love shall not...
"And death shall have no dominion." –Dylan Thomas
WELL, ***ENOUGH*** OF THAT.
I'VE STILL GOT A LOT OF SONGS TO PLAY...

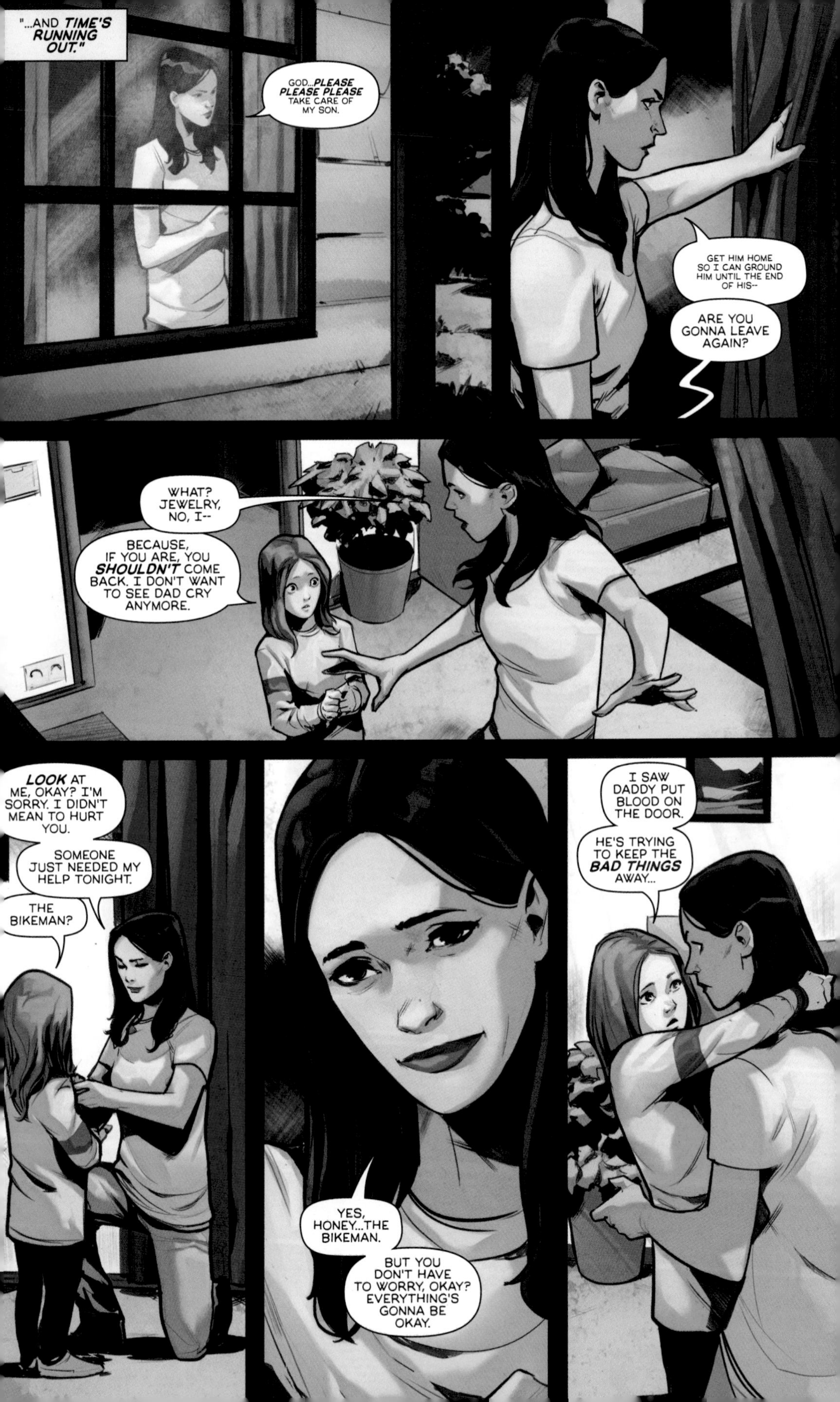
"...AND TIME'S RUNNING OUT."
GOD...PLEASE PLEASE PLEASE TAKE CARE OF MY SON.
GET HIM HOME SO I CAN GROUND HIM UNTIL THE END OF HIS--
ARE YOU GONNA LEAVE AGAIN?
WHAT? JEWELRY, NO, I--
BECAUSE, IF YOU ARE, YOU SHOULDN'T COME BACK. I DON'T WANT TO SEE DAD CRY ANYMORE.
LOOK AT ME, OKAY? I'M SORRY. I DIDN'T MEAN TO HURT YOU.
SOMEONE JUST NEEDED MY HELP TONIGHT.
THE BIKEMAN?
YES, HONEY...THE BIKEMAN.
BUT YOU DON'T HAVE TO WORRY, OKAY? EVERYTHING'S GONNA BE OKAY.
I SAW DADDY PUT BLOOD ON THE DOOR.
HE'S TRYING TO KEEP THE BAD THINGS AWAY...

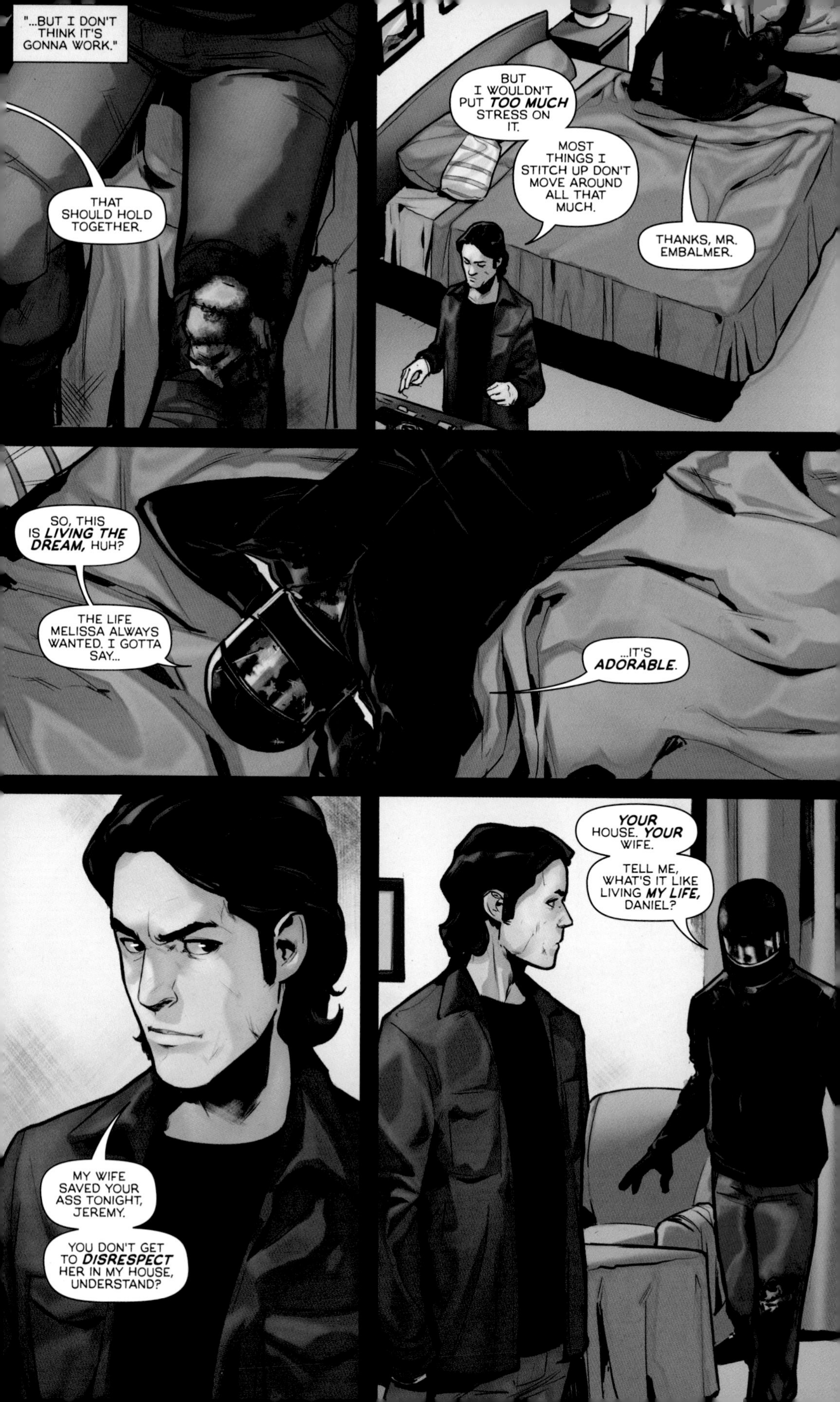
"...BUT I DON'T THINK IT'S GONNA WORK."
THAT SHOULD HOLD TOGETHER.
BUT I WOULDN'T PUT TOO MUCH STRESS ON IT.
MOST THINGS I STITCH UP DON'T MOVE AROUND ALL THAT MUCH.
THANKS, MR. EMBALMER.
SO, THIS IS LIVING THE DREAM, HUH?
THE LIFE MELISSA ALWAYS WANTED. I GOTTA SAY...
...IT'S ADORABLE.
MY WIFE SAVED YOUR ASS TONIGHT, JEREMY.
YOU DON'T GET TO DISRESPECT HER IN MY HOUSE, UNDERSTAND?
YOUR HOUSE. YOUR WIFE.
TELL ME, WHAT'S IT LIKE LIVING MY LIFE, DANIEL?

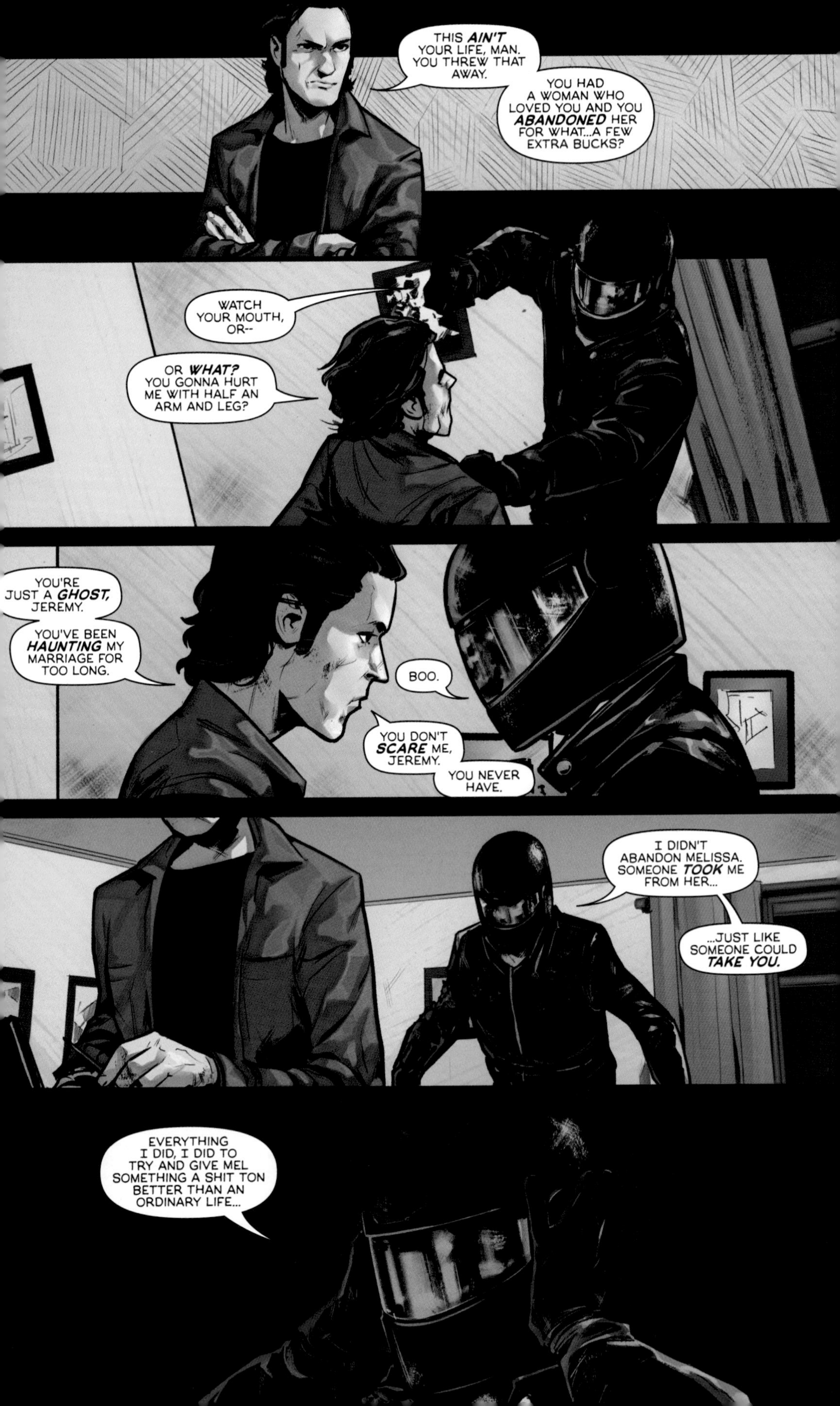
THIS AIN'T YOUR LIFE, MAN. YOU THREW THAT AWAY.
YOU HAD A WOMAN WHO LOVED YOU AND YOU ABANDONED HER FOR WHAT...A FEW EXTRA BUCKS?
WATCH YOUR MOUTH, OR--
OR WHAT? YOU GONNA HURT ME WITH HALF AN ARM AND LEG?
YOU'RE JUST A GHOST, JEREMY.
YOU'VE BEEN HAUNTING MY MARRIAGE FOR TOO LONG.
BOO.
YOU DON'T SCARE ME, JEREMY.
YOU NEVER HAVE.
I DIDN'T ABANDON MELISSA. SOMEONE TOOK ME FROM HER...
...JUST LIKE SOMEONE COULD TAKE YOU.
EVERYTHING I DID, I DID TO TRY AND GIVE MEL SOMETHING A SHIT TON BETTER THAN AN ORDINARY LIFE...

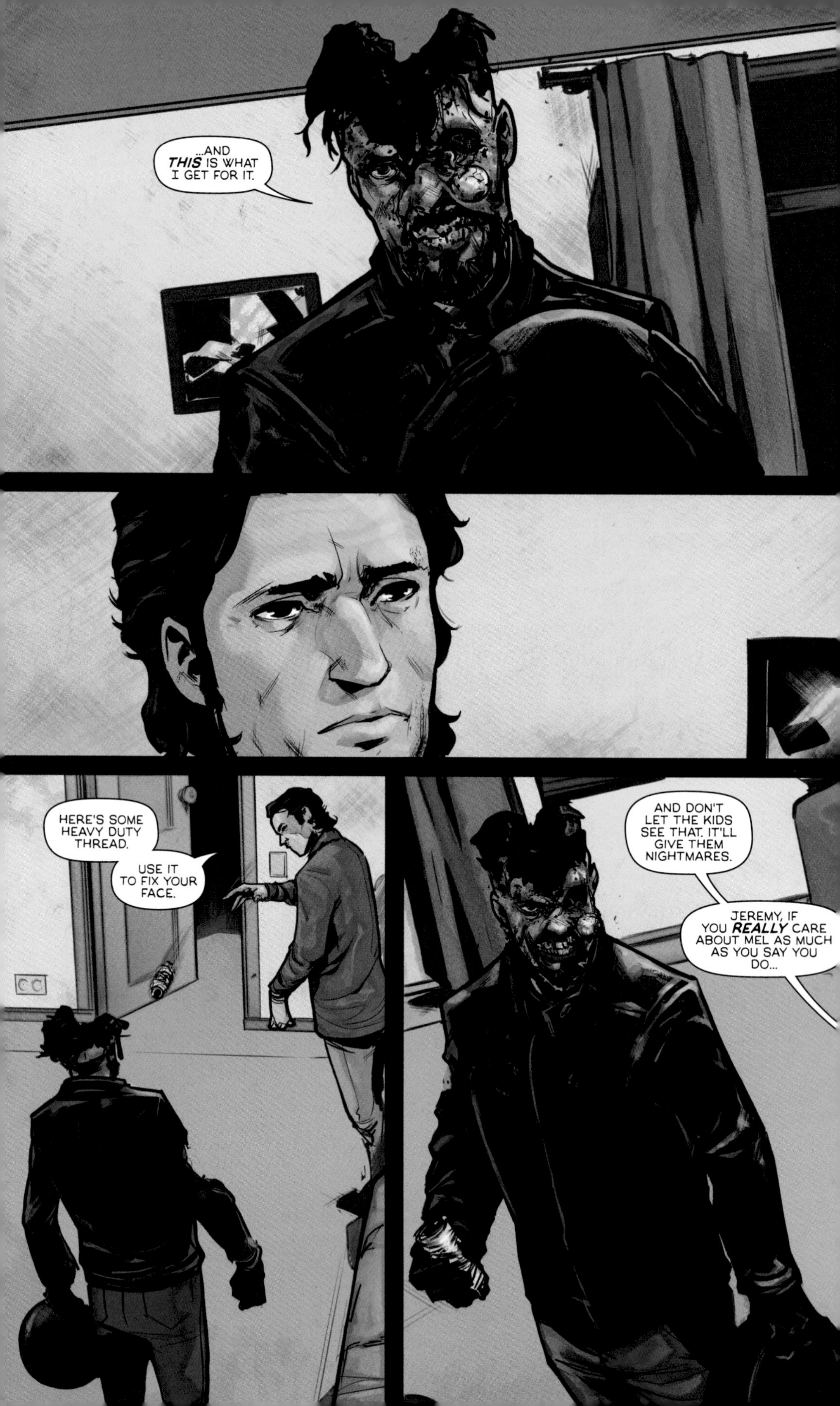
...AND THIS IS WHAT I GET FOR IT.
HERE'S SOME HEAVY DUTY THREAD.
USE IT TO FIX YOUR FACE.
AND DON'T LET THE KIDS SEE THAT. IT'LL GIVE THEM NIGHTMARES.
JEREMY, IF YOU REALLY CARE ABOUT MEL AS MUCH AS YOU SAY YOU DO...

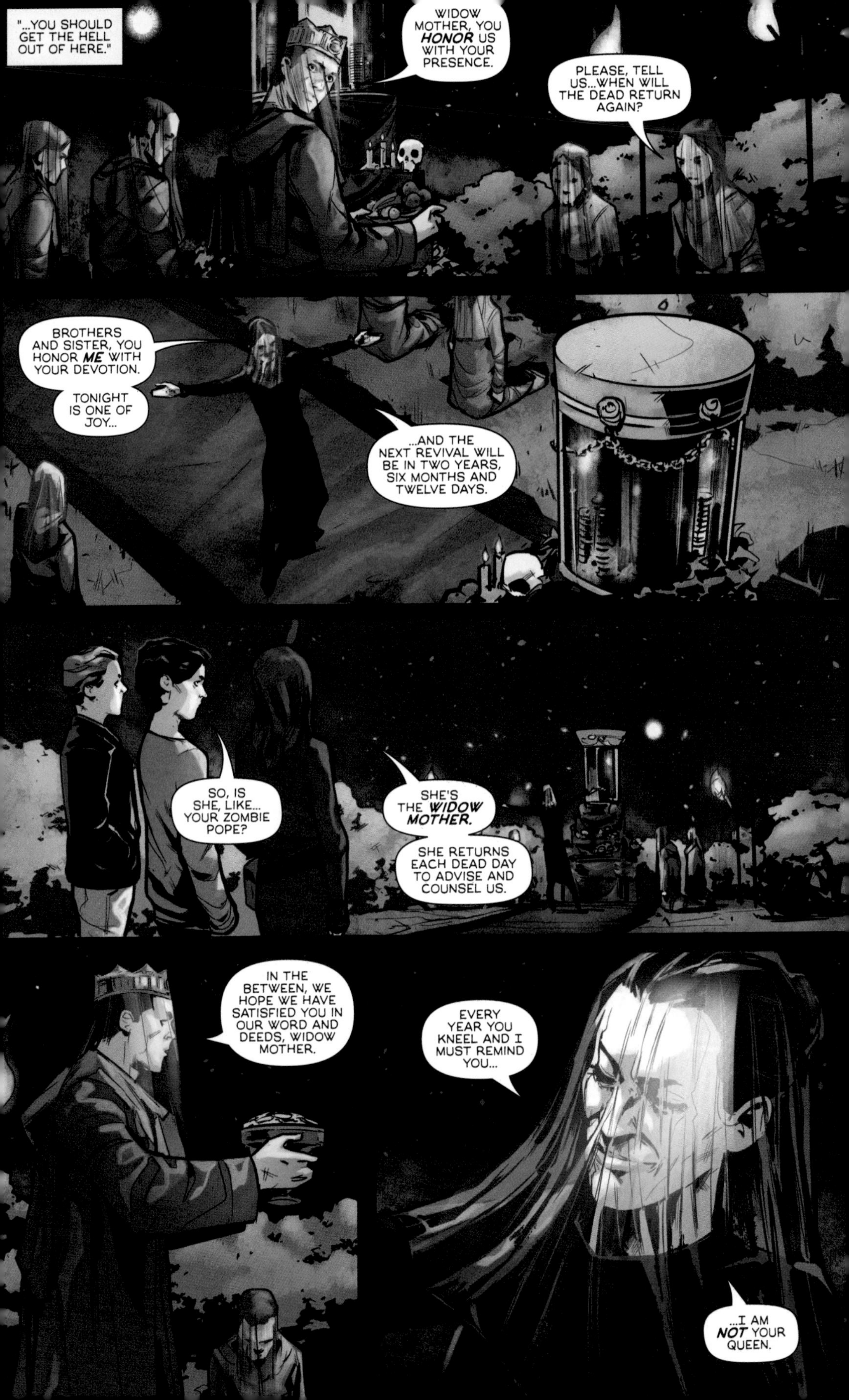
"...YOU SHOULD GET THE HELL OUT OF HERE."
WIDOW MOTHER, YOU HONOR US WITH YOUR PRESENCE.
PLEASE, TELL US...WHEN WILL THE DEAD RETURN AGAIN?
BROTHERS AND SISTER, YOU HONOR ME WITH YOUR DEVOTION.
TONIGHT IS ONE OF JOY...
...AND THE NEXT REVIVAL WILL BE IN TWO YEARS, SIX MONTHS AND TWELVE DAYS.
SO, IS SHE, LIKE... YOUR ZOMBIE POPE?
SHE'S THE WIDOW MOTHER.
SHE RETURNS EACH DEAD DAY TO ADVISE AND COUNSEL US.
IN THE BETWEEN, WE HOPE WE HAVE SATISFIED YOU IN OUR WORD AND DEEDS, WIDOW MOTHER.
EVERY YEAR YOU KNEEL AND I MUST REMIND YOU...
...I AM NOT YOUR QUEEN.

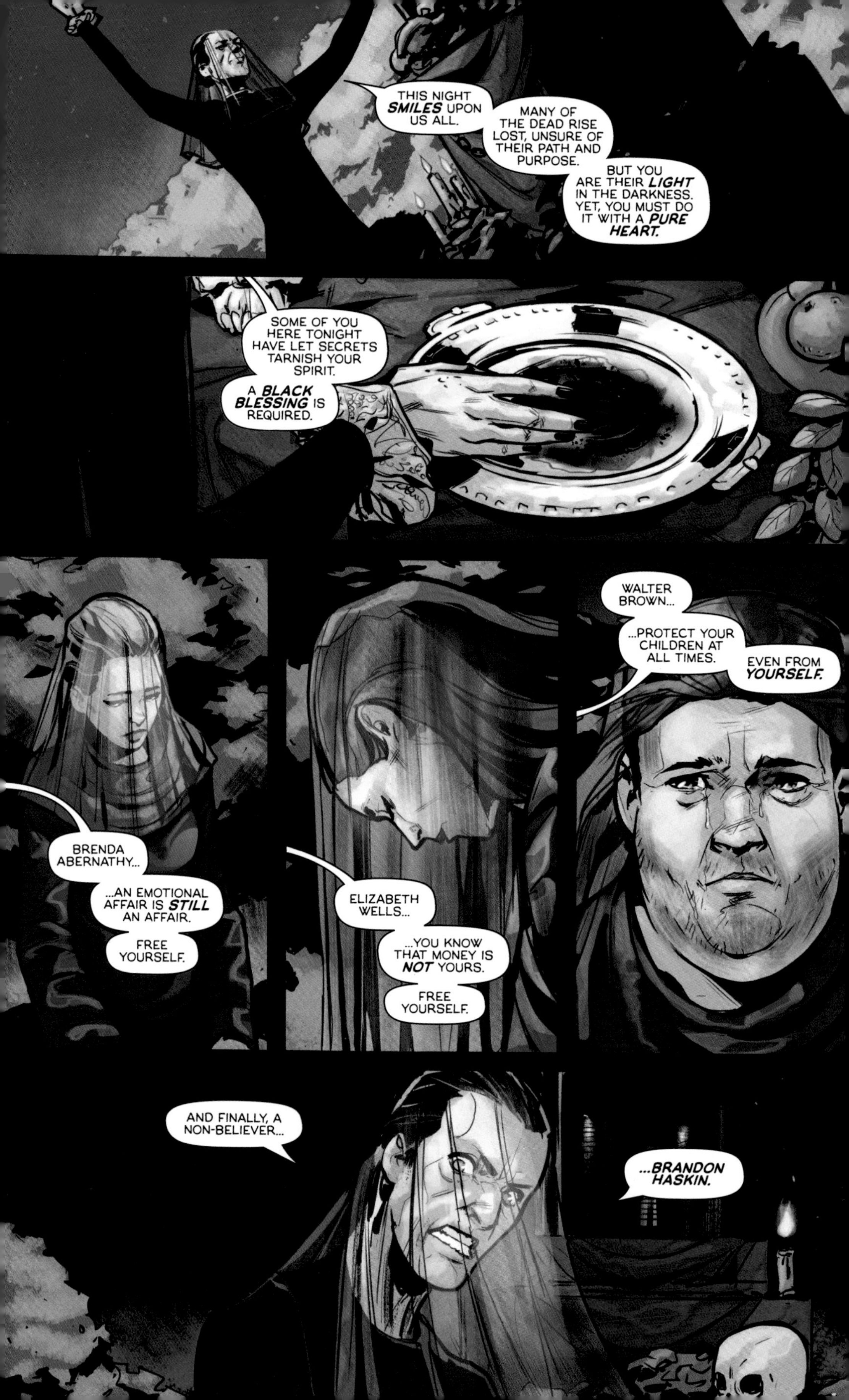
THIS NIGHT SMILES UPON US ALL.
MANY OF THE DEAD RISE LOST, UNSURE OF THEIR PATH AND PURPOSE.
BUT YOU ARE THEIR LIGHT IN THE DARKNESS. YET, YOU MUST DO IT WITH A PURE HEART.
SOME OF YOU HERE TONIGHT HAVE LET SECRETS TARNISH YOUR SPIRIT.
A BLACK BLESSING IS REQUIRED.
BRENDA ABERNATHY...
...AN EMOTIONAL AFFAIR IS STILL AN AFFAIR.
FREE YOURSELF.
ELIZABETH WELLS...
...YOU KNOW THAT MONEY IS NOT YOURS.
FREE YOURSELF.
WALTER BROWN...
...PROTECT YOUR CHILDREN AT ALL TIMES.
EVEN FROM YOURSELF.
AND FINALLY, A NON-BELIEVER...
...BRANDON HASKIN.

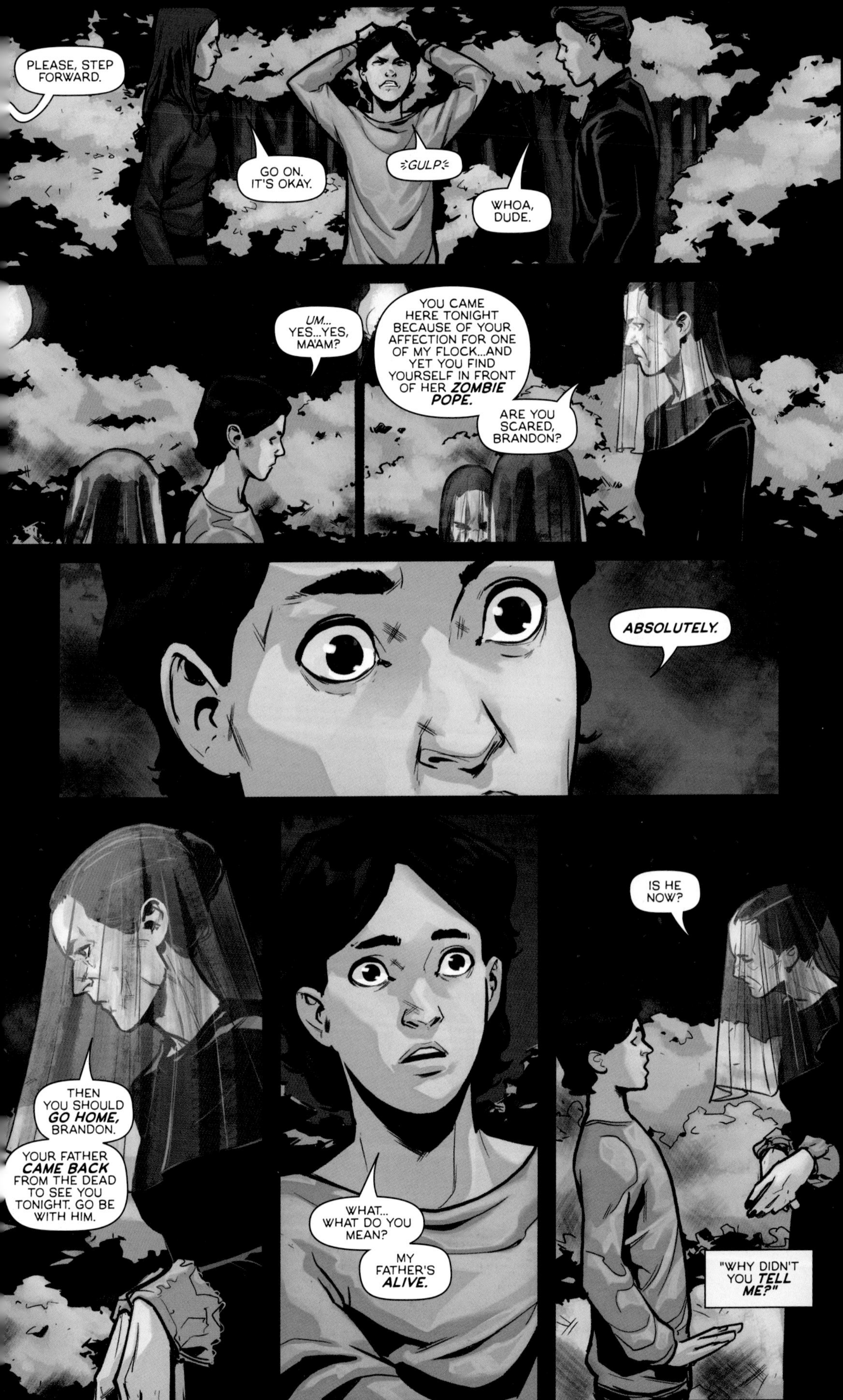
PLEASE, STEP FORWARD.
GO ON. IT'S OKAY.
GULP
WHOA, DUDE.
UM... YES...YES, MA'AM?
YOU CAME HERE TONIGHT BECAUSE OF YOUR AFFECTION FOR ONE OF MY FLOCK...AND YET YOU FIND YOURSELF IN FRONT OF HER ZOMBIE POPE.
ARE YOU SCARED, BRANDON?
ABSOLUTELY.
THEN YOU SHOULD GO HOME, BRANDON.
YOUR FATHER CAME BACK FROM THE DEAD TO SEE YOU TONIGHT. GO BE WITH HIM.
WHAT... WHAT DO YOU MEAN?
MY FATHER'S ALIVE.
IS HE NOW?
"WHY DIDN'T YOU TELL ME?"

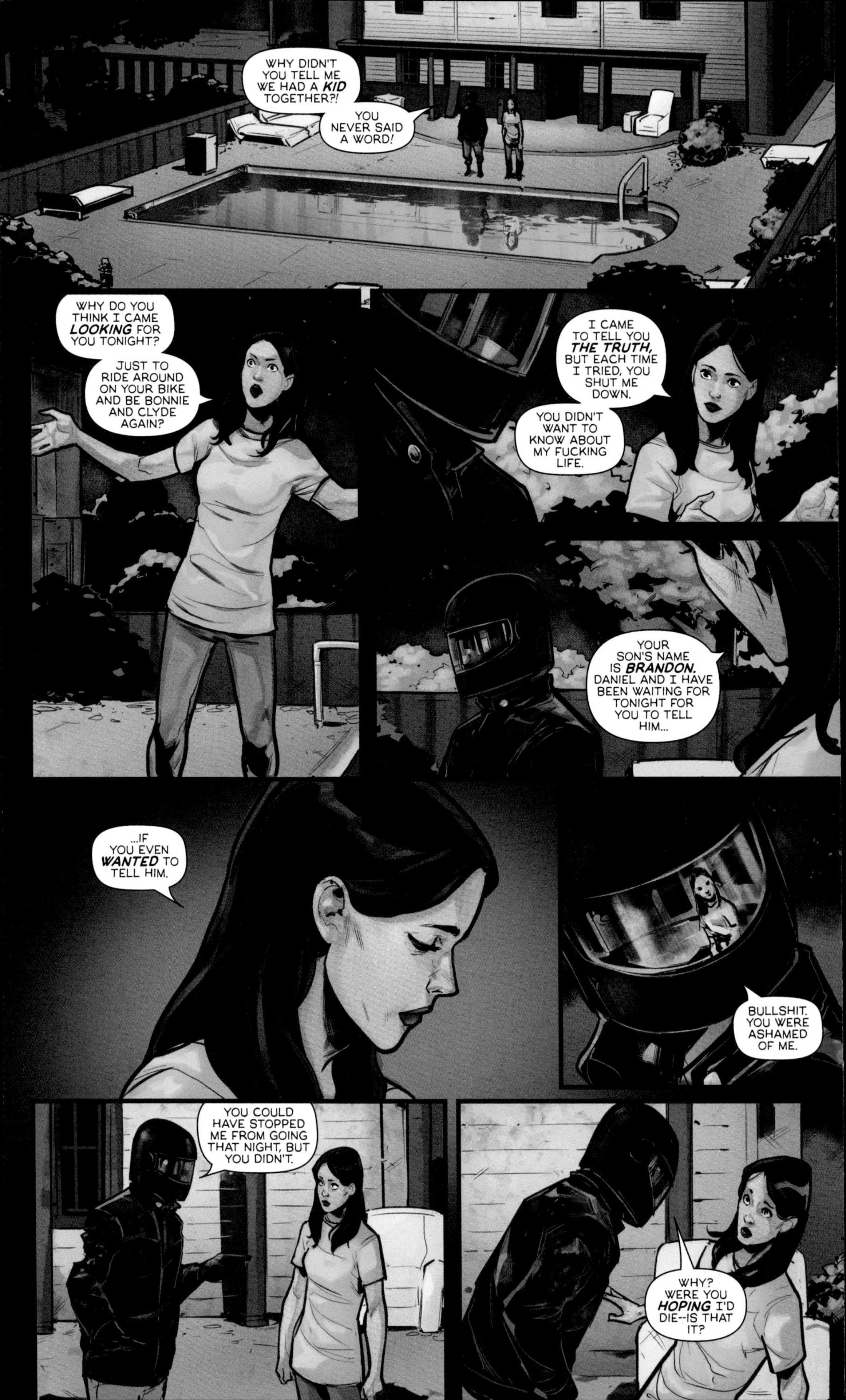
WHY DIDN'T YOU TELL ME WE HAD A *KID* TOGETHER?!
YOU NEVER SAID A WORD!
WHY DO YOU THINK I CAME *LOOKING* FOR YOU TONIGHT?
JUST TO RIDE AROUND ON YOUR BIKE AND BE BONNIE AND CLYDE AGAIN?
I CAME TO TELL YOU *THE TRUTH,* BUT EACH TIME I TRIED, YOU SHUT ME DOWN.
YOU DIDN'T WANT TO KNOW ABOUT MY FUCKING LIFE.
YOUR SON'S NAME IS *BRANDON.* DANIEL AND I HAVE BEEN WAITING FOR TONIGHT FOR YOU TO TELL HIM...
...IF YOU EVEN *WANTED* TO TELL HIM.
BULLSHIT. YOU WERE ASHAMED OF ME.
YOU COULD HAVE STOPPED ME FROM GOING THAT NIGHT, BUT YOU DIDN'T.
WHY? WERE YOU *HOPING* I'D DIE--IS THAT IT?

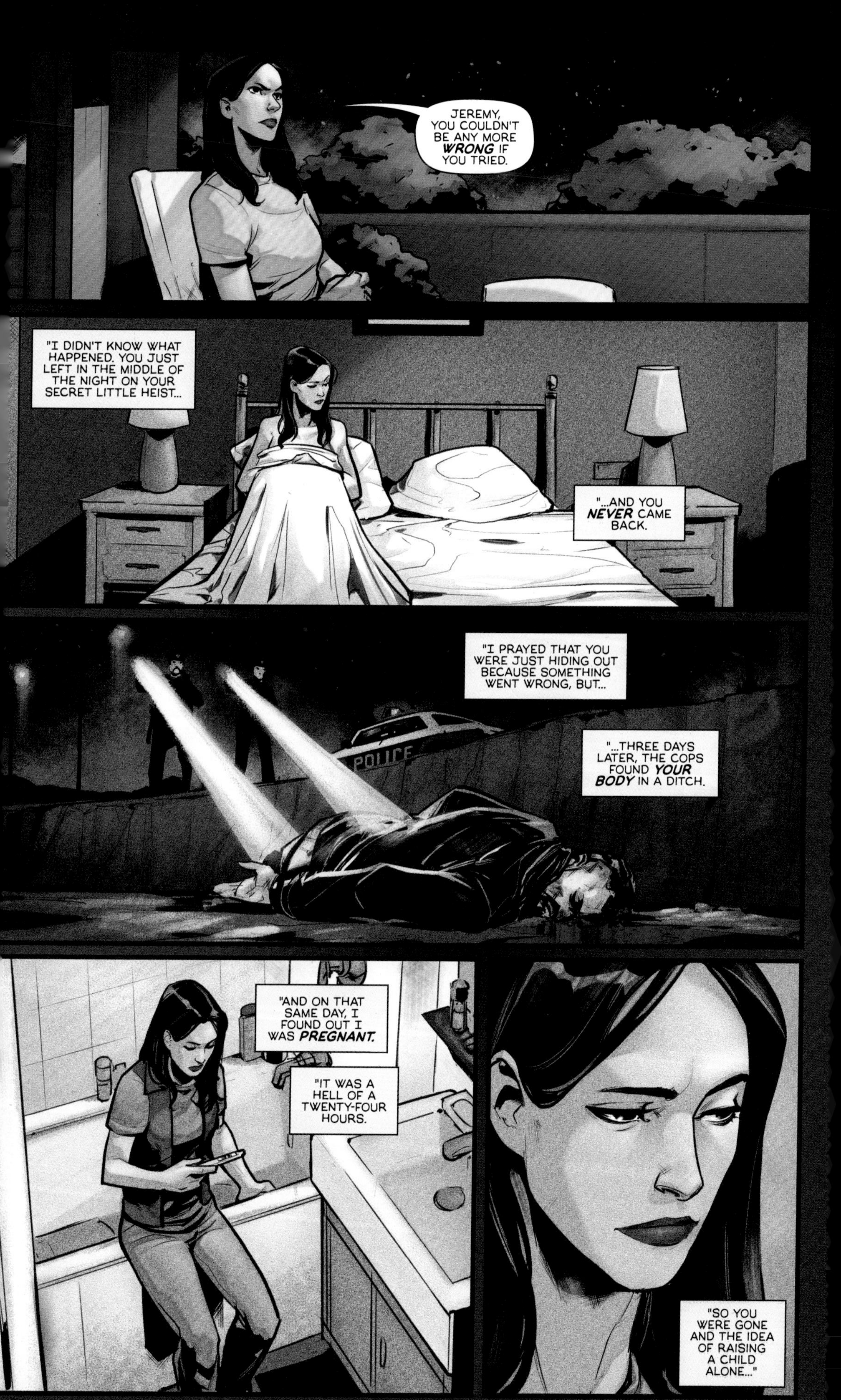

JEREMY, YOU COULDN'T BE ANY MORE WRONG IF YOU TRIED.
"I DIDN'T KNOW WHAT HAPPENED. YOU JUST LEFT IN THE MIDDLE OF THE NIGHT ON YOUR SECRET LITTLE HEIST...
"...AND YOU NEVER CAME BACK.
"I PRAYED THAT YOU WERE JUST HIDING OUT BECAUSE SOMETHING WENT WRONG, BUT...
"...THREE DAYS LATER, THE COPS FOUND YOUR BODY IN A DITCH.
POLICE
"AND ON THAT SAME DAY, I FOUND OUT I WAS PREGNANT.
"IT WAS A HELL OF A TWENTY-FOUR HOURS.
"SO YOU WERE GONE AND THE IDEA OF RAISING A CHILD ALONE..."

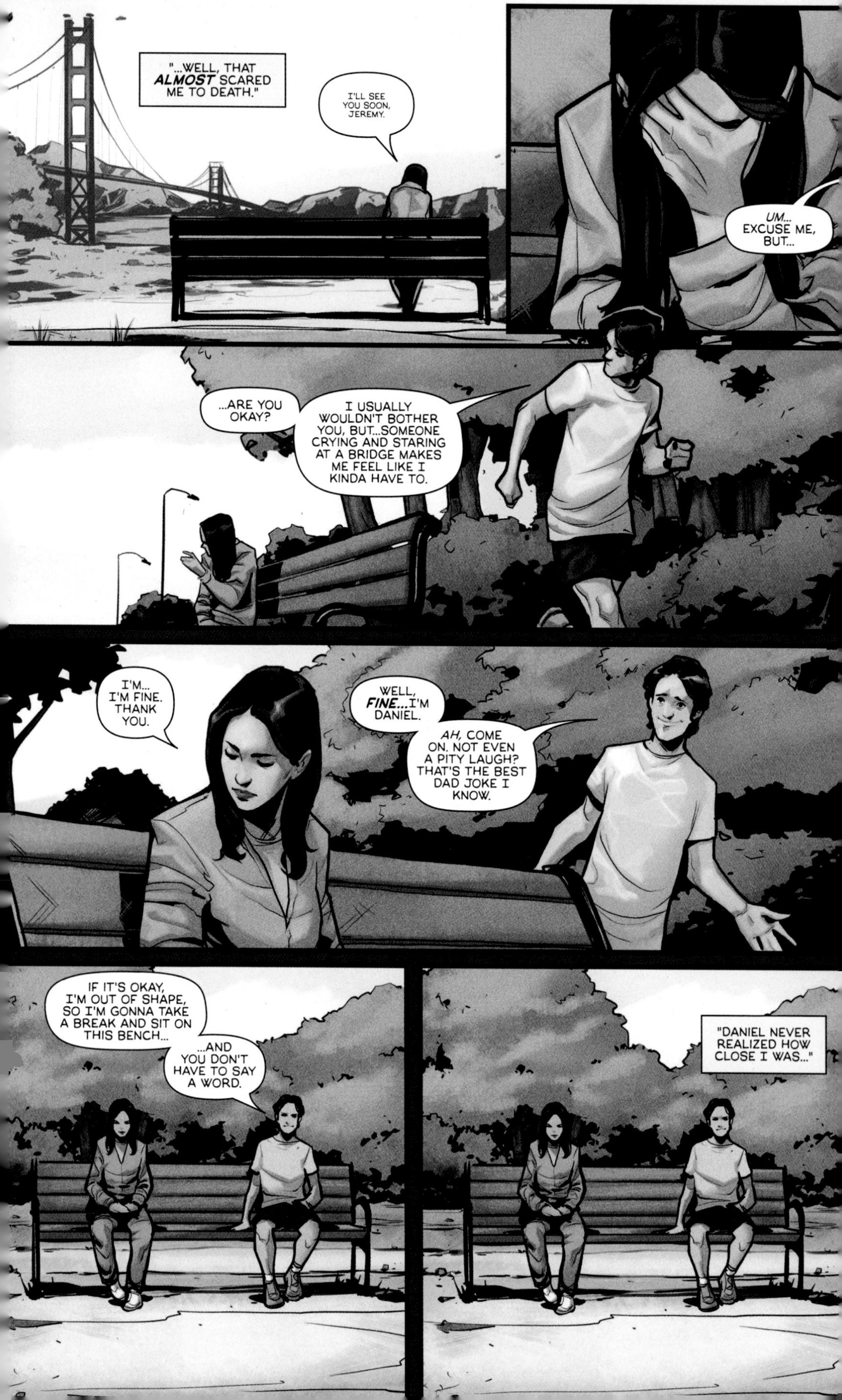

"...WELL, THAT ALMOST SCARED ME TO DEATH."
I'LL SEE YOU SOON, JEREMY.
UM... EXCUSE ME, BUT...
...ARE YOU OKAY?
I USUALLY WOULDN'T BOTHER YOU, BUT...SOMEONE CRYING AND STARING AT A BRIDGE MAKES ME FEEL LIKE I KINDA HAVE TO.
I'M... I'M FINE. THANK YOU.
WELL, FINE...I'M DANIEL.
AH, COME ON. NOT EVEN A PITY LAUGH? THAT'S THE BEST DAD JOKE I KNOW.
IF IT'S OKAY, I'M OUT OF SHAPE, SO I'M GONNA TAKE A BREAK AND SIT ON THIS BENCH...
...AND YOU DON'T HAVE TO SAY A WORD.
"DANIEL NEVER REALIZED HOW CLOSE I WAS..."

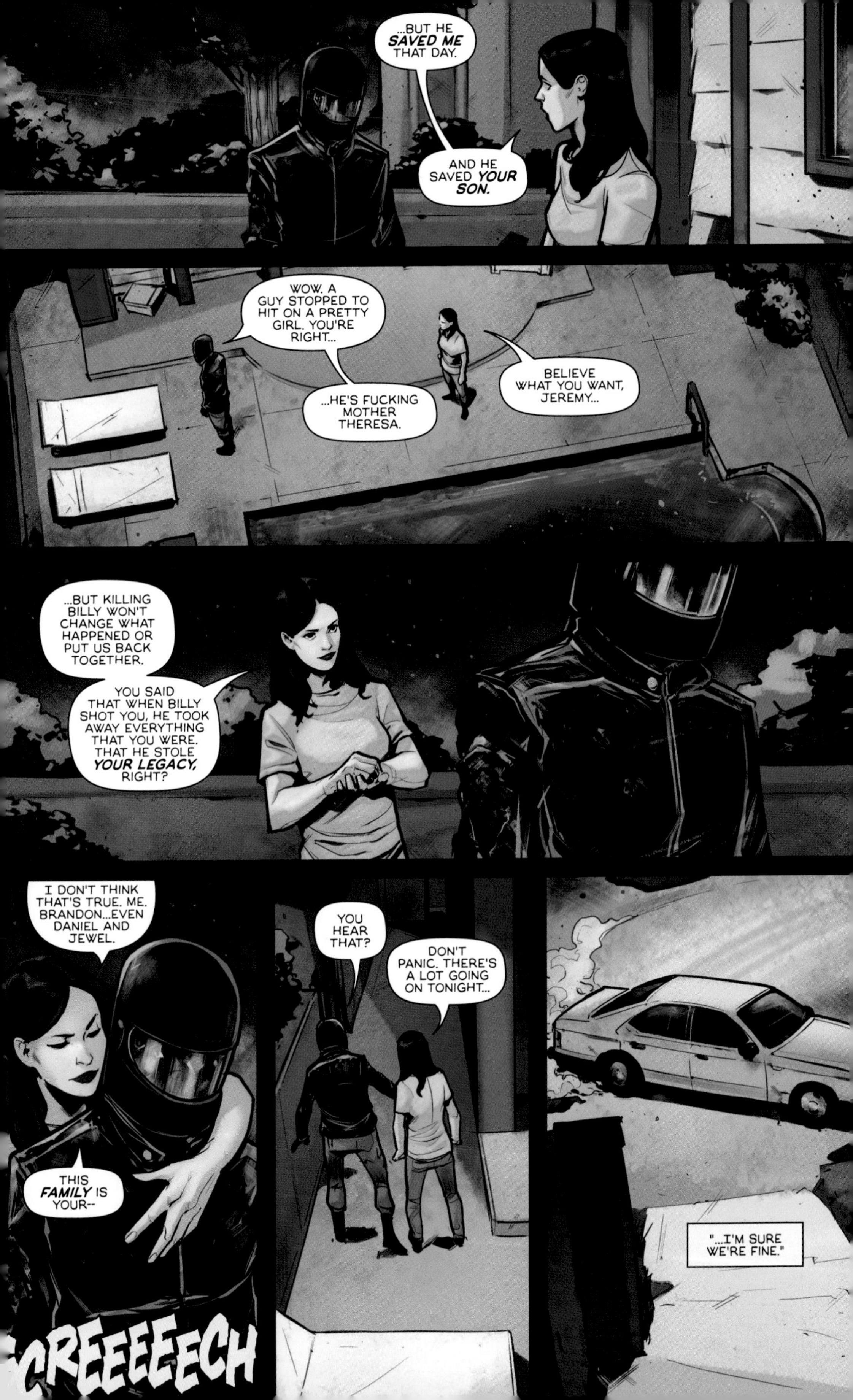
...BUT HE SAVED ME THAT DAY.
AND HE SAVED YOUR SON.
WOW. A GUY STOPPED TO HIT ON A PRETTY GIRL. YOU'RE RIGHT...
...HE'S FUCKING MOTHER THERESA.
BELIEVE WHAT YOU WANT, JEREMY...
...BUT KILLING BILLY WON'T CHANGE WHAT HAPPENED OR PUT US BACK TOGETHER.
YOU SAID THAT WHEN BILLY SHOT YOU, HE TOOK AWAY EVERYTHING THAT YOU WERE. THAT HE STOLE YOUR LEGACY, RIGHT?
I DON'T THINK THAT'S TRUE. ME. BRANDON...EVEN DANIEL AND JEWEL.
THIS FAMILY IS YOUR--
CREEEEECH
YOU HEAR THAT?
DON'T PANIC. THERE'S A LOT GOING ON TONIGHT...
"...I'M SURE WE'RE FINE."

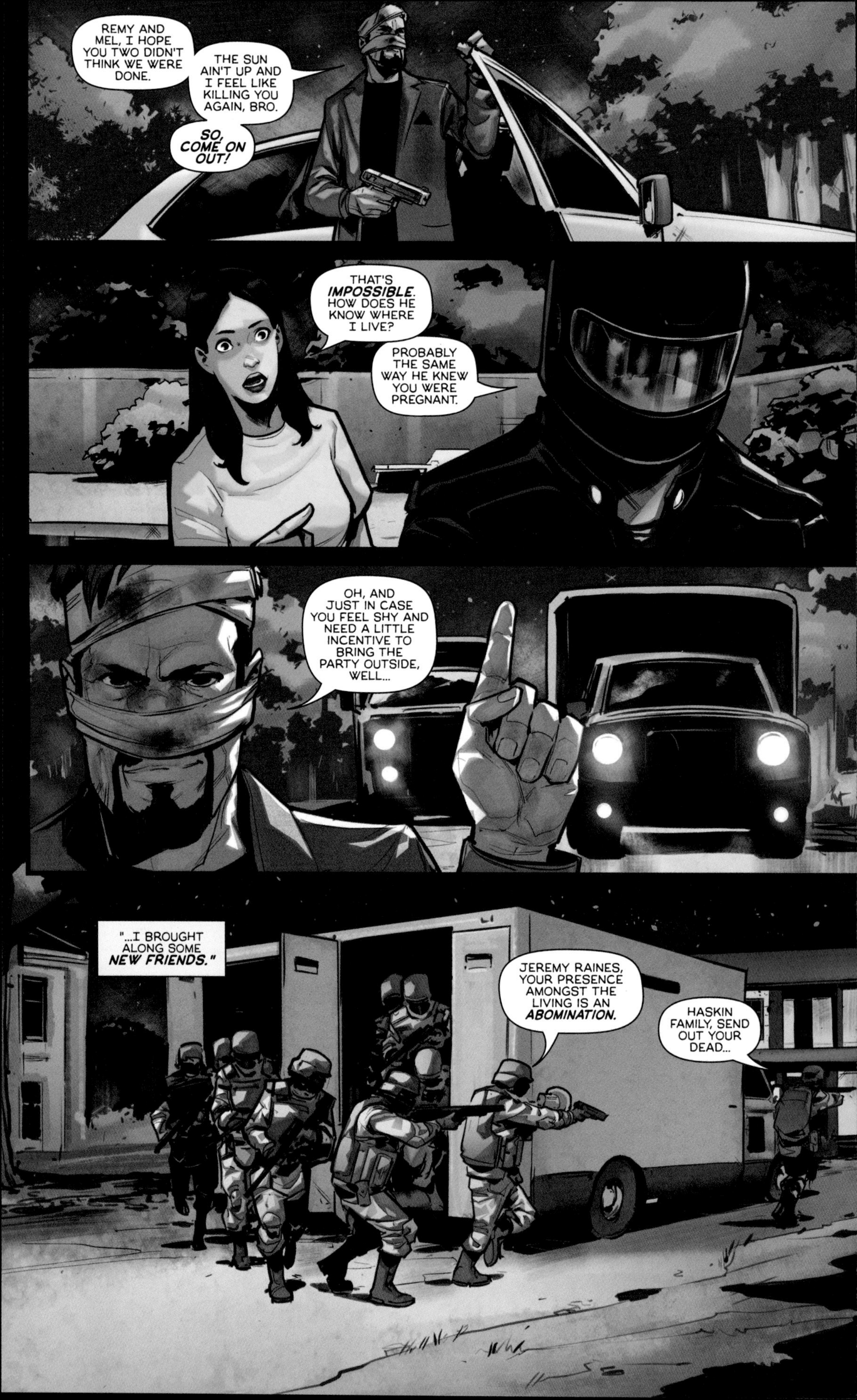
REMY AND MEL, I HOPE YOU TWO DIDN'T THINK WE WERE DONE.
THE SUN AIN'T UP AND I FEEL LIKE KILLING YOU AGAIN, BRO.
SO, COME ON OUT!
THAT'S IMPOSSIBLE. HOW DOES HE KNOW WHERE I LIVE?
PROBABLY THE SAME WAY HE KNEW YOU WERE PREGNANT.
OH, AND JUST IN CASE YOU FEEL SHY AND NEED A LITTLE INCENTIVE TO BRING THE PARTY OUTSIDE, WELL...
"...I BROUGHT ALONG SOME NEW FRIENDS."
JEREMY RAINES, YOUR PRESENCE AMONGST THE LIVING IS AN ABOMINATION.
HASKIN FAMILY, SEND OUT YOUR DEAD...

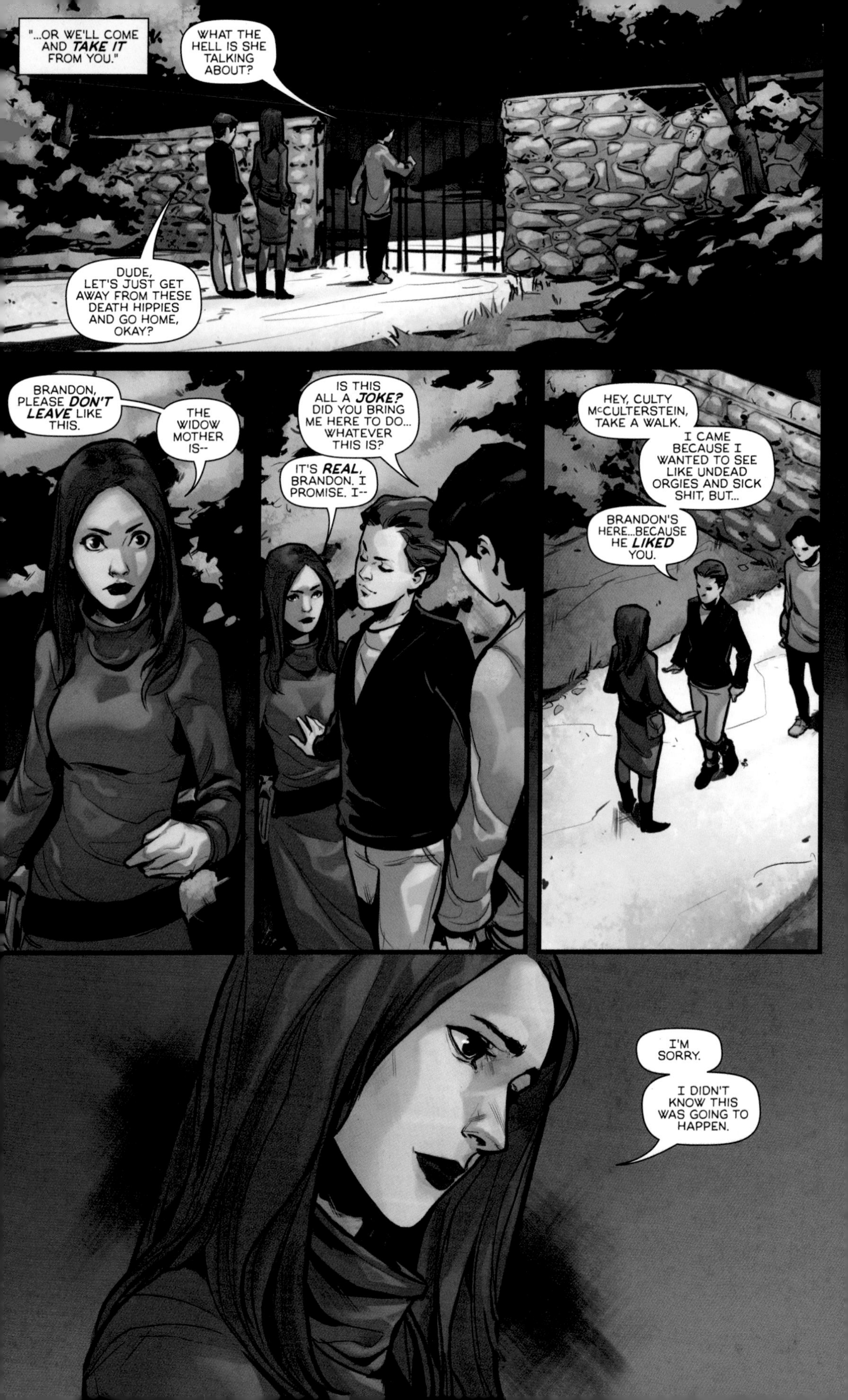
"...OR WE'LL COME AND TAKE IT FROM YOU."
WHAT THE HELL IS SHE TALKING ABOUT?
DUDE, LET'S JUST GET AWAY FROM THESE DEATH HIPPIES AND GO HOME, OKAY?
BRANDON, PLEASE DON'T LEAVE LIKE THIS.
THE WIDOW MOTHER IS--
IS THIS ALL A JOKE? DID YOU BRING ME HERE TO DO... WHATEVER THIS IS?
IT'S REAL, BRANDON. I PROMISE. I--
HEY, CULTY McCULTERSTEIN, TAKE A WALK.
I CAME BECAUSE I WANTED TO SEE LIKE UNDEAD ORGIES AND SICK SHIT, BUT...
BRANDON'S HERE...BECAUSE HE LIKED YOU.
I'M SORRY.
I DIDN'T KNOW THIS WAS GOING TO HAPPEN.

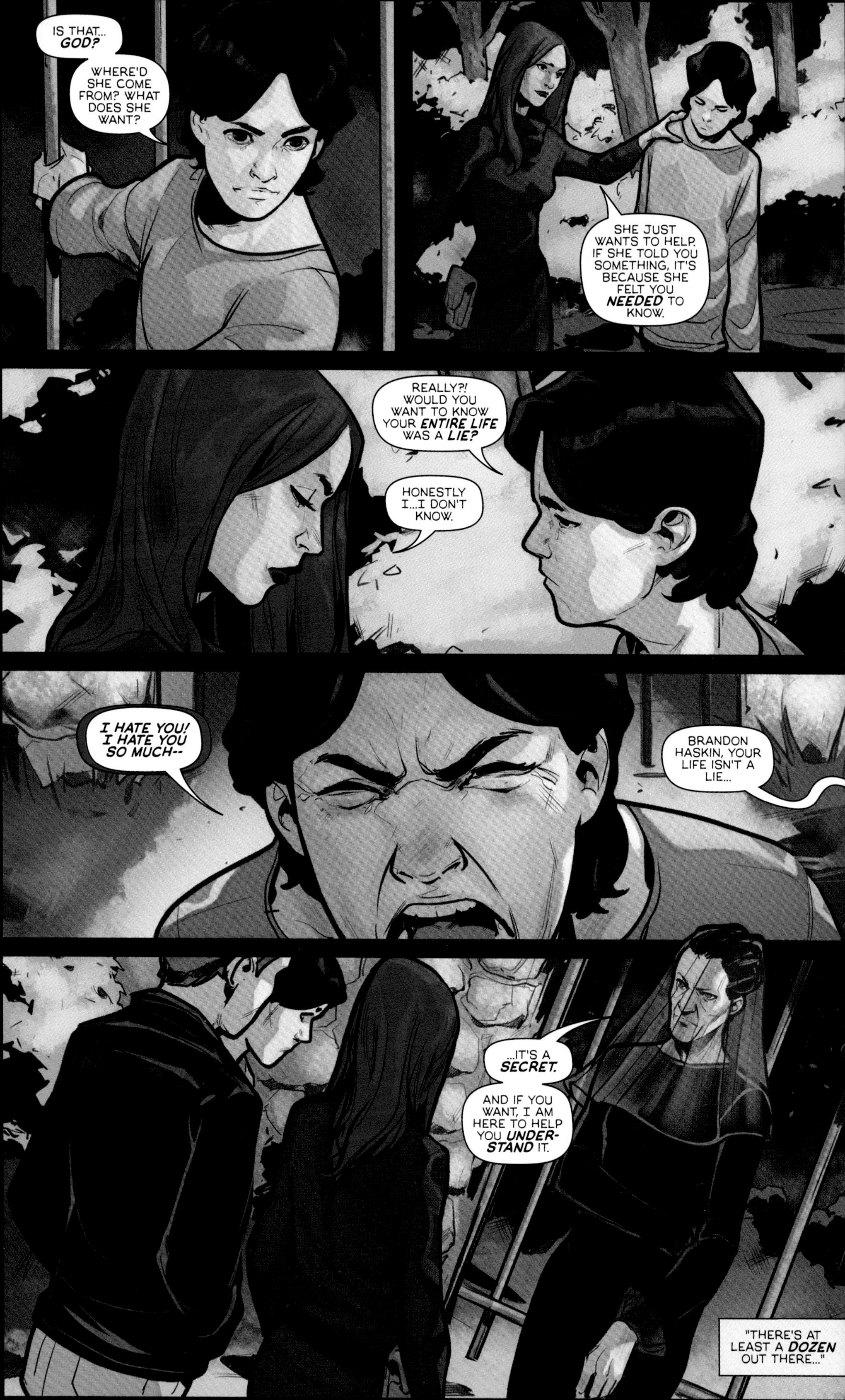
IS THAT... GOD?
WHERE'D SHE COME FROM? WHAT DOES SHE WANT?
SHE JUST WANTS TO HELP. IF SHE TOLD YOU SOMETHING, IT'S BECAUSE SHE FELT YOU NEEDED TO KNOW.
REALLY?! WOULD YOU WANT TO KNOW YOUR ENTIRE LIFE WAS A LIE?
HONESTLY I...I DON'T KNOW.
I HATE YOU! I HATE YOU SO MUCH--
BRANDON HASKIN, YOUR LIFE ISN'T A LIE...
...IT'S A SECRET.
AND IF YOU WANT, I AM HERE TO HELP YOU UNDER-STAND IT.
"THERE'S AT LEAST A DOZEN OUT THERE..."

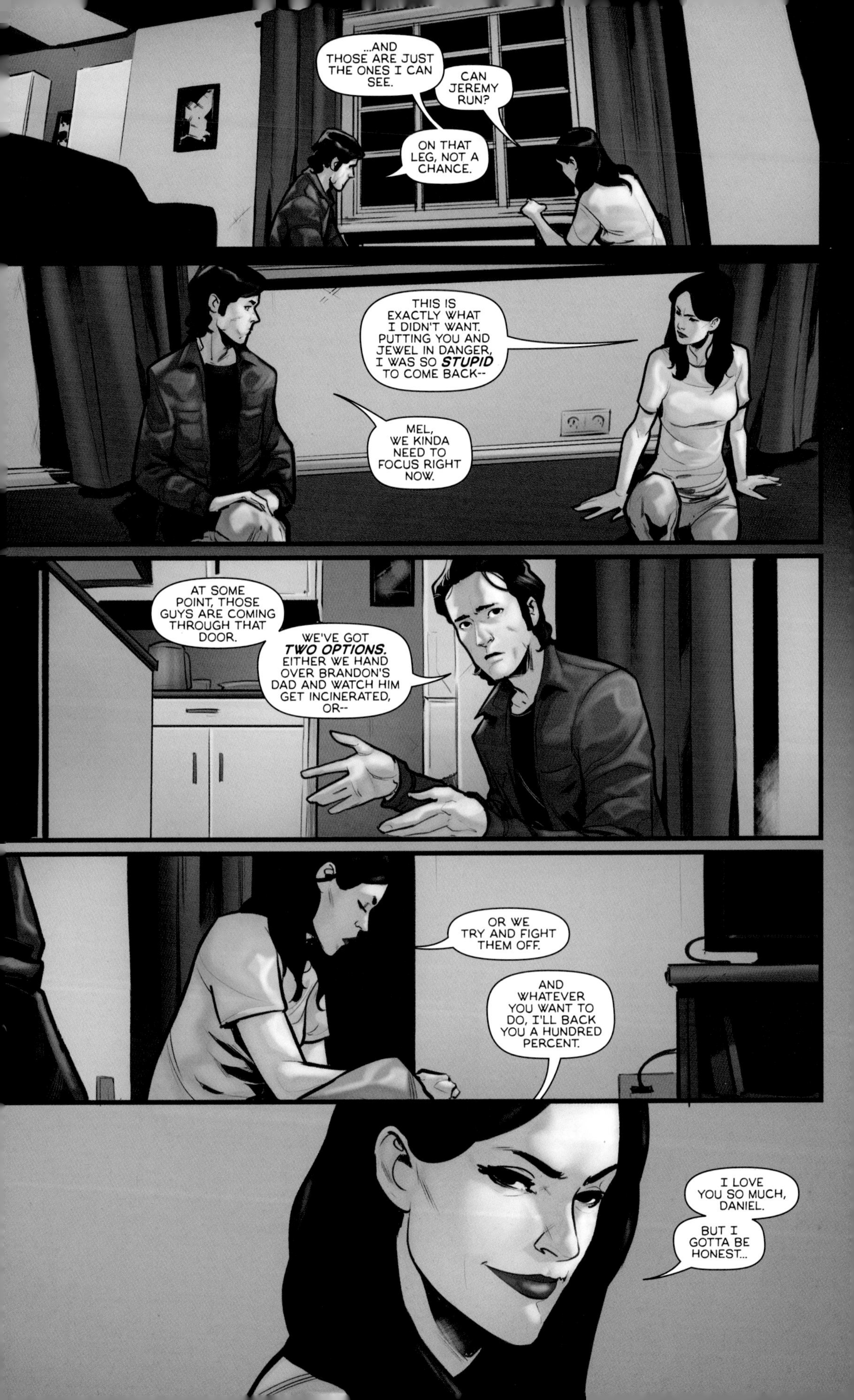
...AND THOSE ARE JUST THE ONES I CAN SEE.
CAN JEREMY RUN?
ON THAT LEG, NOT A CHANCE.
THIS IS EXACTLY WHAT I DIDN'T WANT. PUTTING YOU AND JEWEL IN DANGER, I WAS SO STUPID TO COME BACK--
MEL, WE KINDA NEED TO FOCUS RIGHT NOW.
AT SOME POINT, THOSE GUYS ARE COMING THROUGH THAT DOOR.
WE'VE GOT TWO OPTIONS. EITHER WE HAND OVER BRANDON'S DAD AND WATCH HIM GET INCINERATED, OR--
OR WE TRY AND FIGHT THEM OFF.
AND WHATEVER YOU WANT TO DO, I'LL BACK YOU A HUNDRED PERCENT.
I LOVE YOU SO MUCH, DANIEL.
BUT I GOTTA BE HONEST...

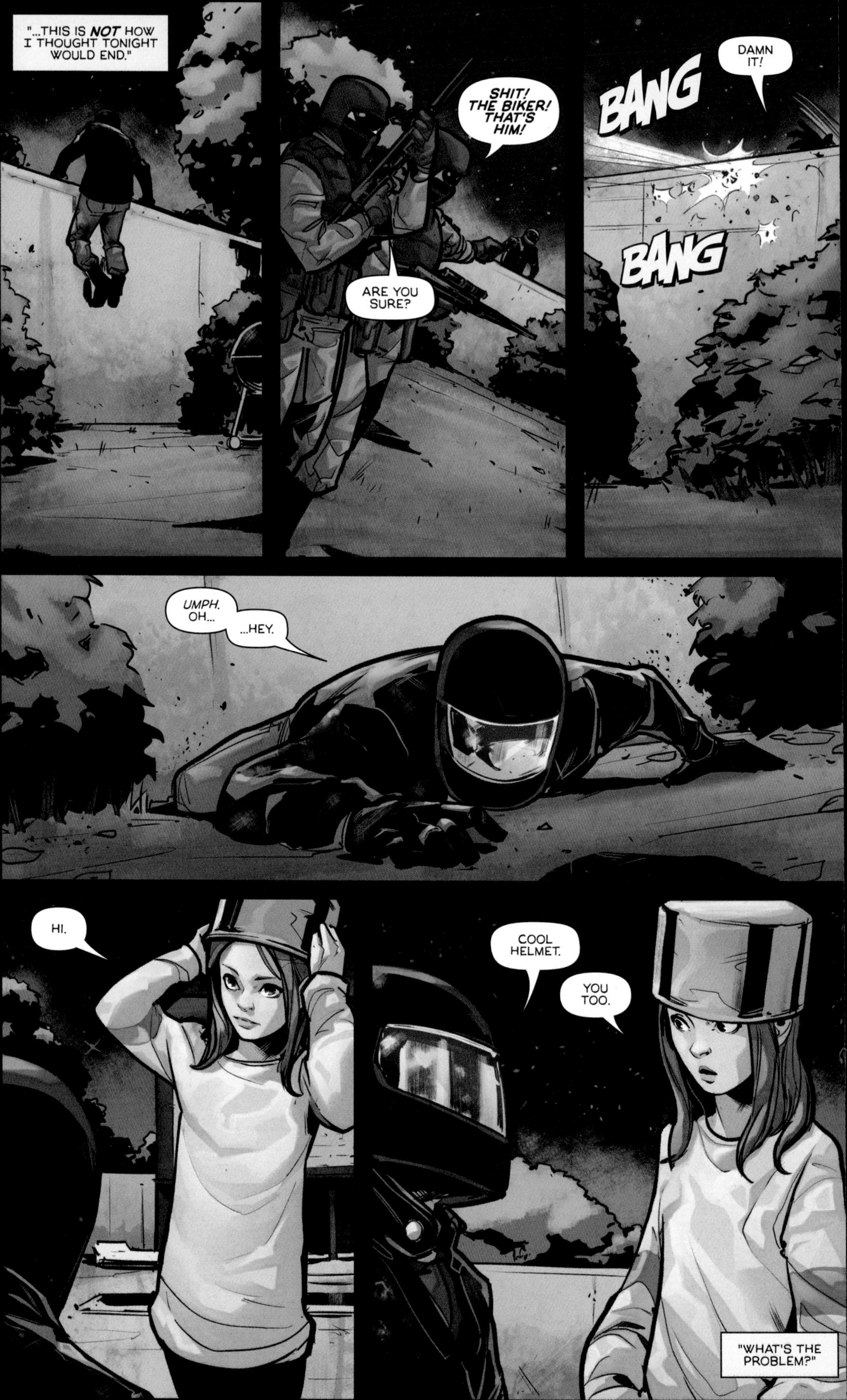
"...THIS IS **NOT** HOW I THOUGHT TONIGHT WOULD END."
SHIT! THE BIKER! THAT'S HIM!
ARE YOU SURE?
BANG
DAMN IT!
BANG
UMPH. OH...
...HEY.
HI.
COOL HELMET.
YOU TOO.
"WHAT'S THE PROBLEM?"

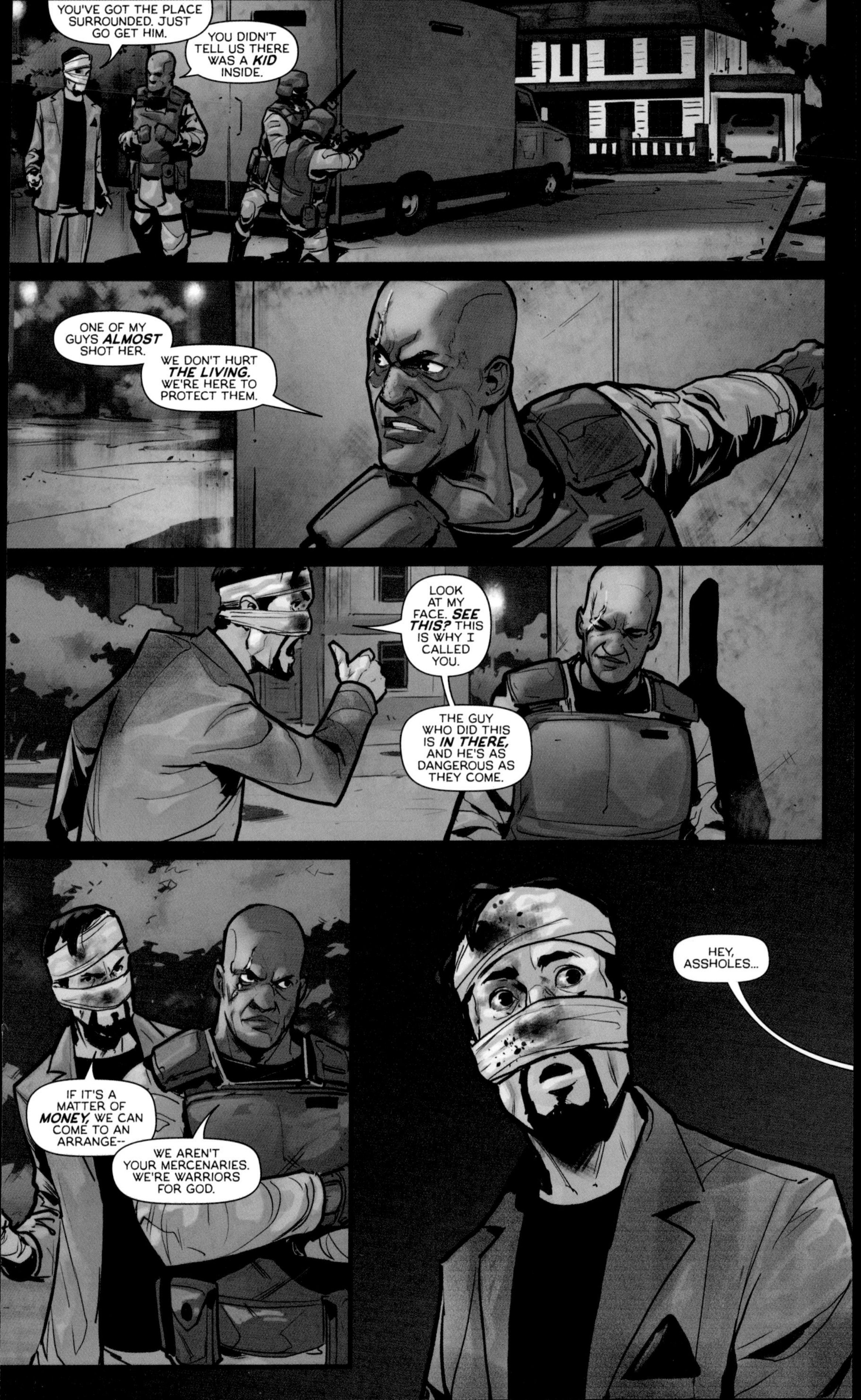
YOU'VE GOT THE PLACE SURROUNDED. JUST GO GET HIM.
YOU DIDN'T TELL US THERE WAS A KID INSIDE.
ONE OF MY GUYS ALMOST SHOT HER.
WE DON'T HURT THE LIVING. WE'RE HERE TO PROTECT THEM.
LOOK AT MY FACE. SEE THIS? THIS IS WHY I CALLED YOU.
THE GUY WHO DID THIS IS IN THERE, AND HE'S AS DANGEROUS AS THEY COME.
IF IT'S A MATTER OF MONEY, WE CAN COME TO AN ARRANGE--
WE AREN'T YOUR MERCENARIES. WE'RE WARRIORS FOR GOD.
HEY, ASSHOLES...

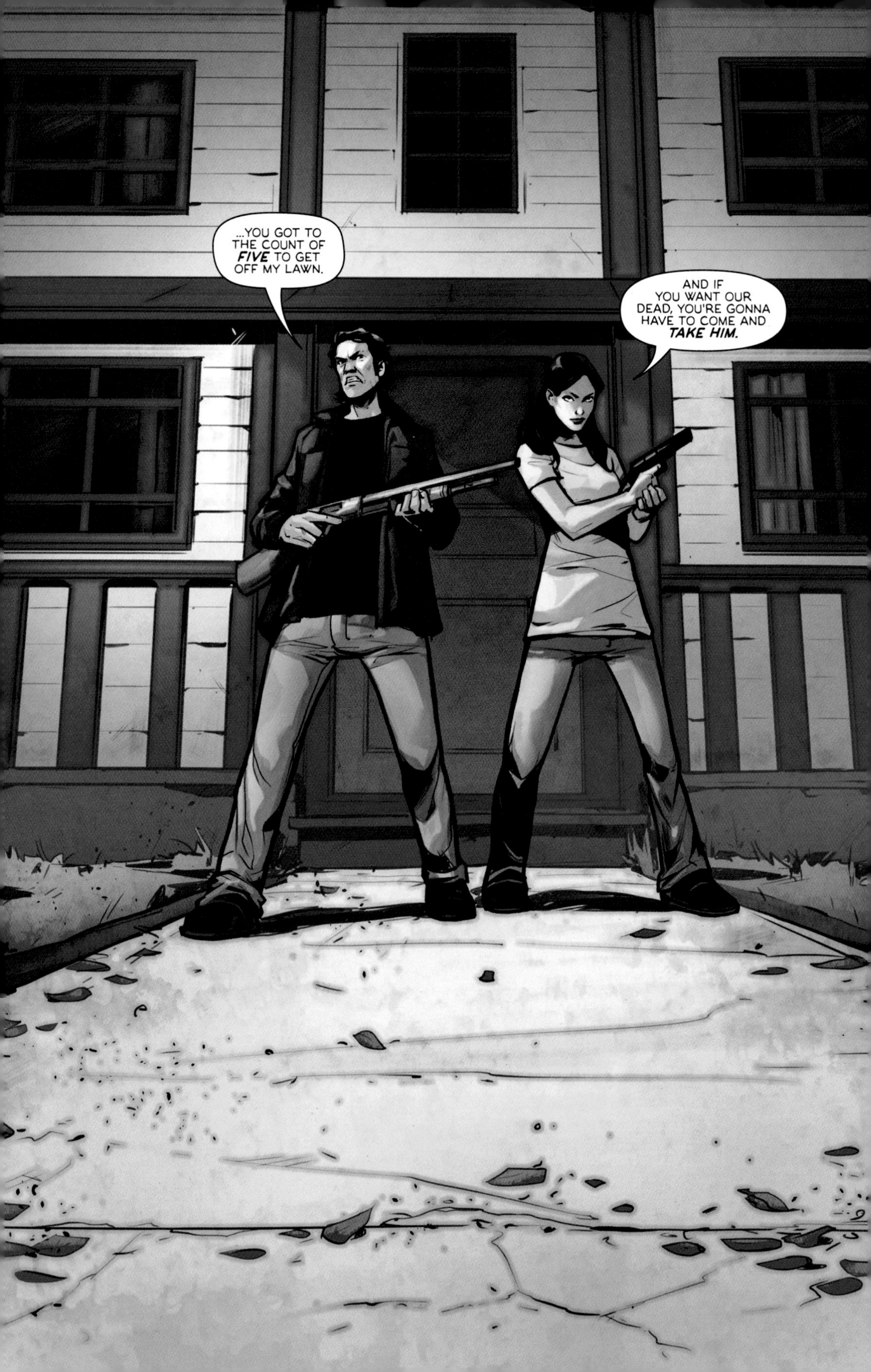
...YOU GOT TO THE COUNT OF FIVE TO GET OFF MY LAWN.
AND IF YOU WANT OUR DEAD, YOU'RE GONNA HAVE TO COME AND TAKE HIM.

5

CHAPTER FIVE

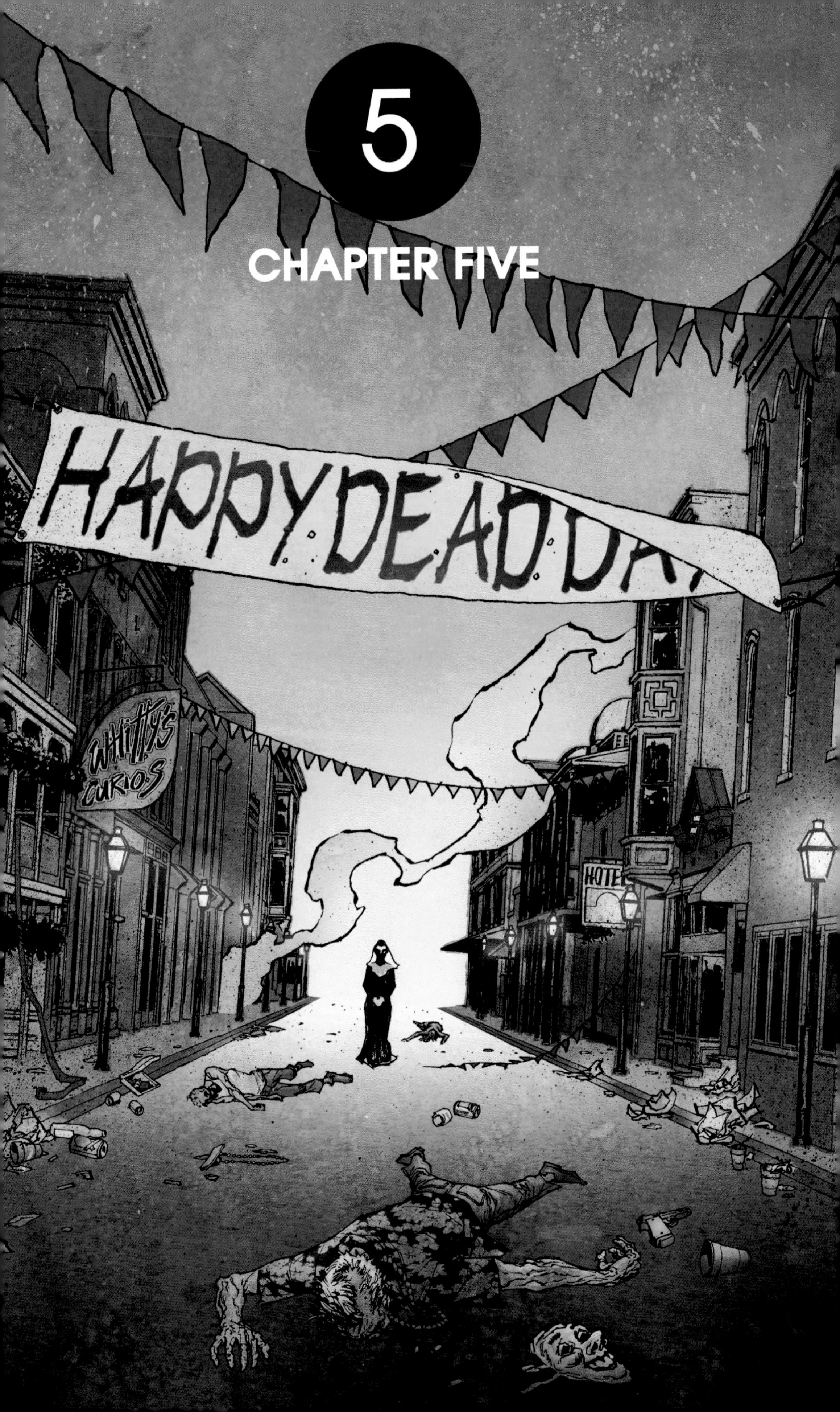
HAPPY DEAD DA
Whitty's
Curios
HOTE

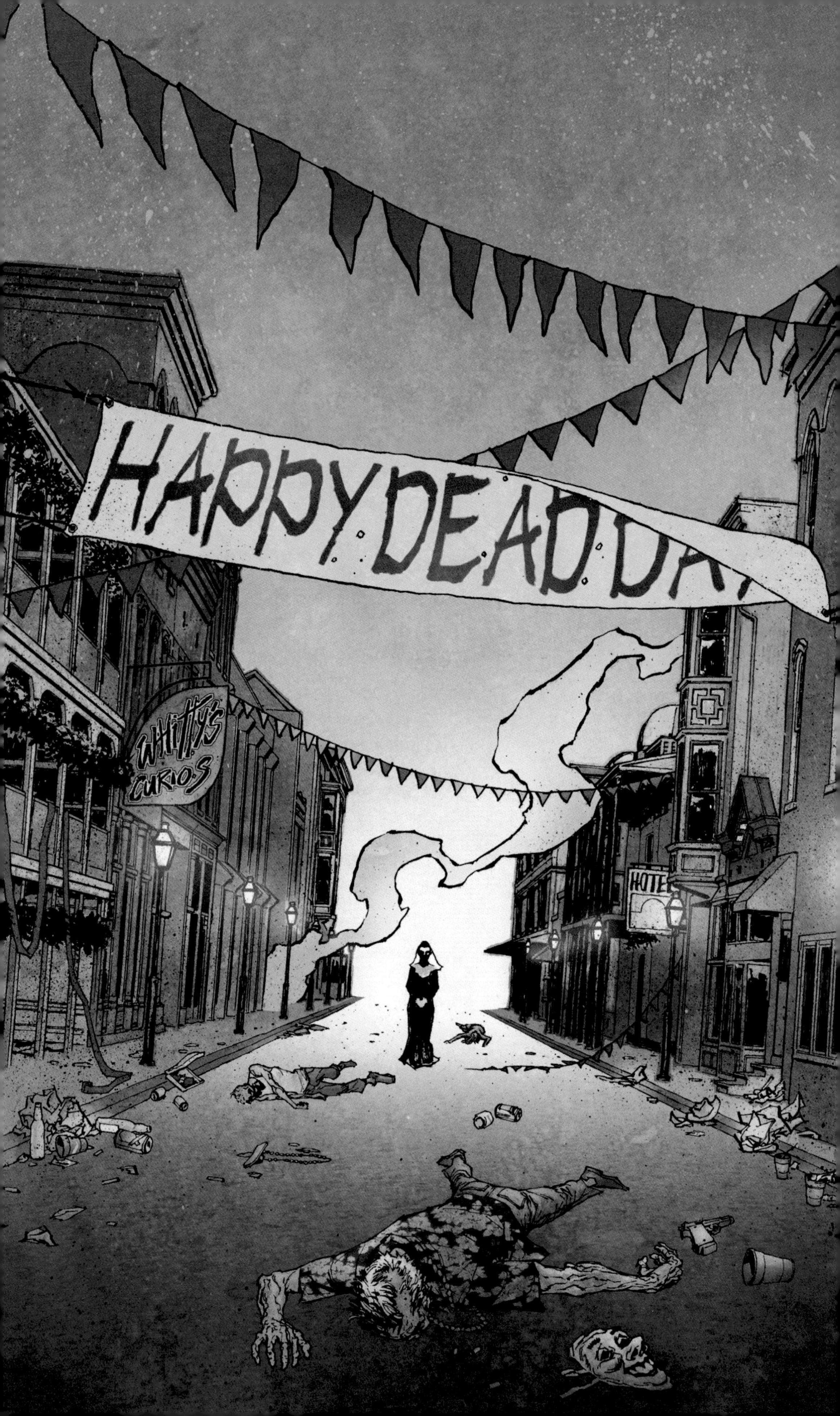
HAPPY DEAD DA
WHITTY'S CURIOS
HOTE

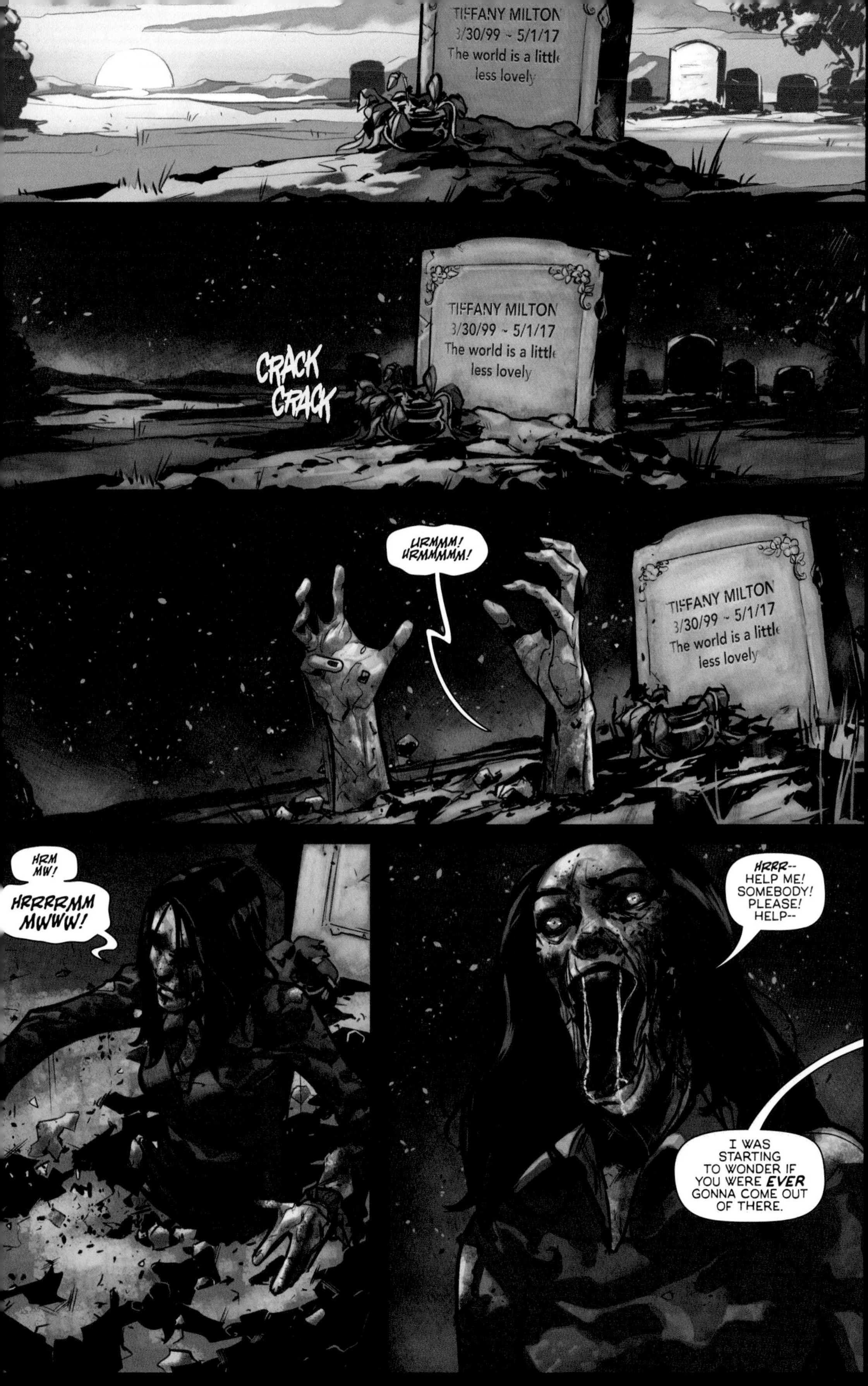
TIFFANY MILTON
3/30/99 ~ 5/1/17
The world is a little
less lovely
CRACK
CRACK
URMMM!
URMMMMM!
HRM
MW!
HRRRRMM
MWWW!
HRRR--
HELP ME!
SOMEBODY!
PLEASE!
HELP--
I WAS STARTING TO WONDER IF YOU WERE *EVER* GONNA COME OUT OF THERE.

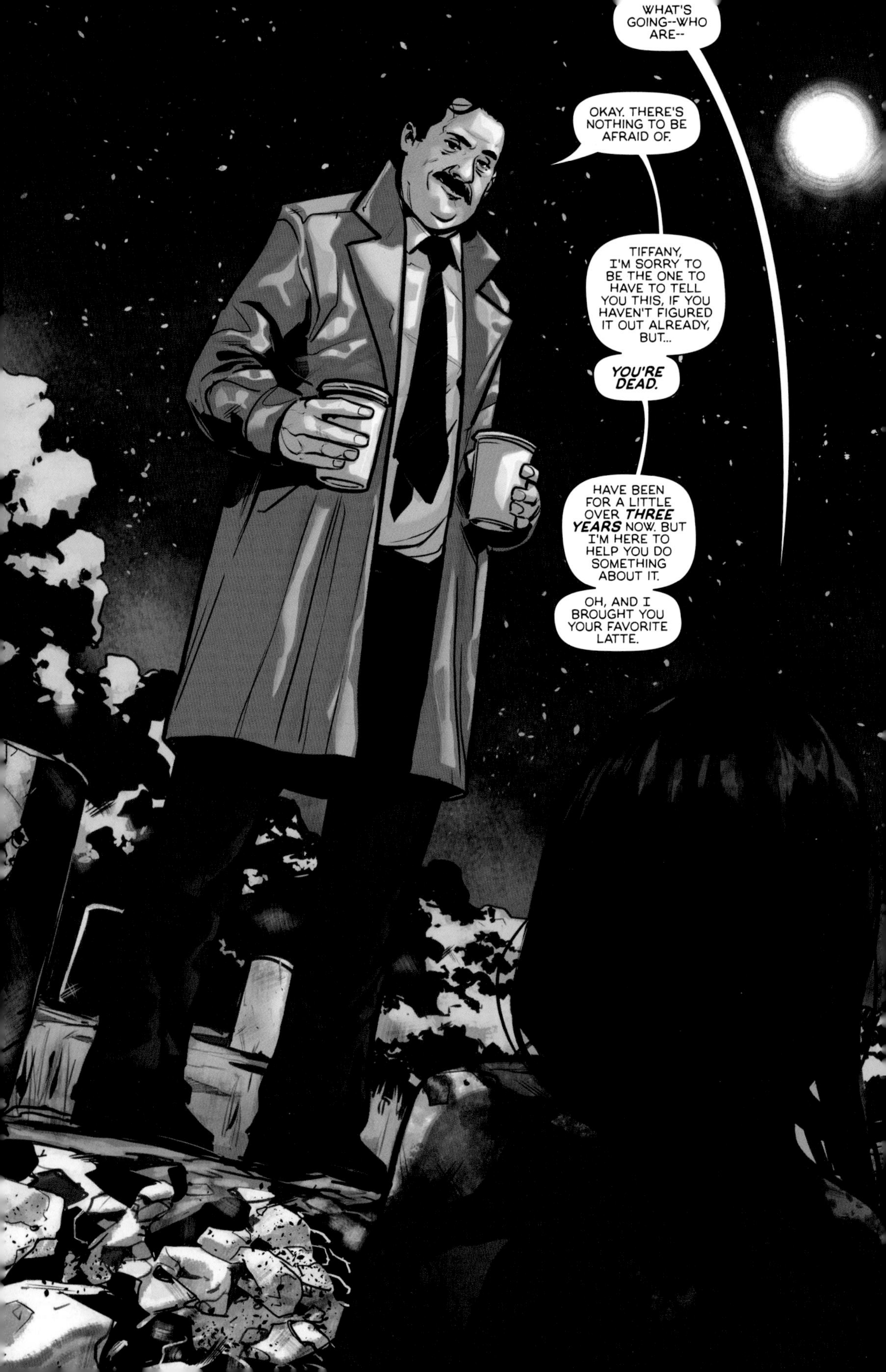
WHAT'S GOING--WHO ARE--
OKAY. THERE'S NOTHING TO BE AFRAID OF.
TIFFANY, I'M SORRY TO BE THE ONE TO HAVE TO TELL YOU THIS, IF YOU HAVEN'T FIGURED IT OUT ALREADY, BUT...
YOU'RE DEAD.
HAVE BEEN FOR A LITTLE OVER THREE YEARS NOW. BUT I'M HERE TO HELP YOU DO SOMETHING ABOUT IT.
OH, AND I BROUGHT YOU YOUR FAVORITE LATTE.

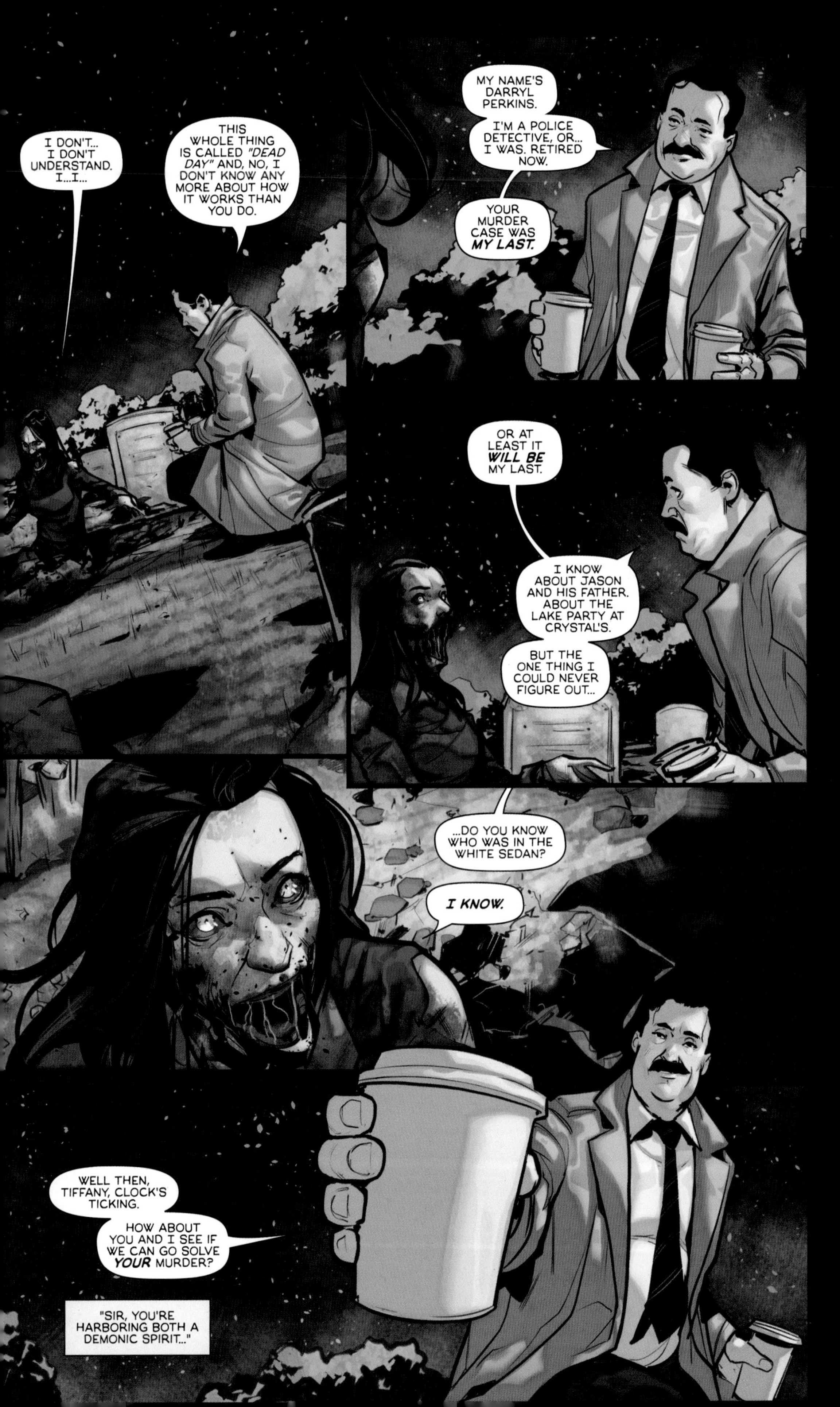

I DON'T... I DON'T UNDERSTAND. I...I...
THIS WHOLE THING IS CALLED "DEAD DAY" AND, NO, I DON'T KNOW ANY MORE ABOUT HOW IT WORKS THAN YOU DO.
MY NAME'S DARRYL PERKINS.
I'M A POLICE DETECTIVE, OR... I WAS. RETIRED NOW.
YOUR MURDER CASE WAS MY LAST.
OR AT LEAST IT WILL BE MY LAST.
I KNOW ABOUT JASON AND HIS FATHER. ABOUT THE LAKE PARTY AT CRYSTAL'S.
BUT THE ONE THING I COULD NEVER FIGURE OUT...
...DO YOU KNOW WHO WAS IN THE WHITE SEDAN?
I KNOW.
WELL THEN, TIFFANY, CLOCK'S TICKING.
HOW ABOUT YOU AND I SEE IF WE CAN GO SOLVE YOUR MURDER?
"SIR, YOU'RE HARBORING BOTH A DEMONIC SPIRIT..."

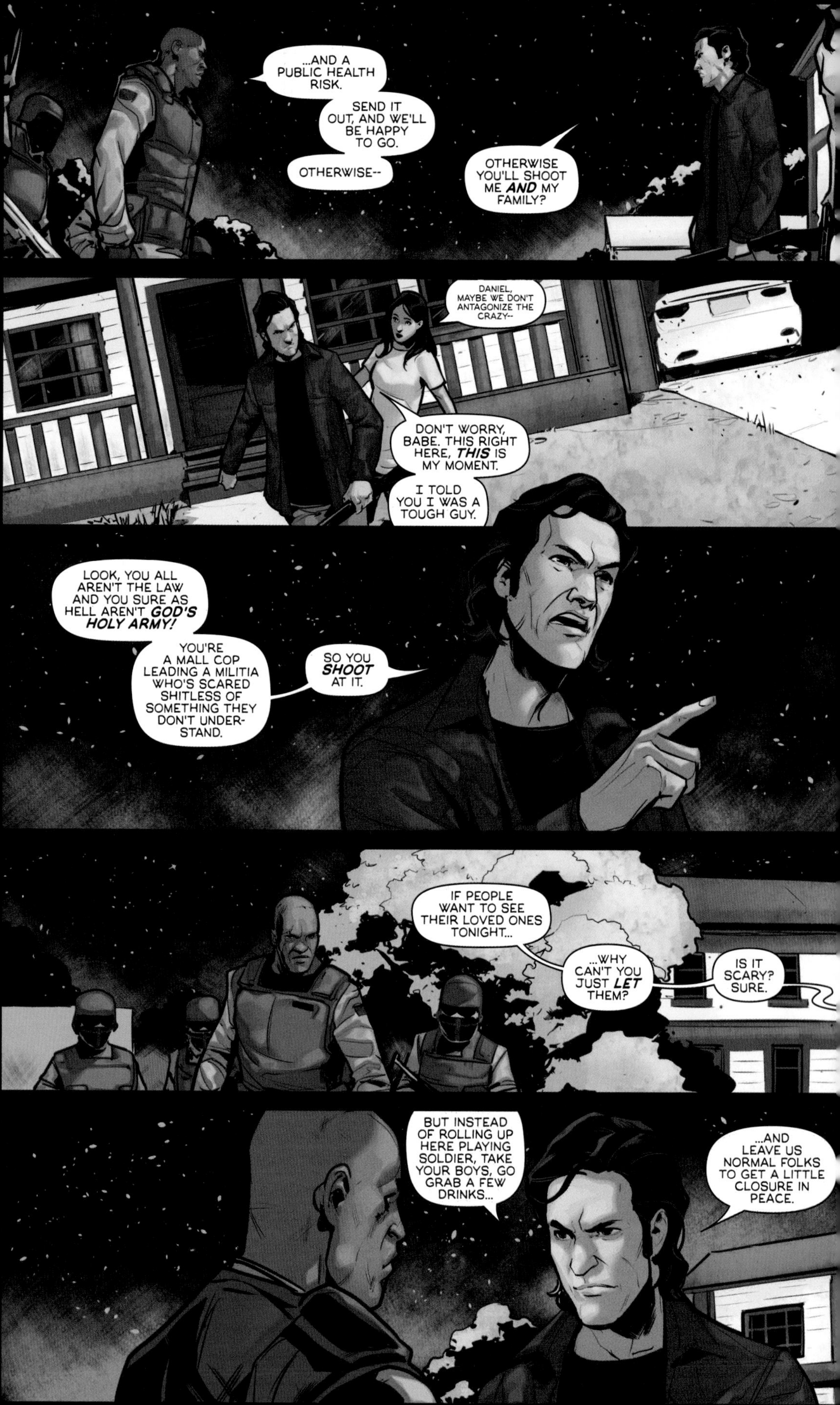
...AND A PUBLIC HEALTH RISK.
SEND IT OUT, AND WE'LL BE HAPPY TO GO.
OTHERWISE--
OTHERWISE YOU'LL SHOOT ME **AND** MY FAMILY?
DANIEL, MAYBE WE DON'T ANTAGONIZE THE CRAZY--
DON'T WORRY, BABE. THIS RIGHT HERE, **THIS** IS MY MOMENT.
I TOLD YOU I WAS A TOUGH GUY.
LOOK, YOU ALL AREN'T THE LAW AND YOU SURE AS HELL AREN'T **GOD'S HOLY ARMY!**
YOU'RE A MALL COP LEADING A MILITIA WHO'S SCARED SHITLESS OF SOMETHING THEY DON'T UNDER-STAND.
SO YOU **SHOOT** AT IT.
IF PEOPLE WANT TO SEE THEIR LOVED ONES TONIGHT...
...WHY CAN'T YOU JUST **LET** THEM?
IS IT SCARY? SURE.
BUT INSTEAD OF ROLLING UP HERE PLAYING SOLDIER, TAKE YOUR BOYS, GO GRAB A FEW DRINKS...
...AND LEAVE US NORMAL FOLKS TO GET A LITTLE CLOSURE IN PEACE.

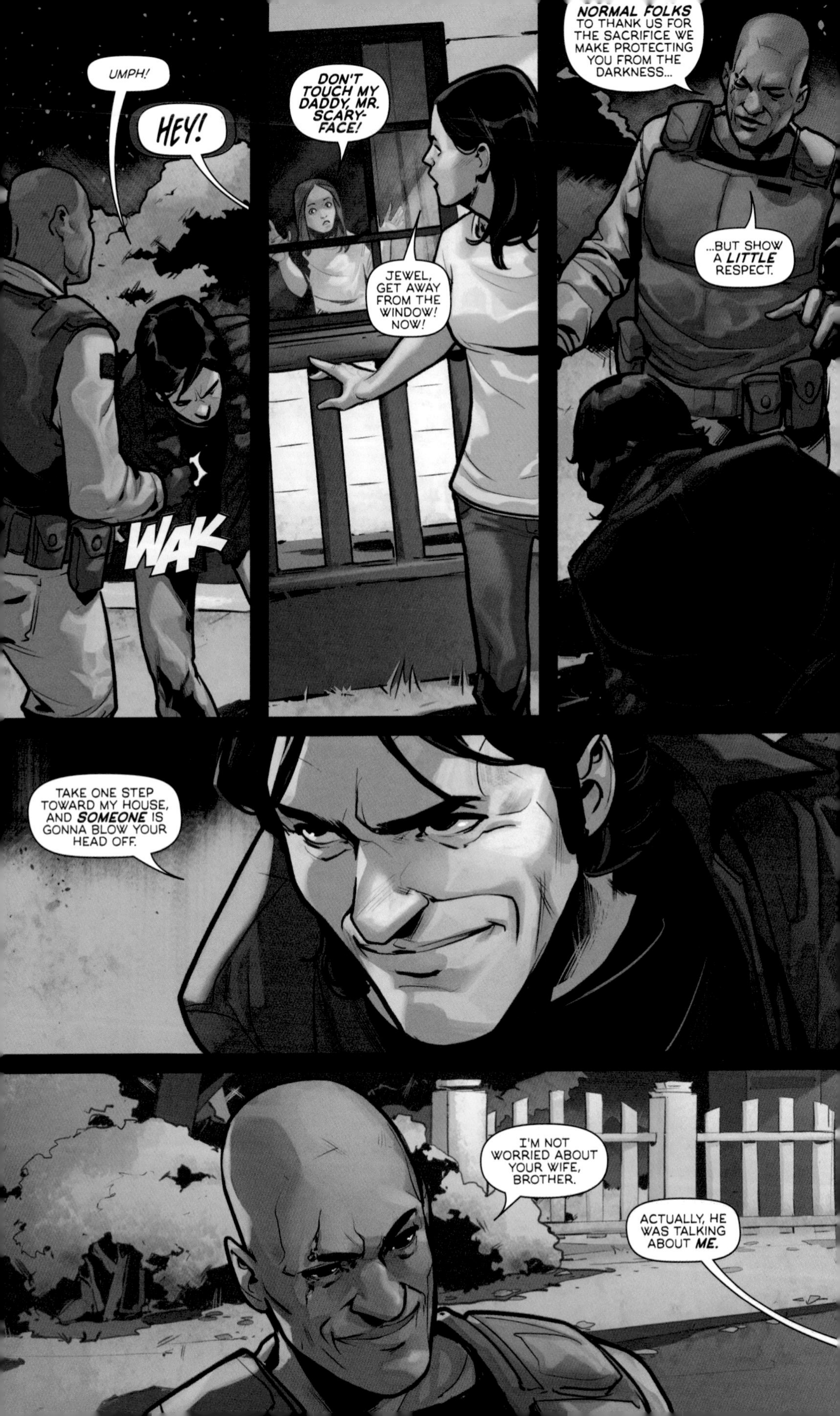
UMPH!
HEY!
WAK
DON'T TOUCH MY DADDY, MR. SCARY-FACE!
JEWEL, GET AWAY FROM THE WINDOW! NOW!
NORMAL FOLKS TO THANK US FOR THE SACRIFICE WE MAKE PROTECTING YOU FROM THE DARKNESS...
...BUT SHOW A LITTLE RESPECT.
TAKE ONE STEP TOWARD MY HOUSE, AND SOMEONE IS GONNA BLOW YOUR HEAD OFF.
I'M NOT WORRIED ABOUT YOUR WIFE, BROTHER.
ACTUALLY, HE WAS TALKING ABOUT ME.

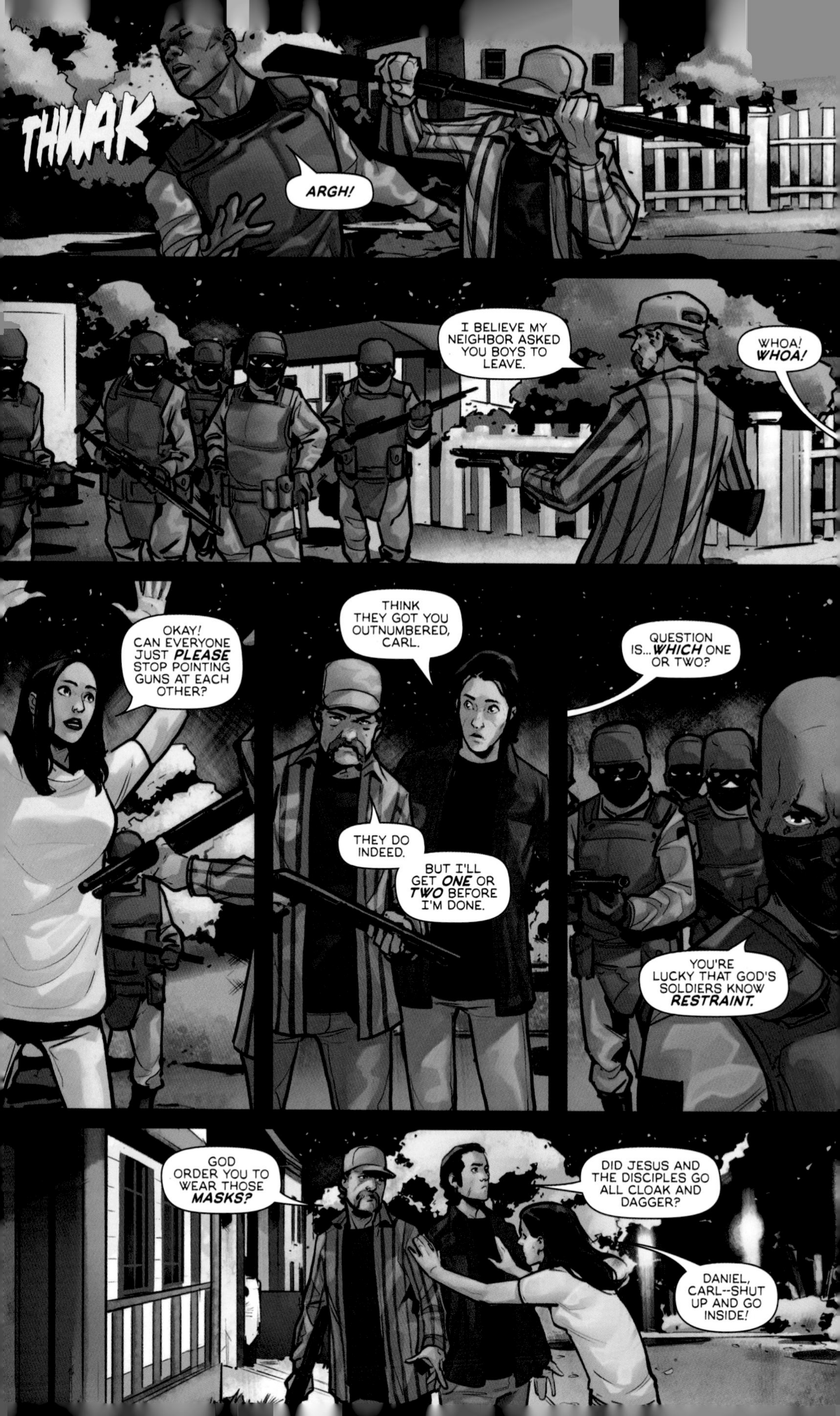
THWAK
ARGH!
I BELIEVE MY NEIGHBOR ASKED YOU BOYS TO LEAVE.
WHOA! WHOA!
OKAY! CAN EVERYONE JUST PLEASE STOP POINTING GUNS AT EACH OTHER?
THINK THEY GOT YOU OUTNUMBERED, CARL.
THEY DO INDEED.
BUT I'LL GET ONE OR TWO BEFORE I'M DONE.
QUESTION IS...WHICH ONE OR TWO?
YOU'RE LUCKY THAT GOD'S SOLDIERS KNOW RESTRAINT.
GOD ORDER YOU TO WEAR THOSE MASKS?
DID JESUS AND THE DISCIPLES GO ALL CLOAK AND DAGGER?
DANIEL, CARL--SHUT UP AND GO INSIDE!

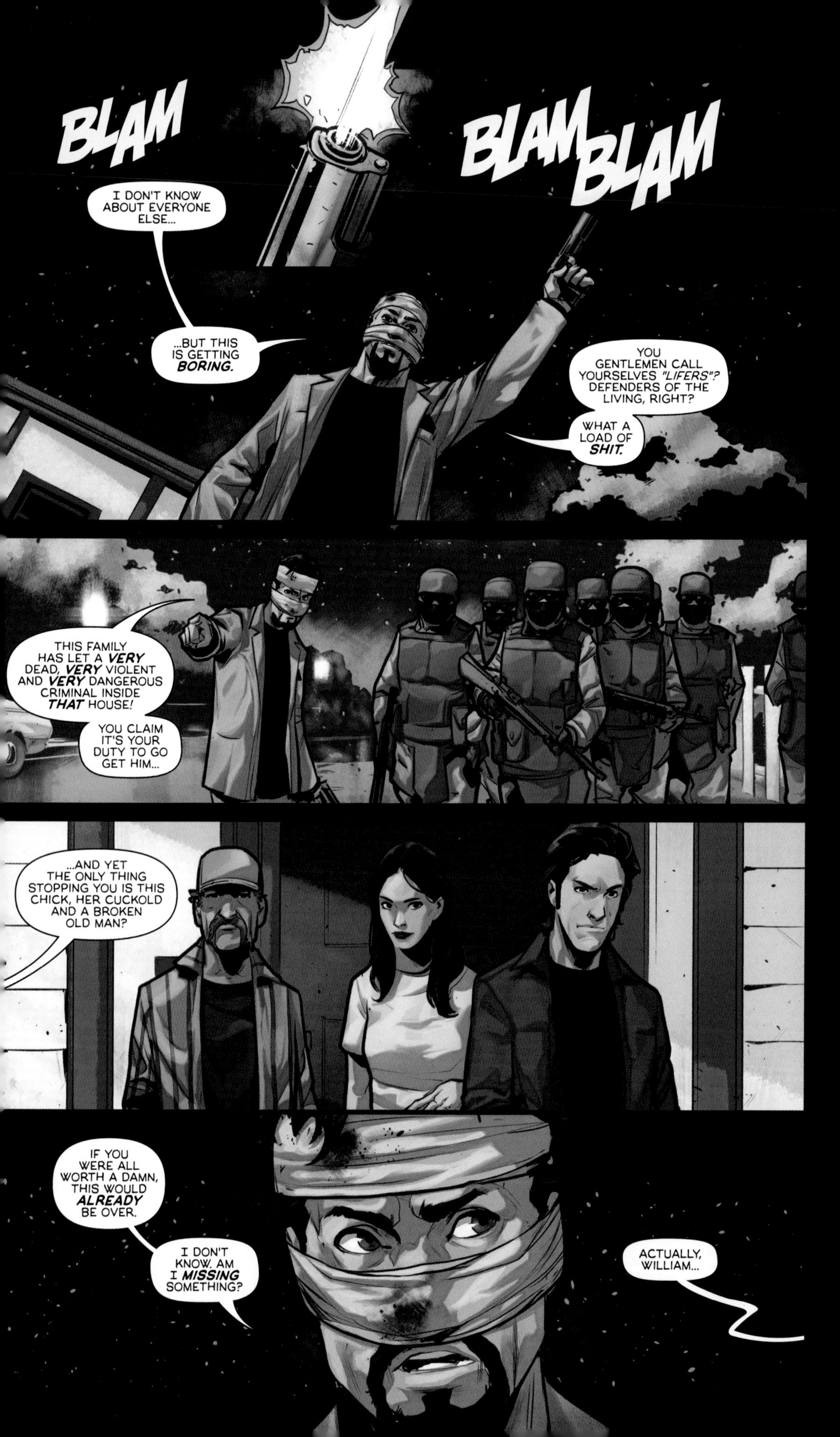
BLAM
BLAM BLAM
I DON'T KNOW ABOUT EVERYONE ELSE...
...BUT THIS IS GETTING BORING.
YOU GENTLEMEN CALL YOURSELVES "LIFERS"? DEFENDERS OF THE LIVING, RIGHT?
WHAT A LOAD OF SHIT.
THIS FAMILY HAS LET A VERY DEAD, VERY VIOLENT AND VERY DANGEROUS CRIMINAL INSIDE THAT HOUSE!
YOU CLAIM IT'S YOUR DUTY TO GO GET HIM...
...AND YET THE ONLY THING STOPPING YOU IS THIS CHICK, HER CUCKOLD AND A BROKEN OLD MAN?
IF YOU WERE ALL WORTH A DAMN, THIS WOULD ALREADY BE OVER.
I DON'T KNOW. AM I MISSING SOMETHING?
ACTUALLY, WILLIAM...

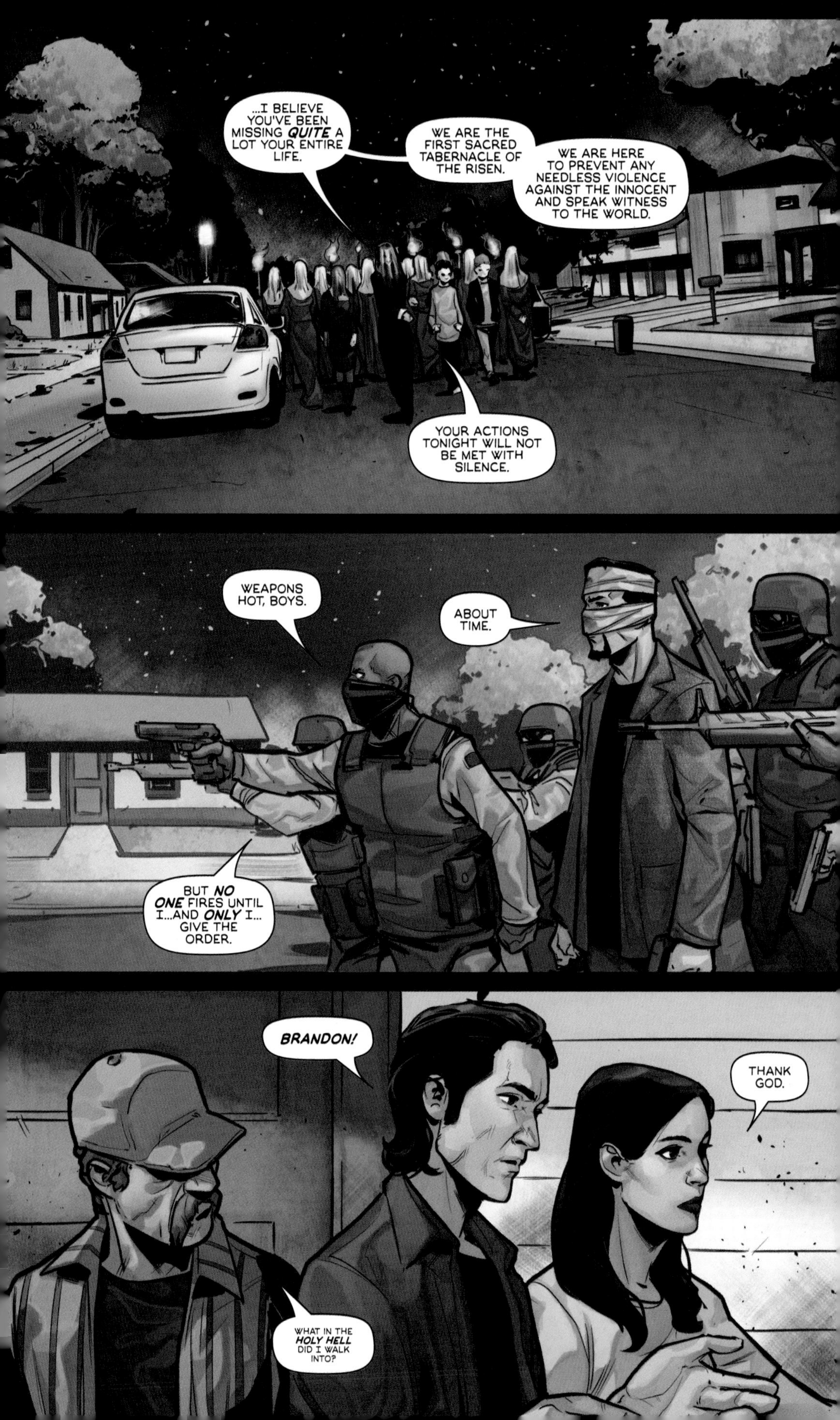

...I BELIEVE YOU'VE BEEN MISSING *QUITE* A LOT YOUR ENTIRE LIFE.
WE ARE THE FIRST SACRED TABERNACLE OF THE RISEN.
WE ARE HERE TO PREVENT ANY NEEDLESS VIOLENCE AGAINST THE INNOCENT AND SPEAK WITNESS TO THE WORLD.
YOUR ACTIONS TONIGHT WILL NOT BE MET WITH SILENCE.
WEAPONS HOT, BOYS.
ABOUT TIME.
BUT *NO ONE* FIRES UNTIL I...AND *ONLY* I... GIVE THE ORDER.
BRANDON!
THANK GOD.
WHAT IN THE *HOLY HELL* DID I WALK INTO?

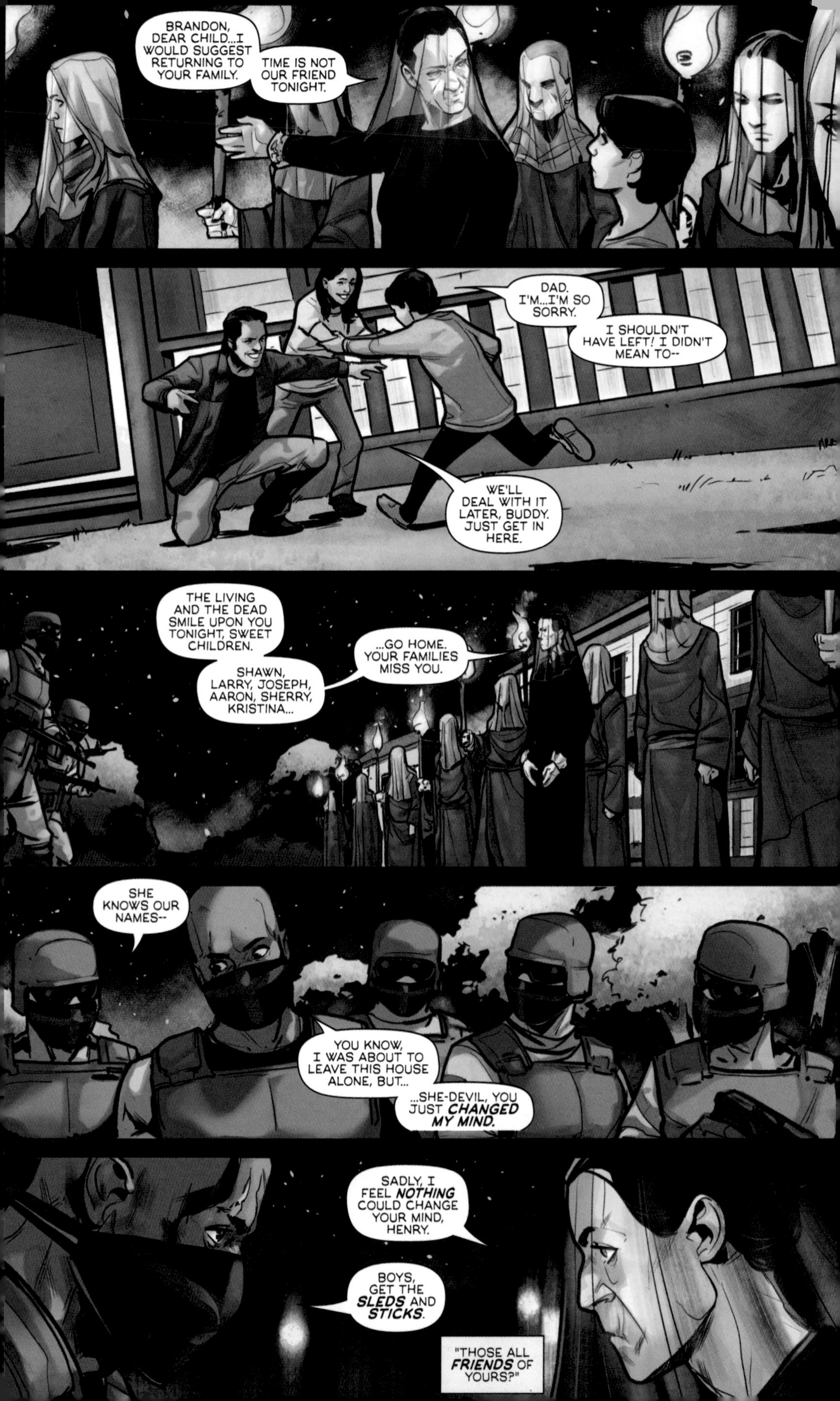

BRANDON, DEAR CHILD...I WOULD SUGGEST RETURNING TO YOUR FAMILY.
TIME IS NOT OUR FRIEND TONIGHT.
DAD. I'M...I'M SO SORRY.
I SHOULDN'T HAVE LEFT! I DIDN'T MEAN TO--
WE'LL DEAL WITH IT LATER, BUDDY. JUST GET IN HERE.
THE LIVING AND THE DEAD SMILE UPON YOU TONIGHT, SWEET CHILDREN.
SHAWN, LARRY, JOSEPH, AARON, SHERRY, KRISTINA...
...GO HOME. YOUR FAMILIES MISS YOU.
SHE KNOWS OUR NAMES--
YOU KNOW, I WAS ABOUT TO LEAVE THIS HOUSE ALONE, BUT...
...SHE-DEVIL, YOU JUST CHANGED MY MIND.
SADLY, I FEEL NOTHING COULD CHANGE YOUR MIND, HENRY.
BOYS, GET THE SLEDS AND STICKS.
"THOSE ALL FRIENDS OF YOURS?"

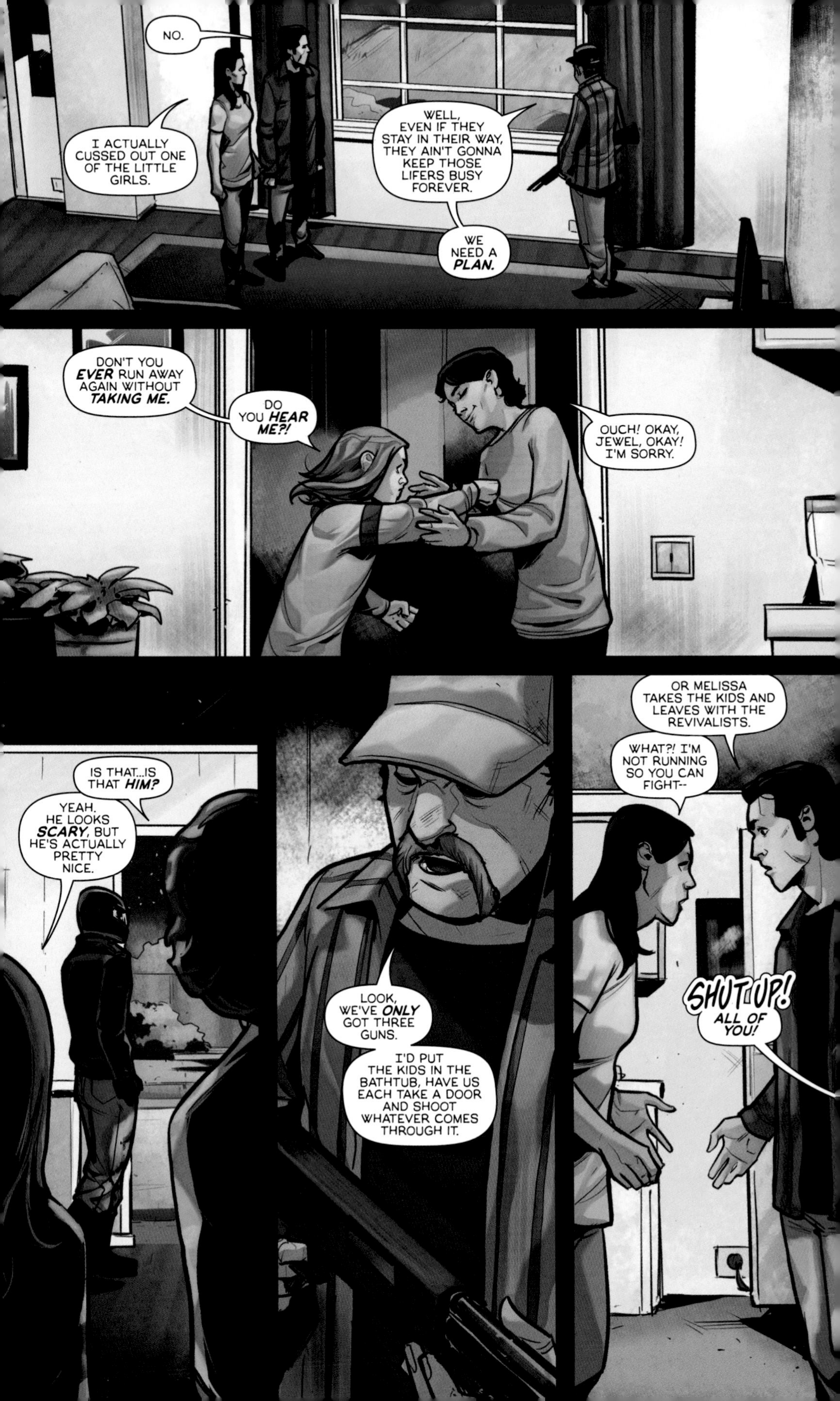
NO.
I ACTUALLY CUSSED OUT ONE OF THE LITTLE GIRLS.
WELL, EVEN IF THEY STAY IN THEIR WAY, THEY AIN'T GONNA KEEP THOSE LIFERS BUSY FOREVER.
WE NEED A PLAN.
DON'T YOU EVER RUN AWAY AGAIN WITHOUT TAKING ME.
DO YOU HEAR ME?!
OUCH! OKAY, JEWEL, OKAY! I'M SORRY.
IS THAT...IS THAT HIM?
YEAH. HE LOOKS SCARY, BUT HE'S ACTUALLY PRETTY NICE.
LOOK, WE'VE ONLY GOT THREE GUNS.
I'D PUT THE KIDS IN THE BATHTUB, HAVE US EACH TAKE A DOOR AND SHOOT WHATEVER COMES THROUGH IT.
OR MELISSA TAKES THE KIDS AND LEAVES WITH THE REVIVALISTS.
WHAT?! I'M NOT RUNNING SO YOU CAN FIGHT--
SHUT UP! ALL OF YOU!

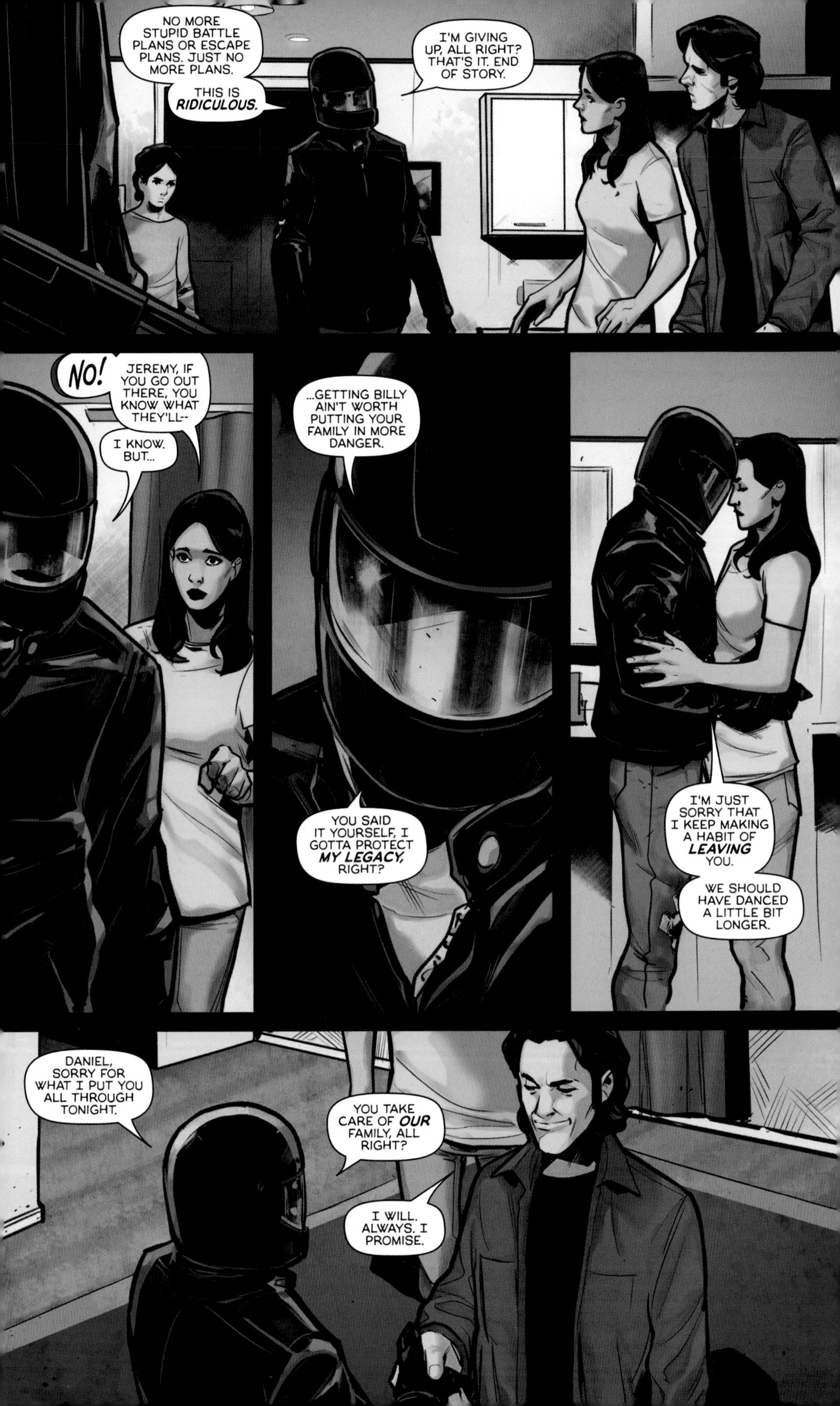

NO MORE STUPID BATTLE PLANS OR ESCAPE PLANS. JUST NO MORE PLANS.
THIS IS *RIDICULOUS.*
I'M GIVING UP, ALL RIGHT? THAT'S IT. END OF STORY.
NO!
JEREMY, IF YOU GO OUT THERE, YOU KNOW WHAT THEY'LL--
I KNOW. BUT...
...GETTING BILLY AIN'T WORTH PUTTING YOUR FAMILY IN MORE DANGER.
YOU SAID IT YOURSELF, I GOTTA PROTECT *MY LEGACY,* RIGHT?
I'M JUST SORRY THAT I KEEP MAKING A HABIT OF *LEAVING* YOU.
WE SHOULD HAVE DANCED A LITTLE BIT LONGER.
DANIEL, SORRY FOR WHAT I PUT YOU ALL THROUGH TONIGHT.
YOU TAKE CARE OF *OUR* FAMILY, ALL RIGHT?
I WILL. ALWAYS. I PROMISE.

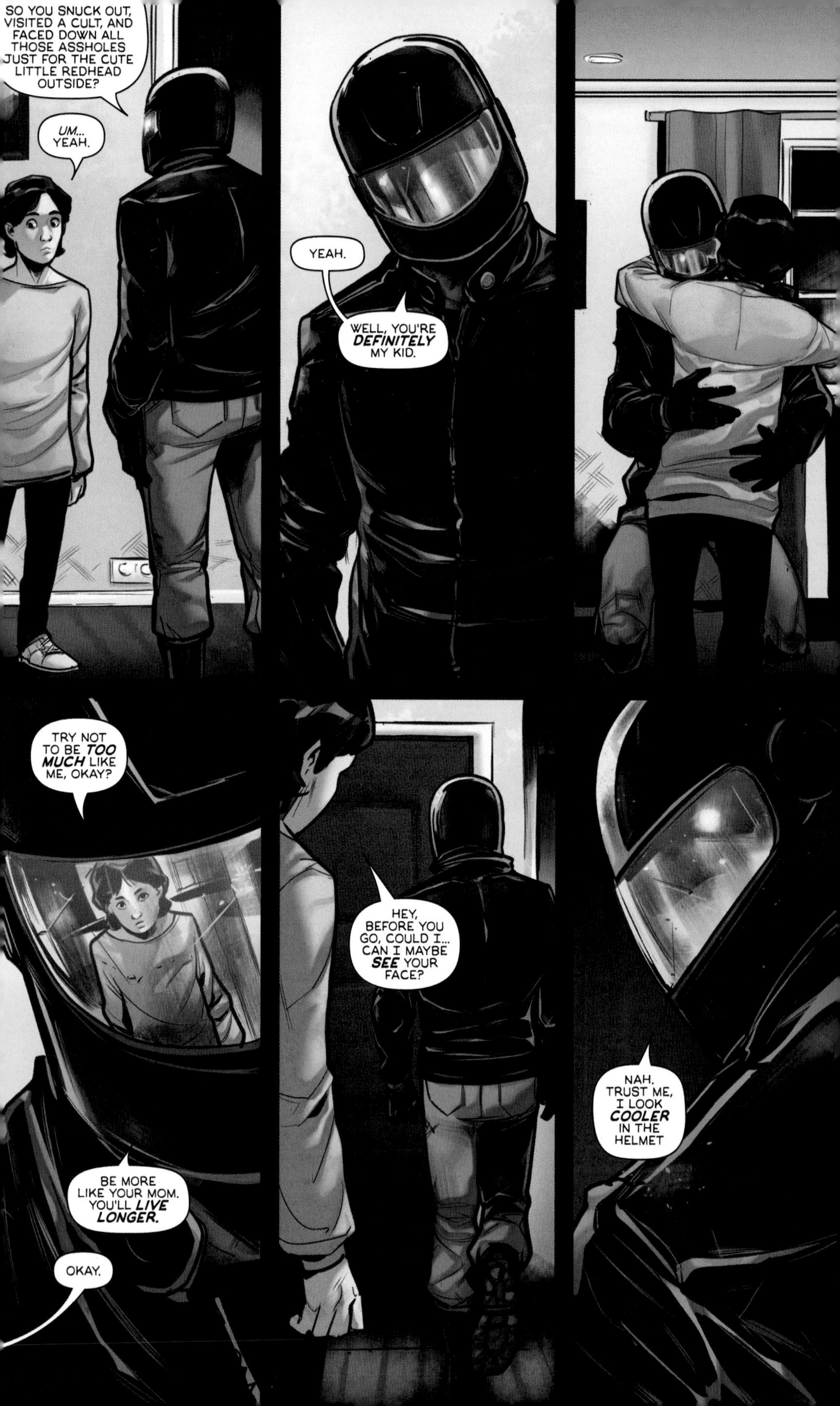

SO YOU SNUCK OUT, VISITED A CULT, AND FACED DOWN ALL THOSE ASSHOLES JUST FOR THE CUTE LITTLE REDHEAD OUTSIDE?
UM... YEAH.
YEAH.
WELL, YOU'RE DEFINITELY MY KID.
TRY NOT TO BE TOO MUCH LIKE ME, OKAY?
BE MORE LIKE YOUR MOM. YOU'LL LIVE LONGER.
OKAY.
HEY, BEFORE YOU GO, COULD I... CAN I MAYBE SEE YOUR FACE?
NAH. TRUST ME, I LOOK COOLER IN THE HELMET

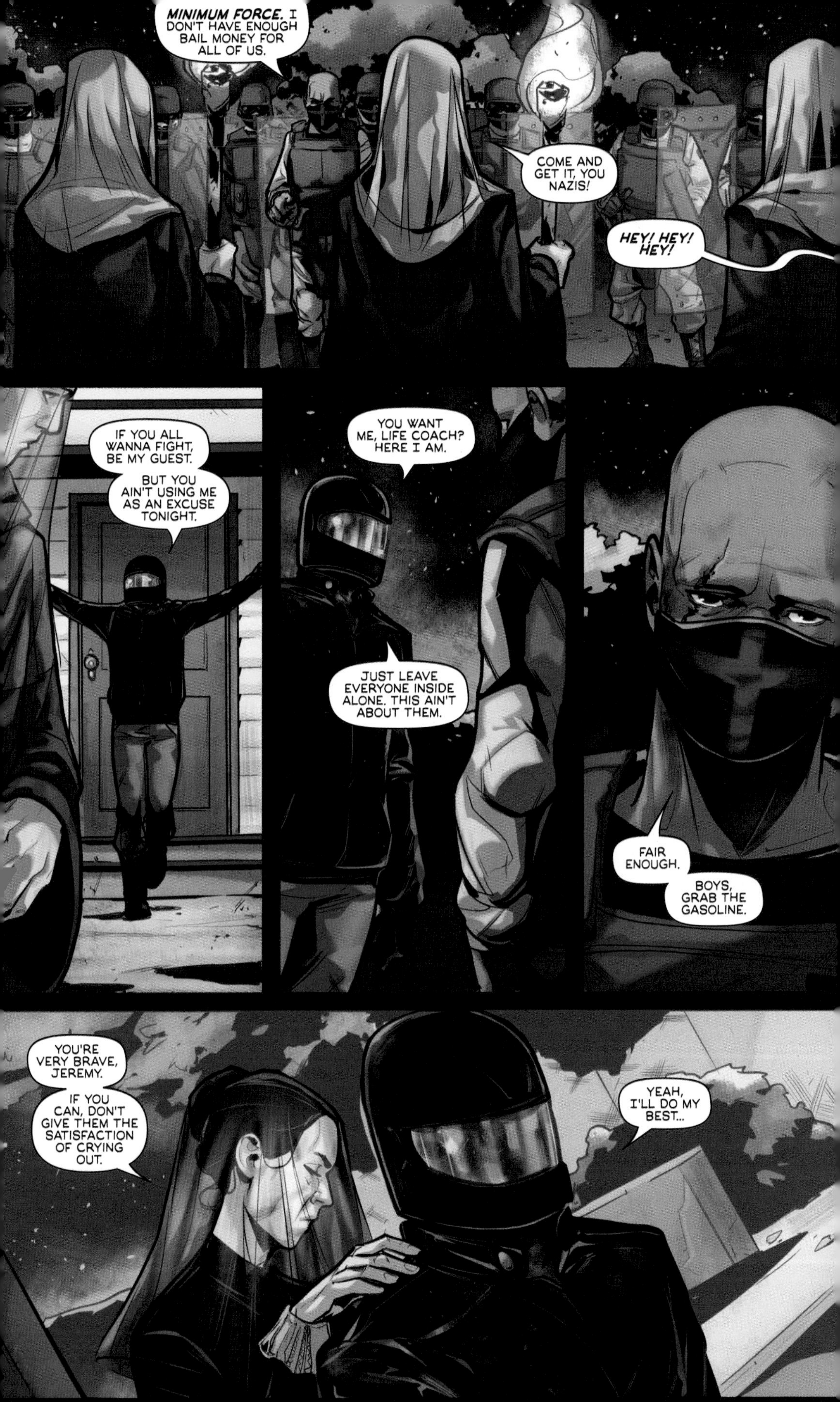
MINIMUM FORCE. I DON'T HAVE ENOUGH BAIL MONEY FOR ALL OF US.
COME AND GET IT, YOU NAZIS!
HEY! HEY! HEY!
IF YOU ALL WANNA FIGHT, BE MY GUEST.
BUT YOU AIN'T USING ME AS AN EXCUSE TONIGHT.
YOU WANT ME, LIFE COACH? HERE I AM.
JUST LEAVE EVERYONE INSIDE ALONE. THIS AIN'T ABOUT THEM.
FAIR ENOUGH.
BOYS, GRAB THE GASOLINE.
YOU'RE VERY BRAVE, JEREMY.
IF YOU CAN, DON'T GIVE THEM THE SATISFACTION OF CRYING OUT.
YEAH, I'LL DO MY BEST...

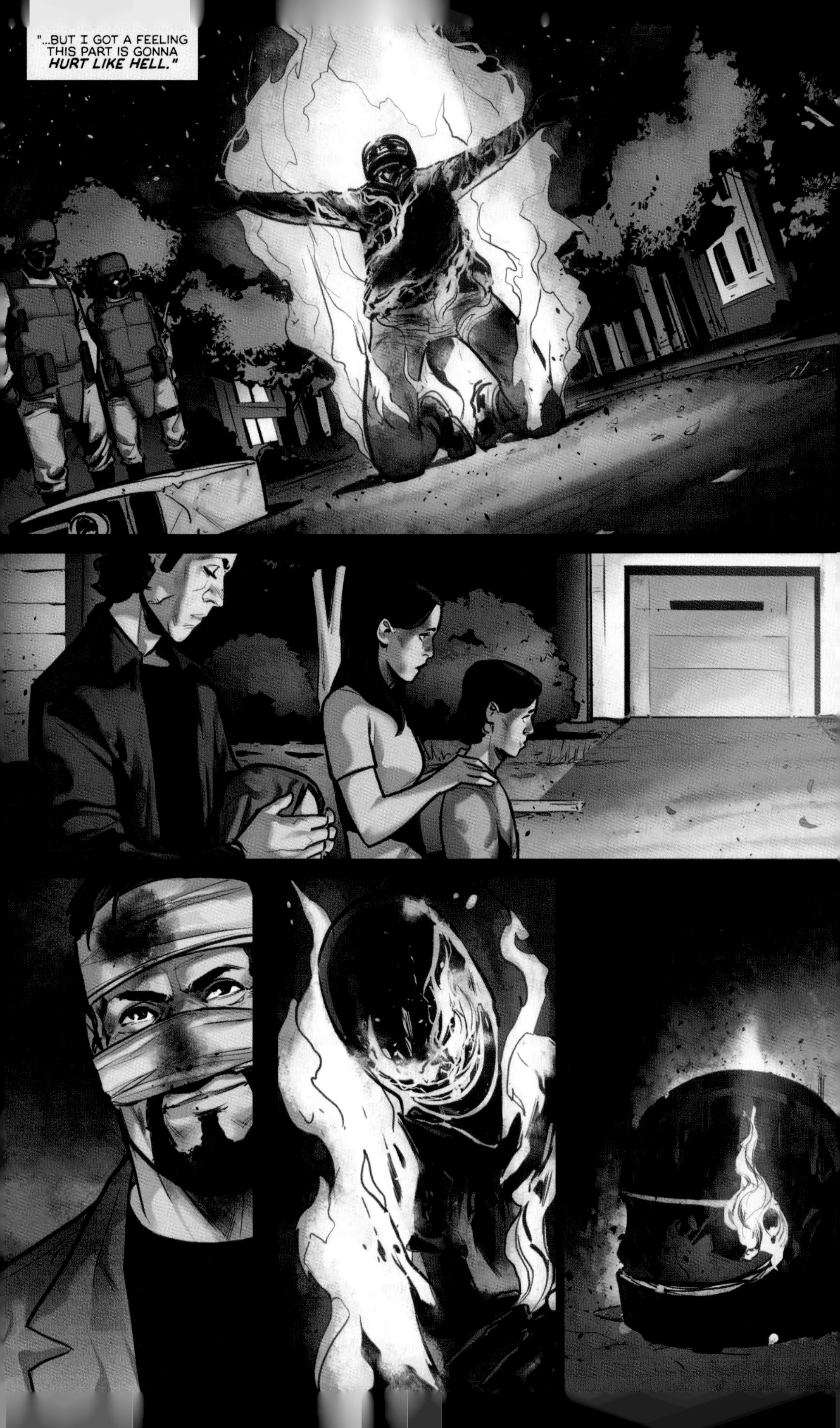
"...BUT I GOT A FEELING THIS PART IS GONNA HURT LIKE HELL."

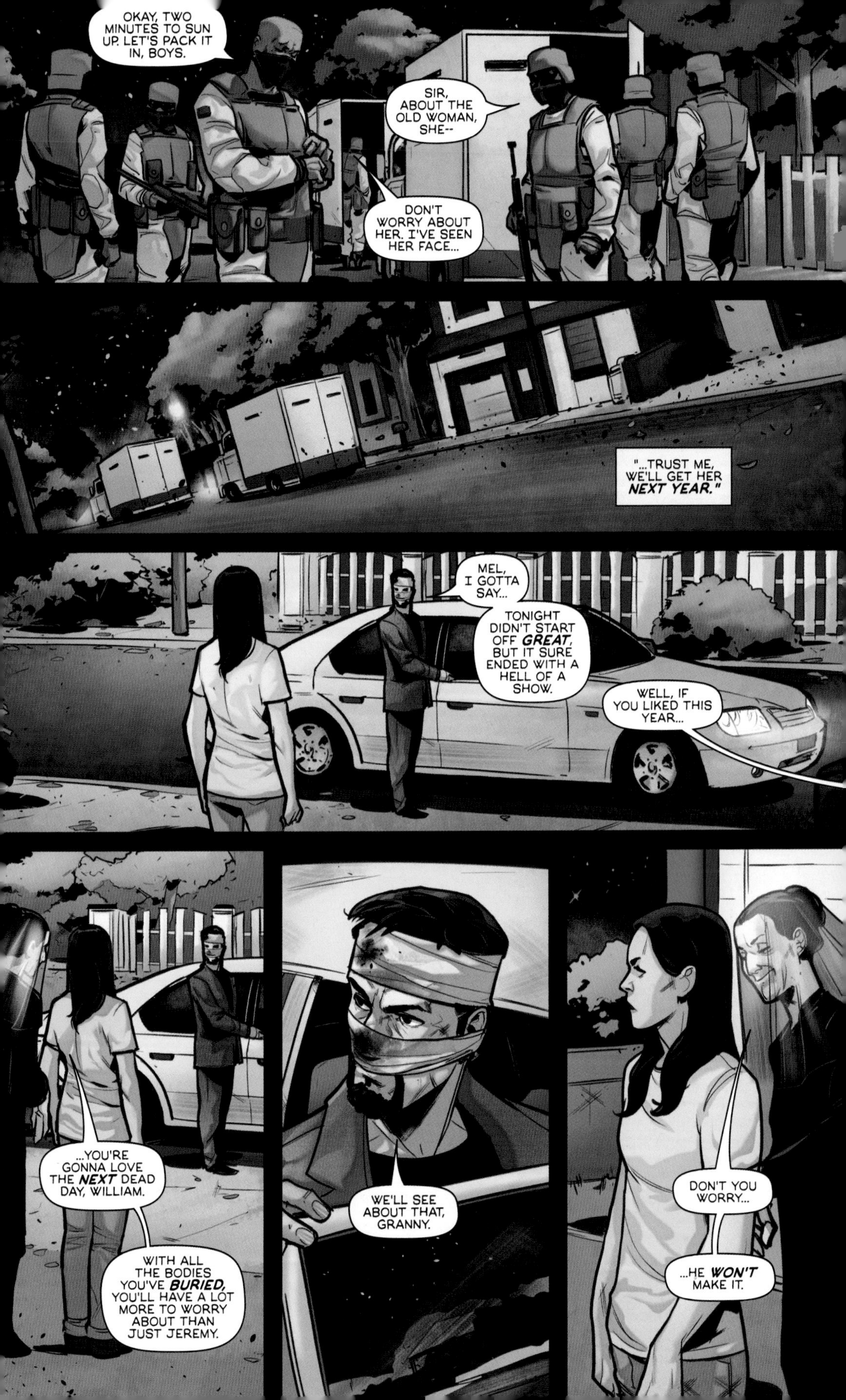
OKAY, TWO MINUTES TO SUN UP. LET'S PACK IT IN, BOYS.
SIR, ABOUT THE OLD WOMAN, SHE--
DON'T WORRY ABOUT HER. I'VE SEEN HER FACE...
"...TRUST ME, WE'LL GET HER NEXT YEAR."
MEL, I GOTTA SAY...
TONIGHT DIDN'T START OFF GREAT, BUT IT SURE ENDED WITH A HELL OF A SHOW.
WELL, IF YOU LIKED THIS YEAR...
...YOU'RE GONNA LOVE THE NEXT DEAD DAY, WILLIAM.
WITH ALL THE BODIES YOU'VE BURIED, YOU'LL HAVE A LOT MORE TO WORRY ABOUT THAN JUST JEREMY.
WE'LL SEE ABOUT THAT, GRANNY.
DON'T YOU WORRY...
...HE WON'T MAKE IT.

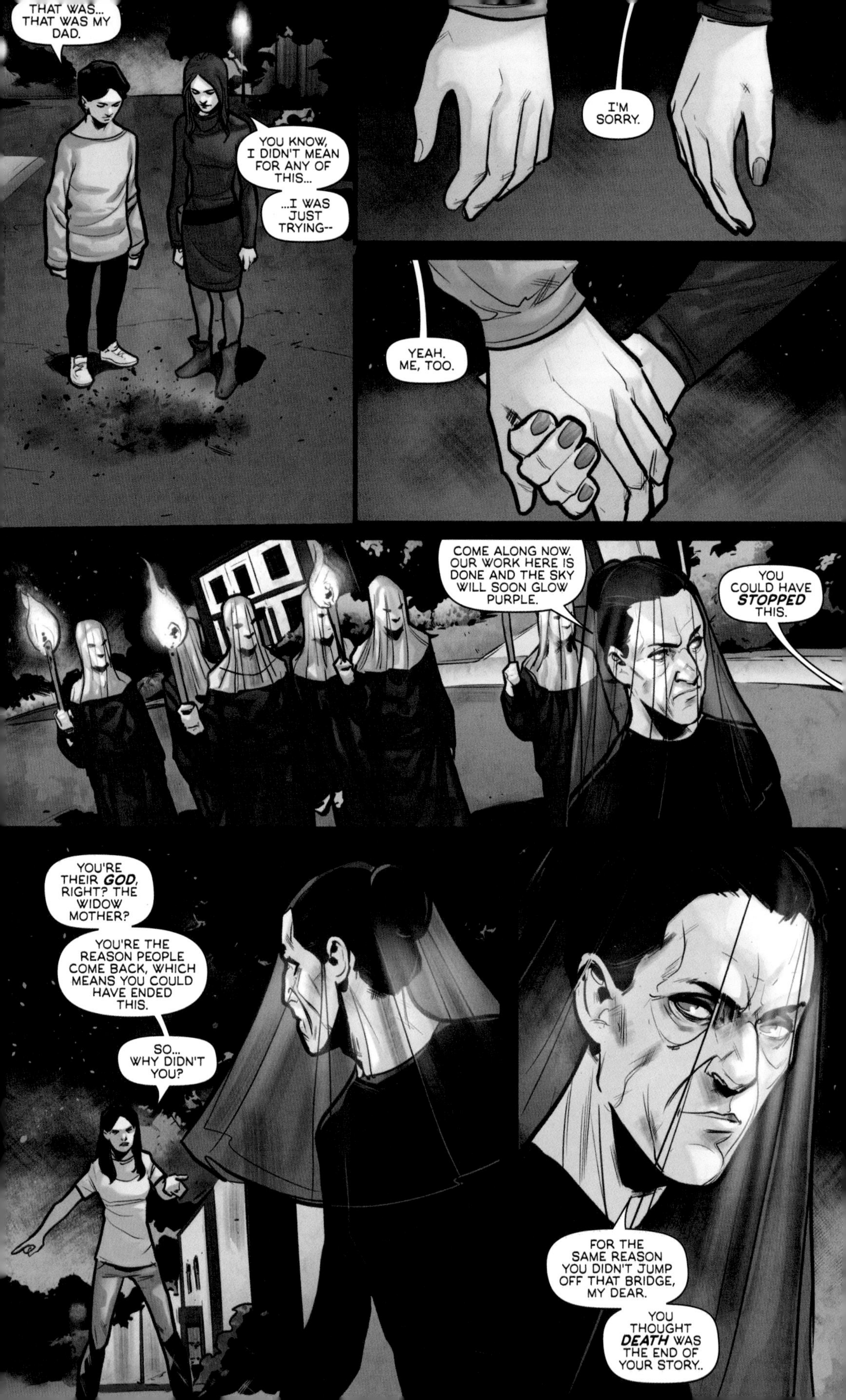
THAT WAS... THAT WAS MY DAD.
YOU KNOW, I DIDN'T MEAN FOR ANY OF THIS...
...I WAS JUST TRYING--
I'M SORRY.
YEAH. ME, TOO.
COME ALONG NOW. OUR WORK HERE IS DONE AND THE SKY WILL SOON GLOW PURPLE.
YOU COULD HAVE ***STOPPED*** THIS.
YOU'RE THEIR ***GOD***, RIGHT? THE WIDOW MOTHER?
YOU'RE THE REASON PEOPLE COME BACK, WHICH MEANS YOU COULD HAVE ENDED THIS.
SO... WHY DIDN'T YOU?
FOR THE SAME REASON YOU DIDN'T JUMP OFF THAT BRIDGE, MY DEAR.
YOU THOUGHT ***DEATH*** WAS THE END OF YOUR STORY..

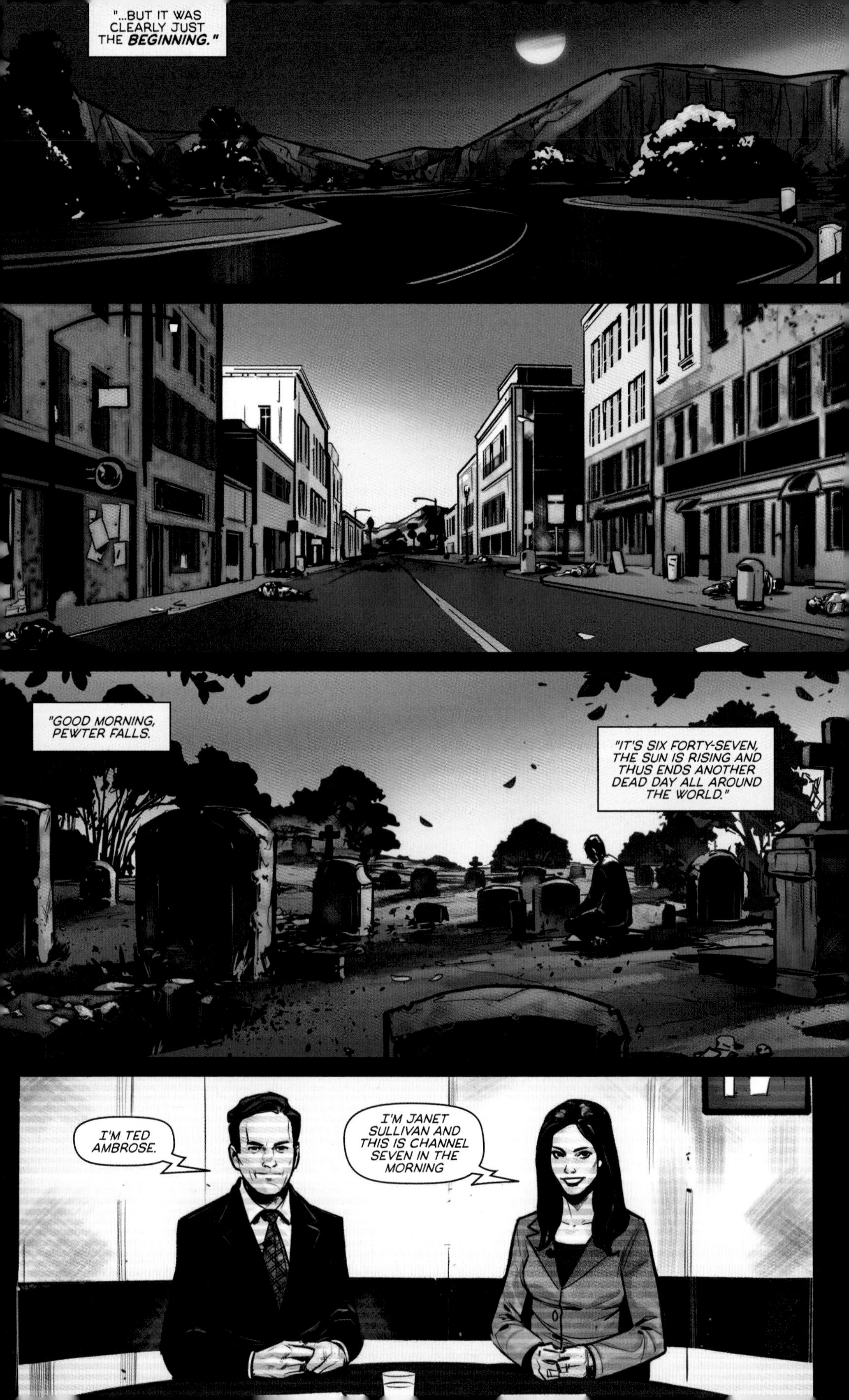
"...BUT IT WAS CLEARLY JUST THE BEGINNING."
"GOOD MORNING, PEWTER FALLS.
"IT'S SIX FORTY-SEVEN, THE SUN IS RISING AND THUS ENDS ANOTHER DEAD DAY ALL AROUND THE WORLD."
I'M TED AMBROSE.
I'M JANET SULLIVAN AND THIS IS CHANNEL SEVEN IN THE MORNING

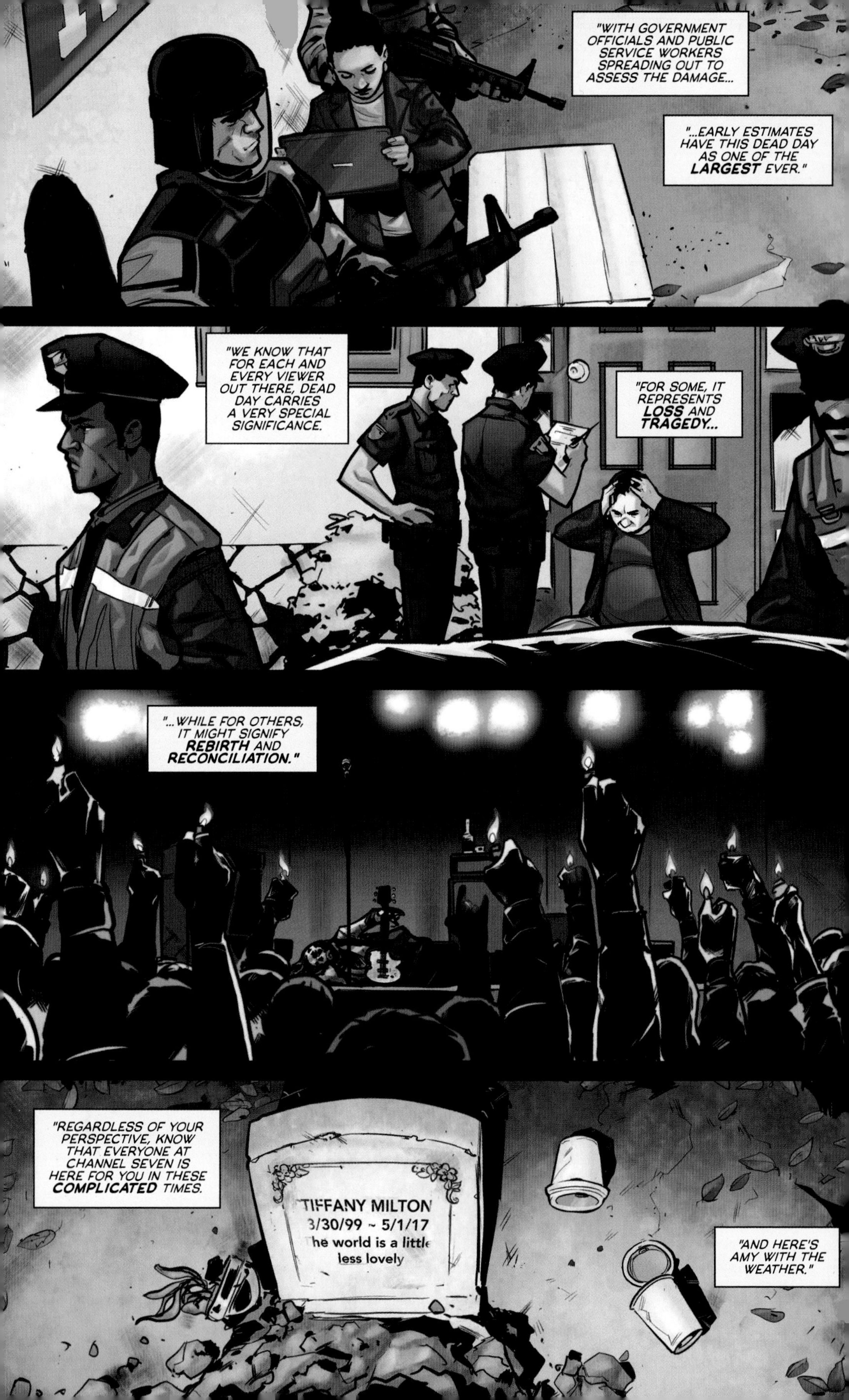
"WITH GOVERNMENT OFFICIALS AND PUBLIC SERVICE WORKERS SPREADING OUT TO ASSESS THE DAMAGE...
"...EARLY ESTIMATES HAVE THIS DEAD DAY AS ONE OF THE **LARGEST** EVER."
"WE KNOW THAT FOR EACH AND EVERY VIEWER OUT THERE, DEAD DAY CARRIES A VERY SPECIAL SIGNIFICANCE.
"FOR SOME, IT REPRESENTS **LOSS** AND **TRAGEDY**...
"...WHILE FOR OTHERS, IT MIGHT SIGNIFY **REBIRTH** AND **RECONCILIATION.**"
"REGARDLESS OF YOUR PERSPECTIVE, KNOW THAT EVERYONE AT CHANNEL SEVEN IS HERE FOR YOU IN THESE **COMPLICATED** TIMES.
TIFFANY MILTON
3/30/99 ~ 5/1/17
The world is a little less lovely
"AND HERE'S AMY WITH THE WEATHER."

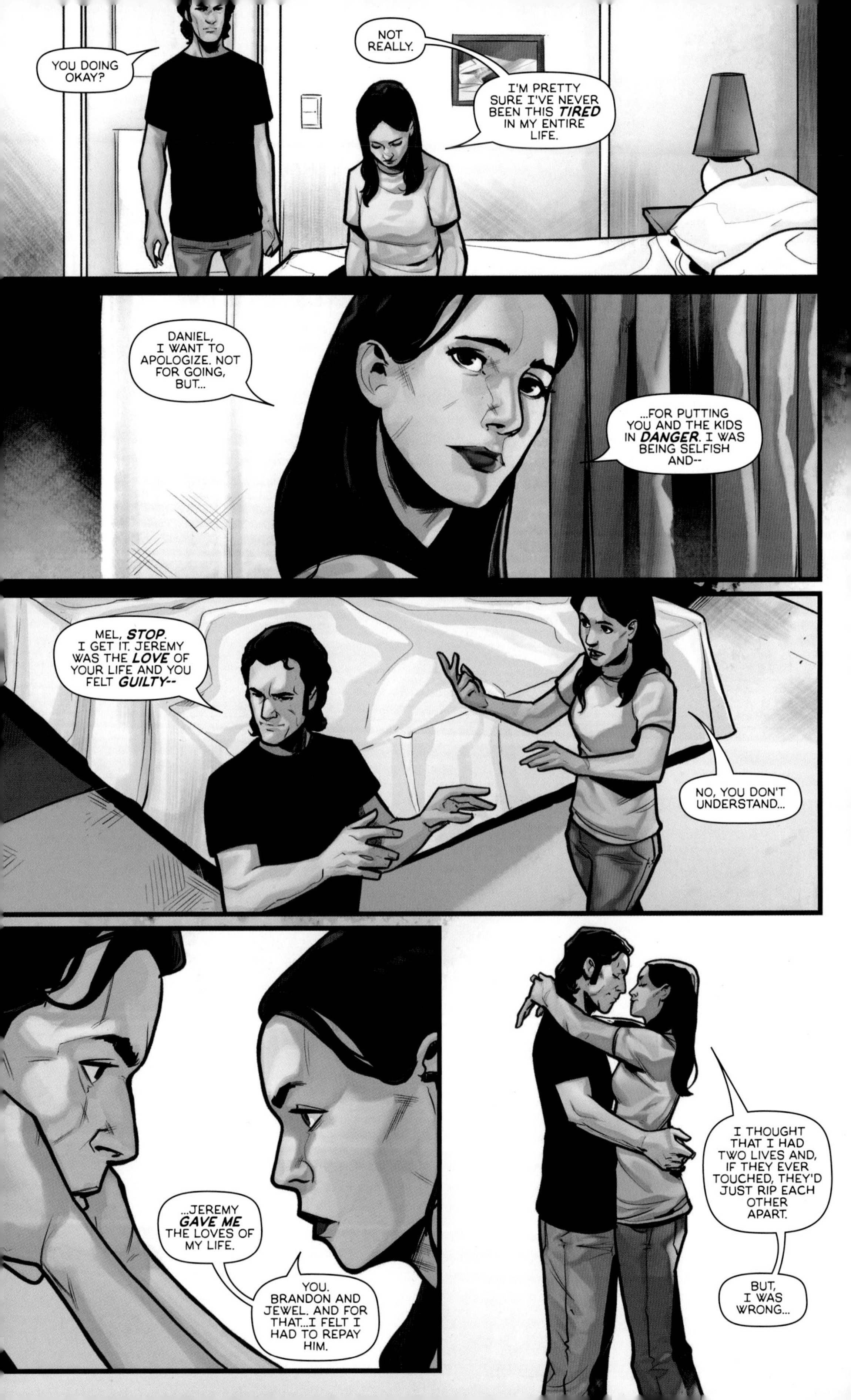
YOU DOING OKAY?
NOT REALLY.
I'M PRETTY SURE I'VE NEVER BEEN THIS TIRED IN MY ENTIRE LIFE.
DANIEL, I WANT TO APOLOGIZE. NOT FOR GOING, BUT...
...FOR PUTTING YOU AND THE KIDS IN DANGER. I WAS BEING SELFISH AND--
MEL, STOP. I GET IT. JEREMY WAS THE LOVE OF YOUR LIFE AND YOU FELT GUILTY--
NO, YOU DON'T UNDERSTAND...
...JEREMY GAVE ME THE LOVES OF MY LIFE.
YOU. BRANDON AND JEWEL. AND FOR THAT...I FELT I HAD TO REPAY HIM.
I THOUGHT THAT I HAD TWO LIVES AND, IF THEY EVER TOUCHED, THEY'D JUST RIP EACH OTHER APART.
BUT, I WAS WRONG...

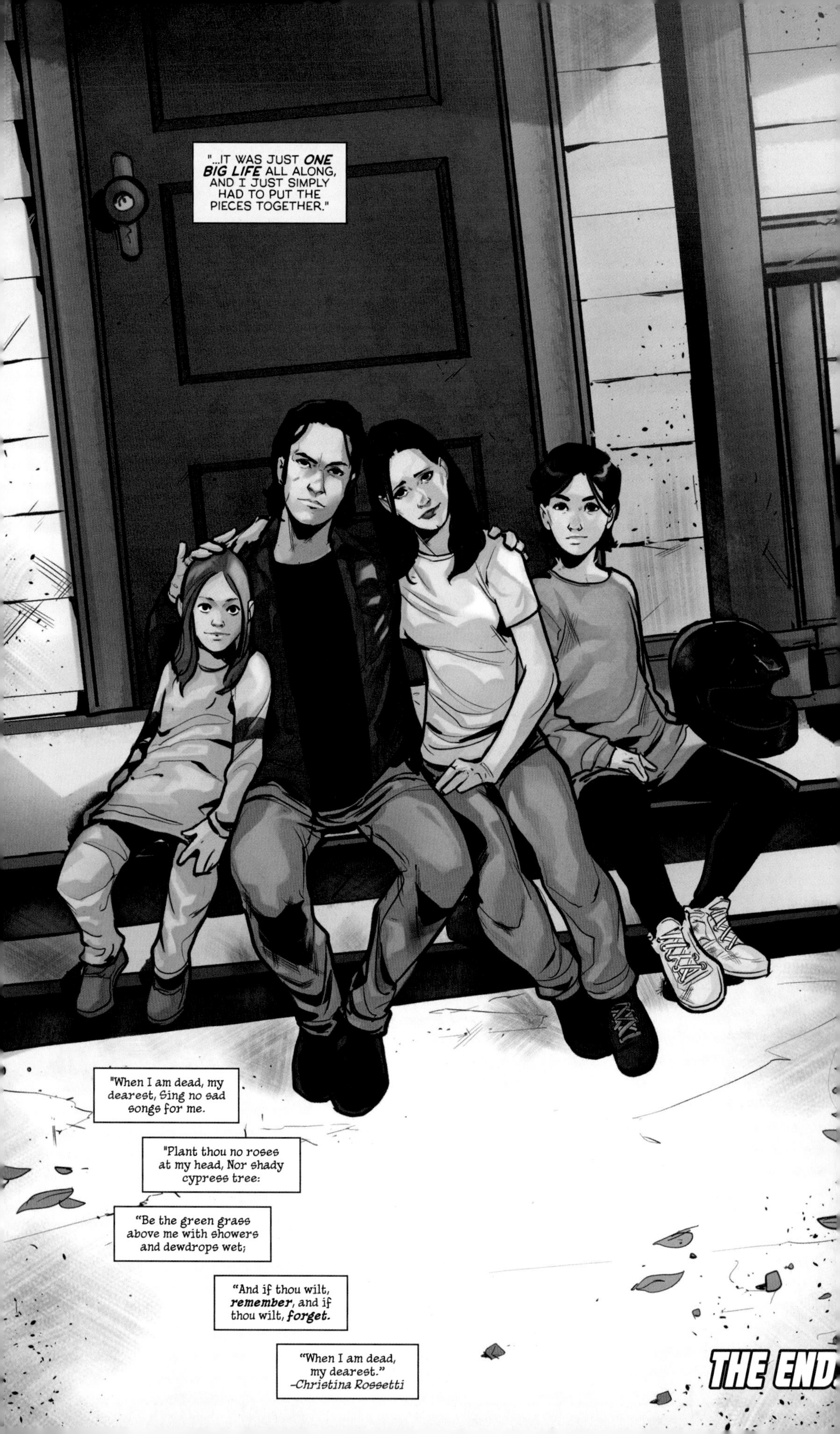
"...IT WAS JUST ONE BIG LIFE ALL ALONG, AND I JUST SIMPLY HAD TO PUT THE PIECES TOGETHER."
"When I am dead, my dearest, Sing no sad songs for me.
"Plant thou no roses at my head, Nor shady cypress tree:
"Be the green grass above me with showers and dewdrops wet;
"And if thou wilt, remember, and if thou wilt, forget.
"When I am dead, my dearest." –Christina Rossetti
THE END.

DEAD DAY™

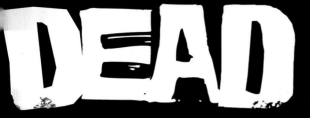

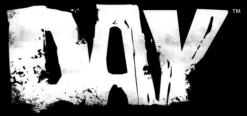

COVER GALLERY & EXTRAS

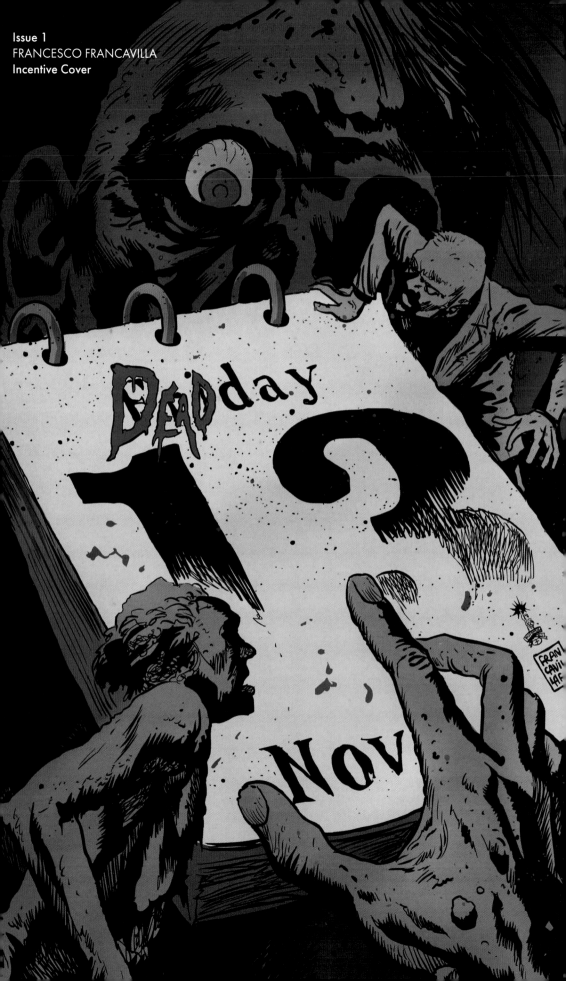

Issue 1
FRANCESCO FRANCAVILLA
Incentive Cover

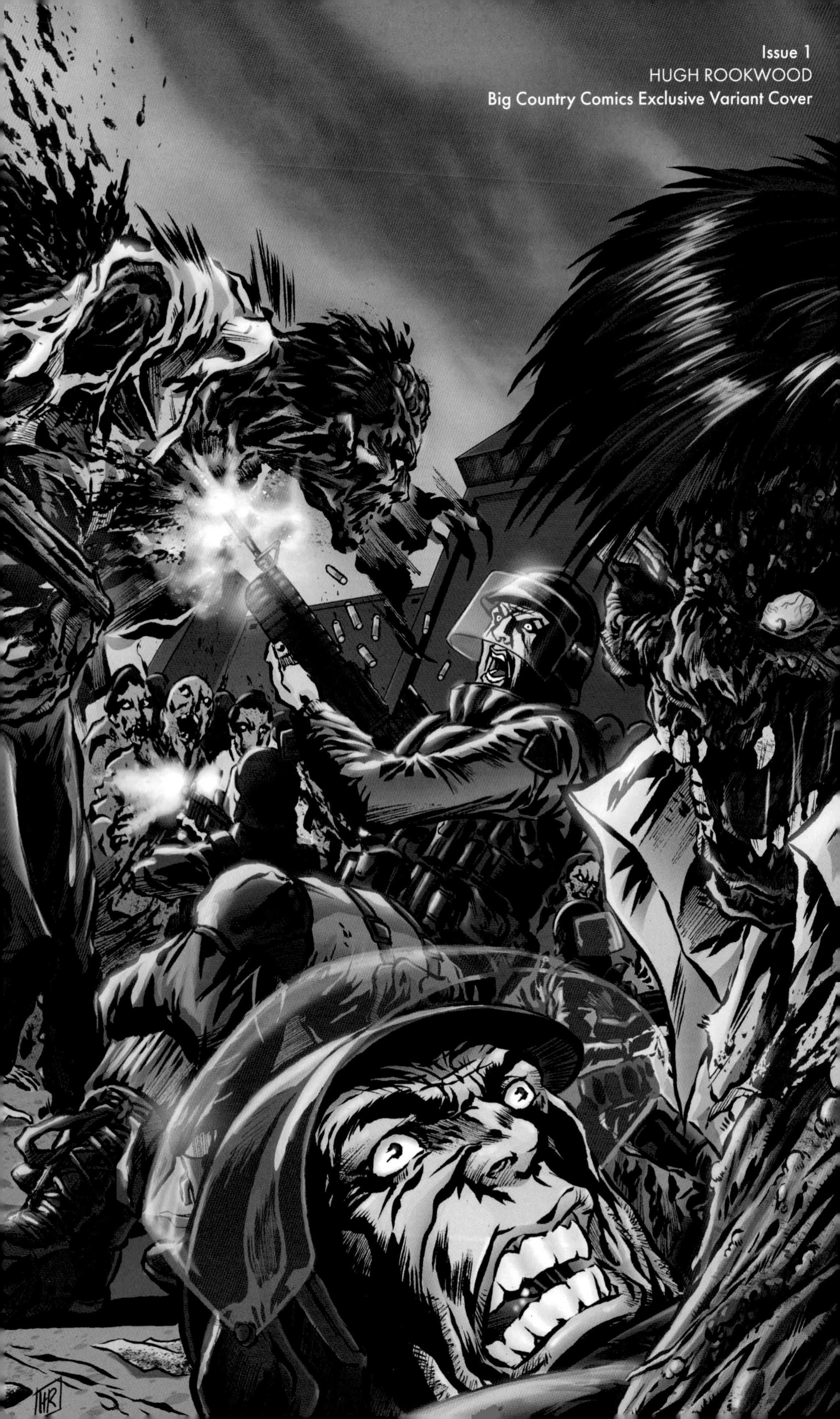

Issue 1
HUGH ROOKWOOD
Big Country Comics Exclusive Variant Cover

Issue 1
ALAN QUAH
Comic Kingdom of Canada Cover

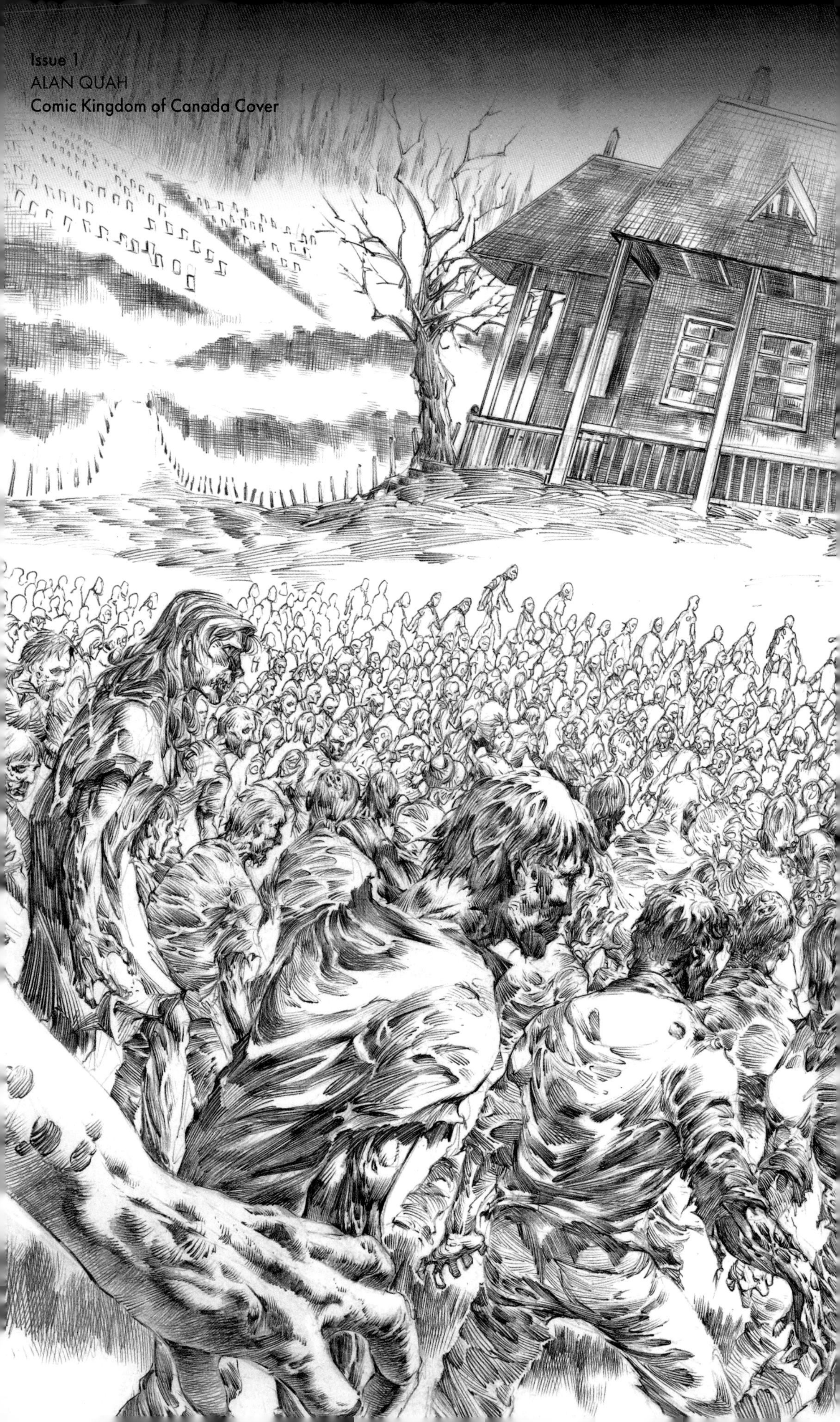

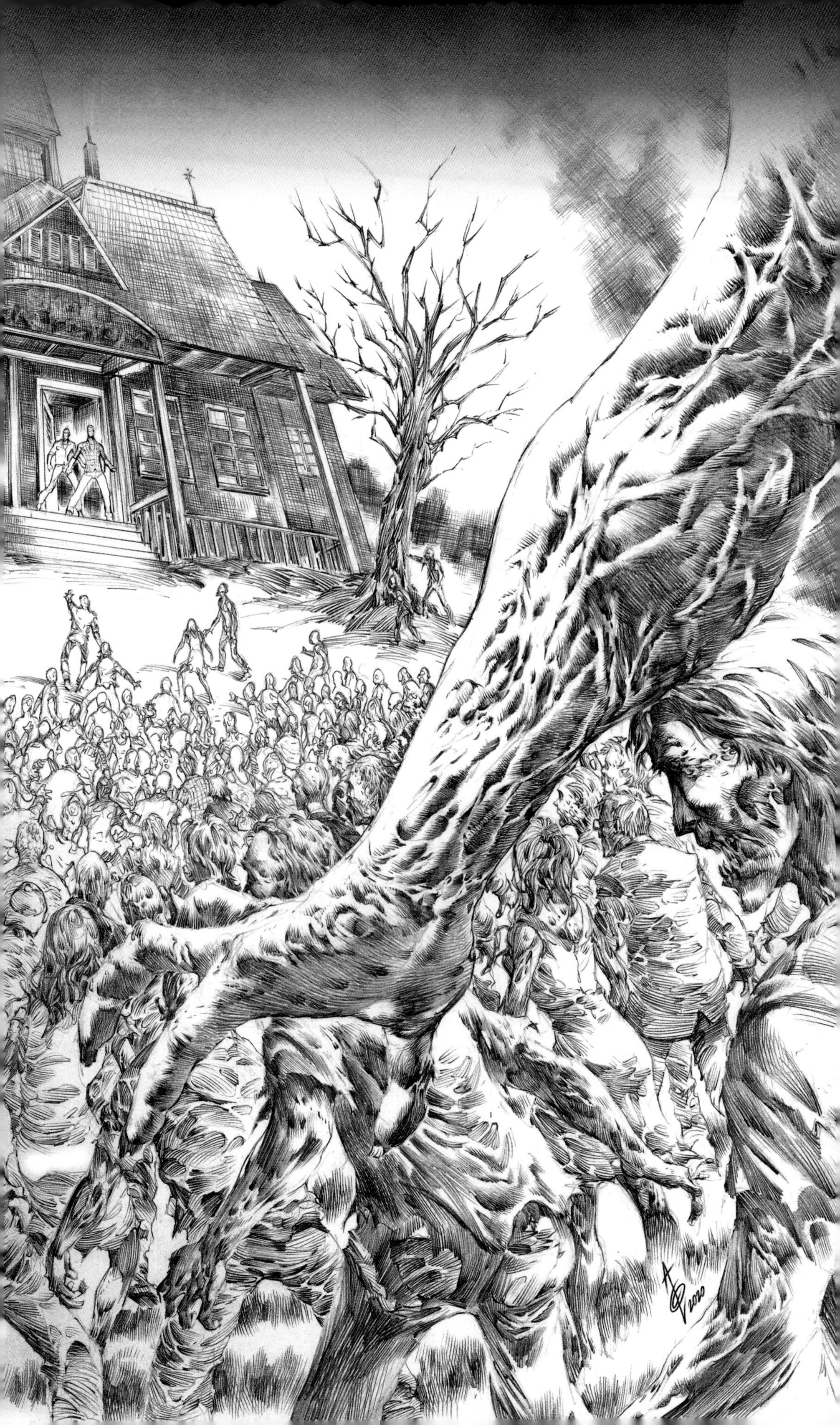

Issue 1
ALAN QUAH
Comic Kingdom of Canada Cover

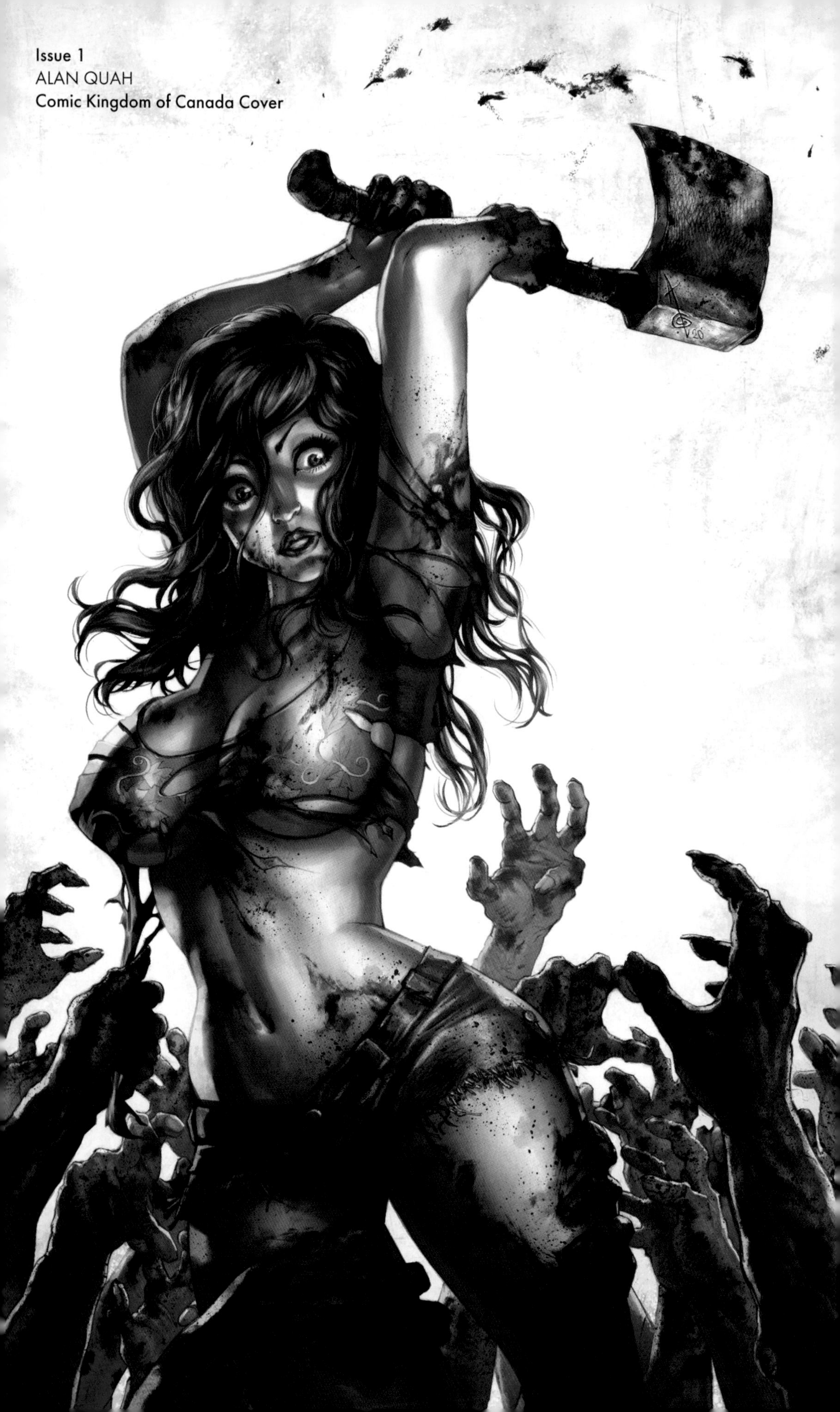

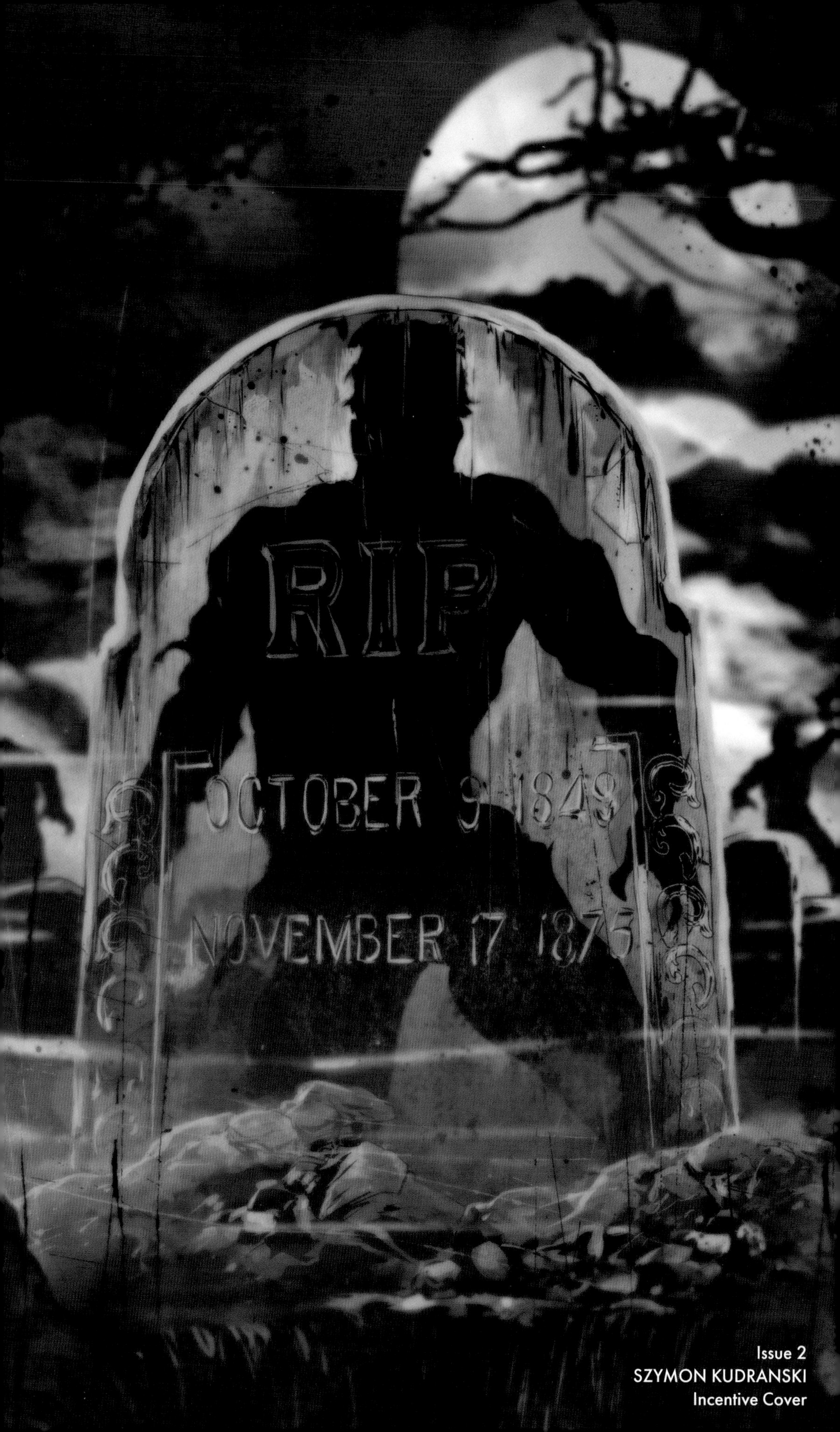
RIP
OCTOBER 9 1849
NOVEMBER 17 1875

Issue 2
SZYMON KUDRANSKI
Incentive Cover

DEAD DAY™

ANDY CLARKE

cover sketches

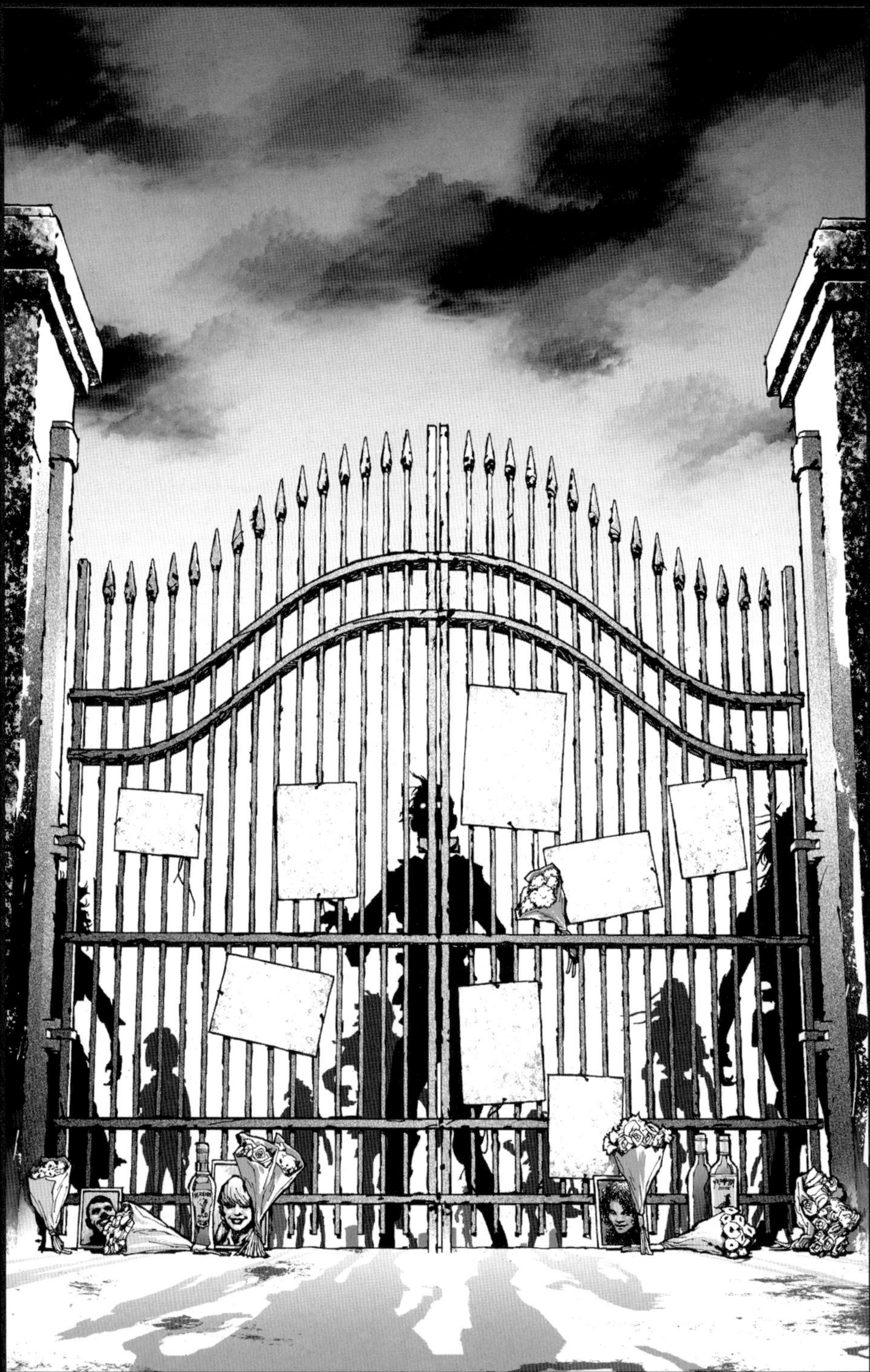

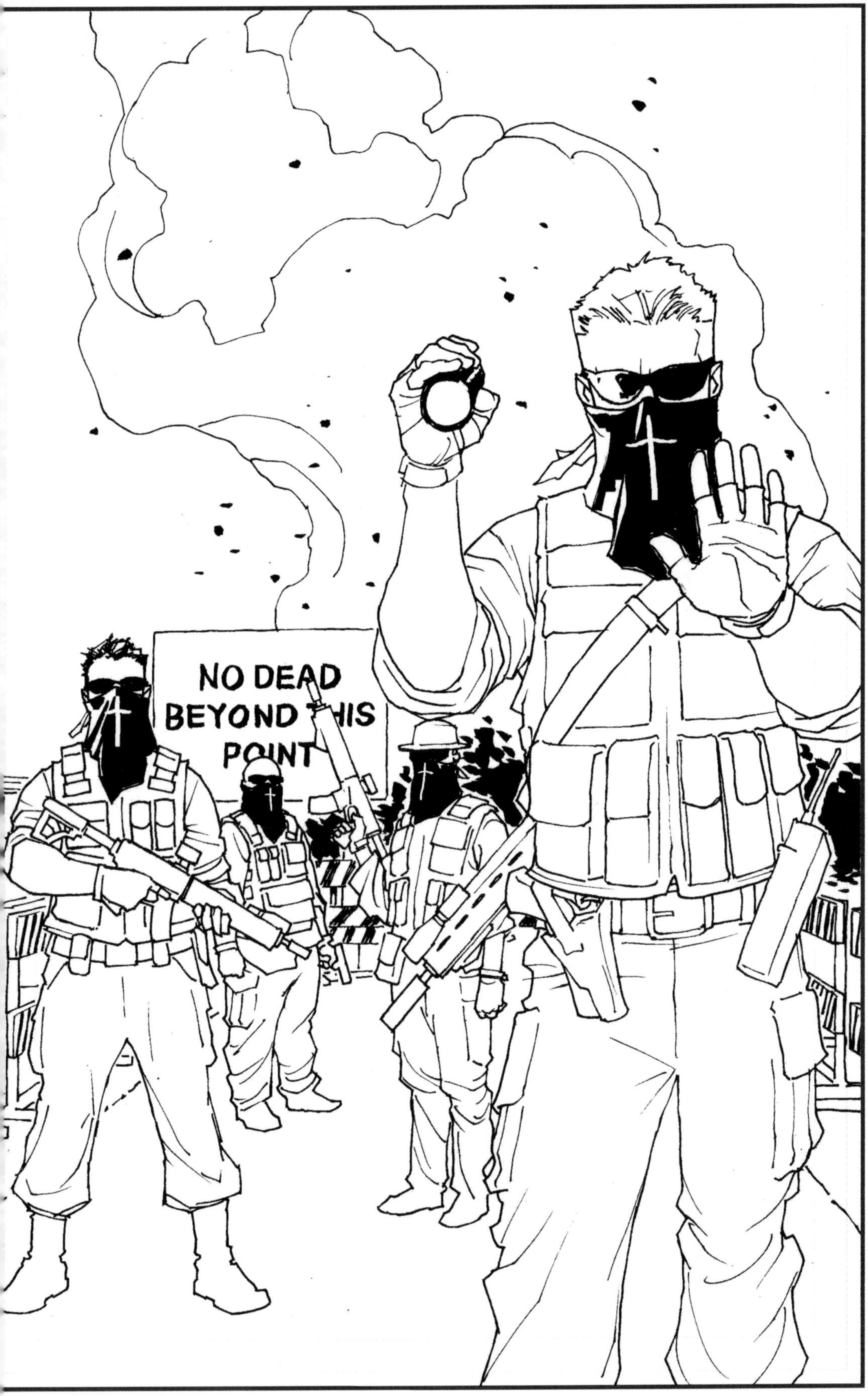
NO DEAD BEYOND THIS POINT

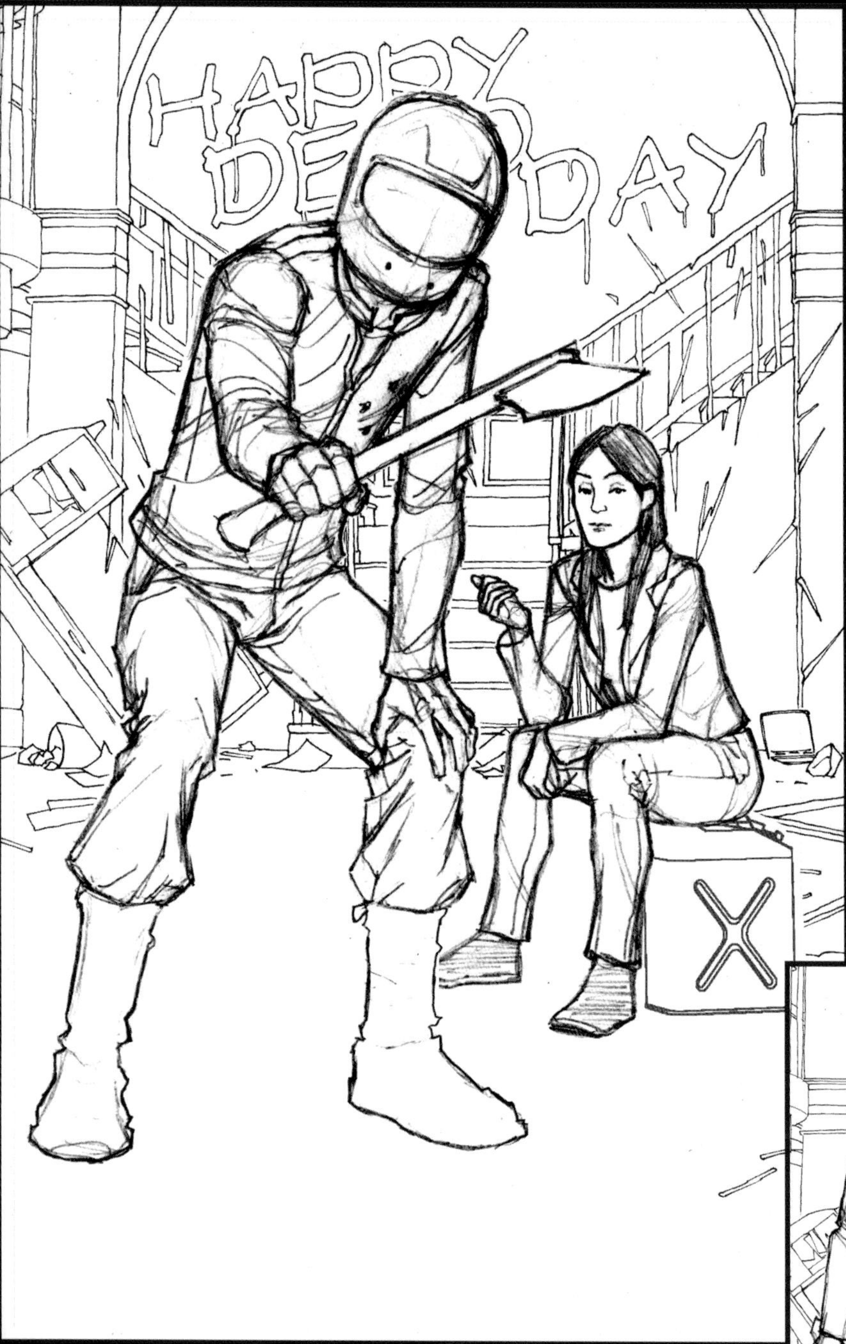
HAPPY
DAY

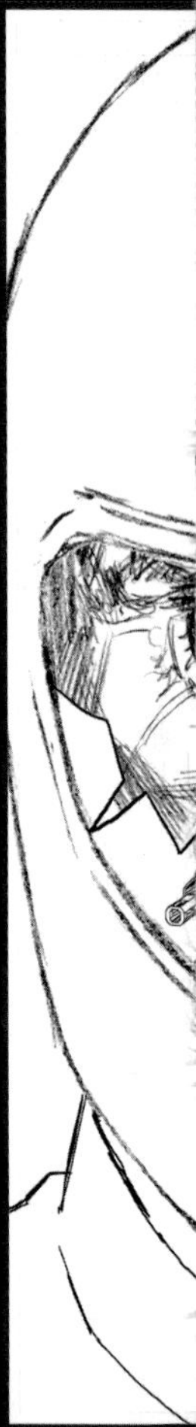

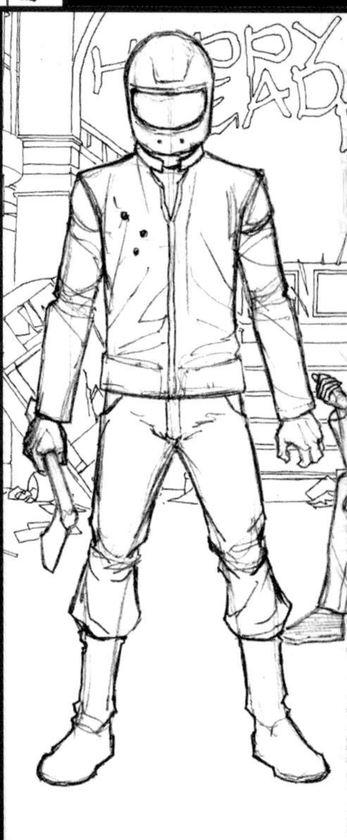

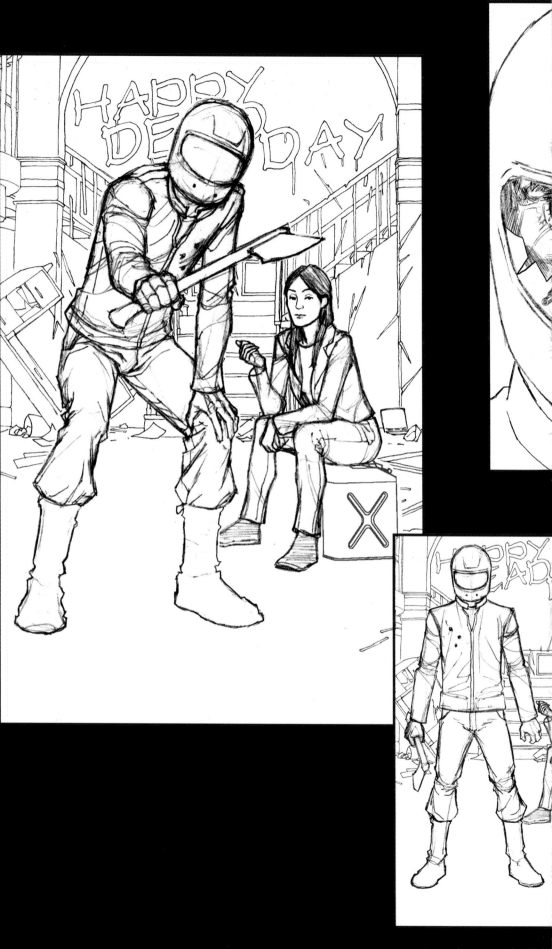

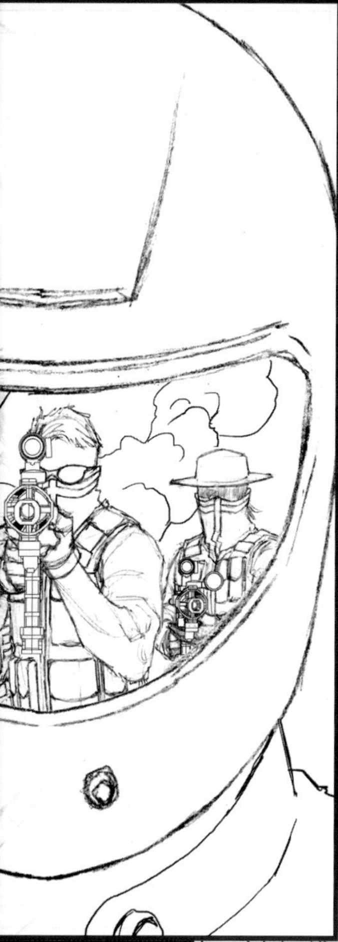

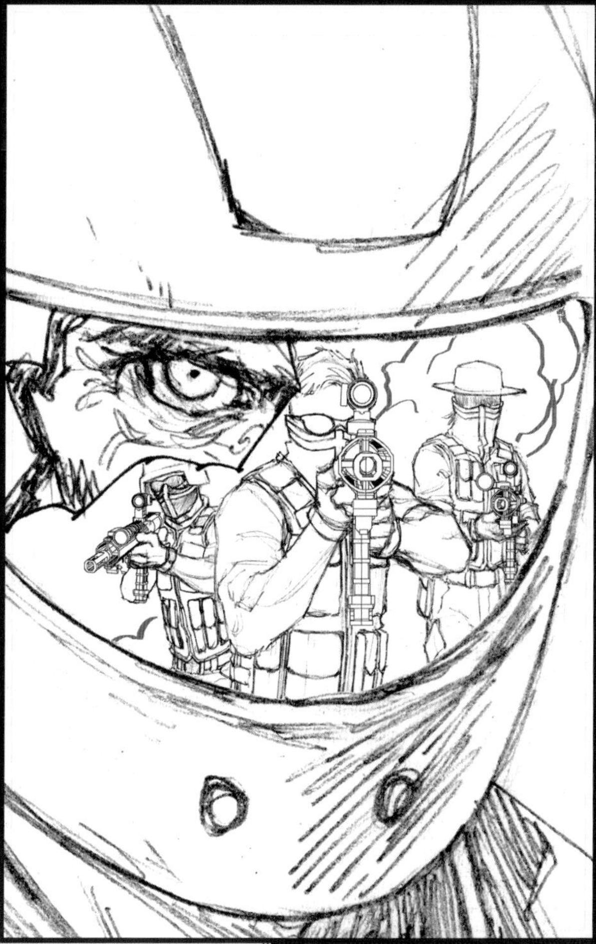

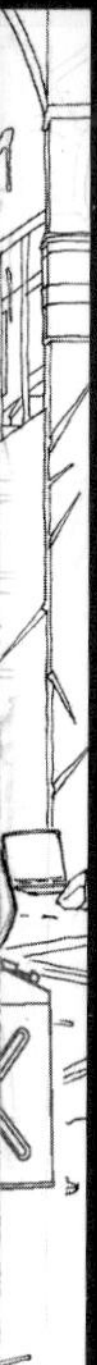

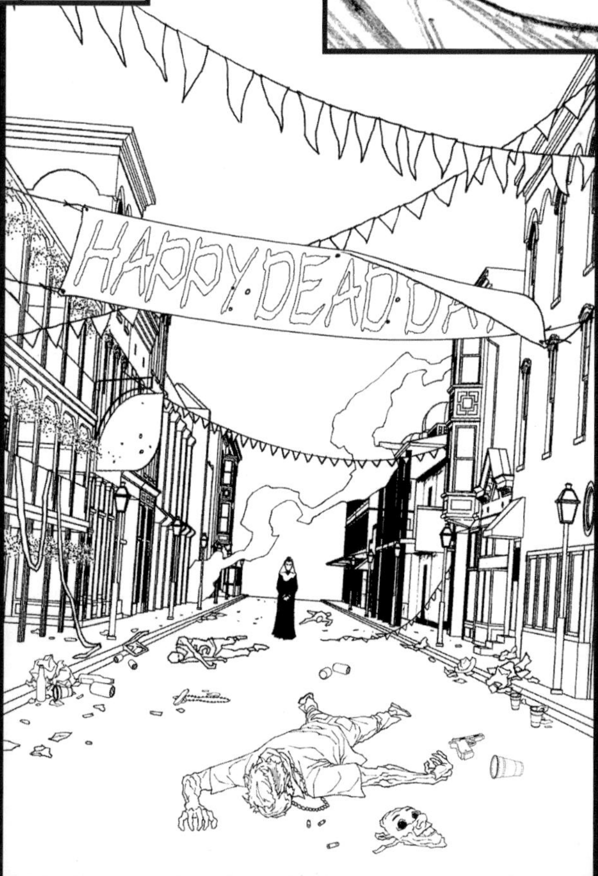
HAPPY DEAD DA

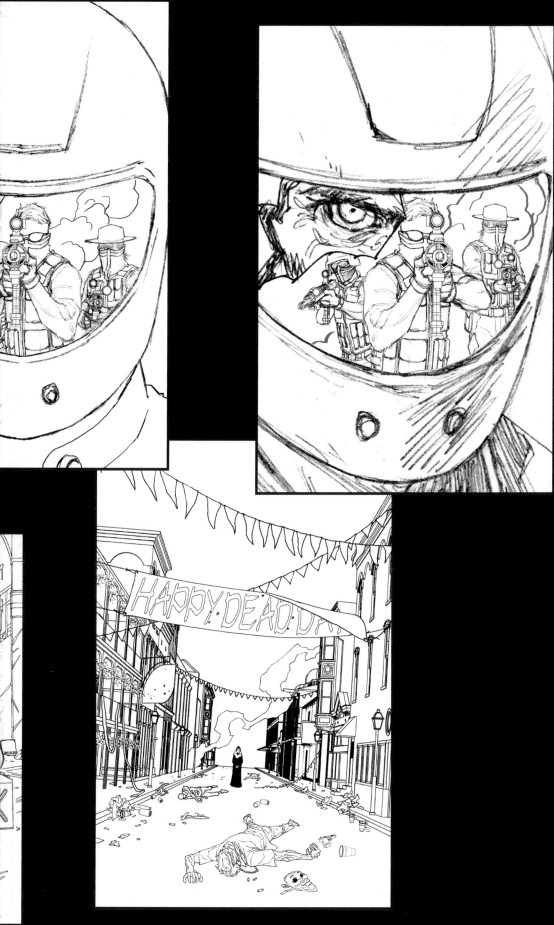

DEAD DAY

EVGENIY BORNYAKOV
character sketches

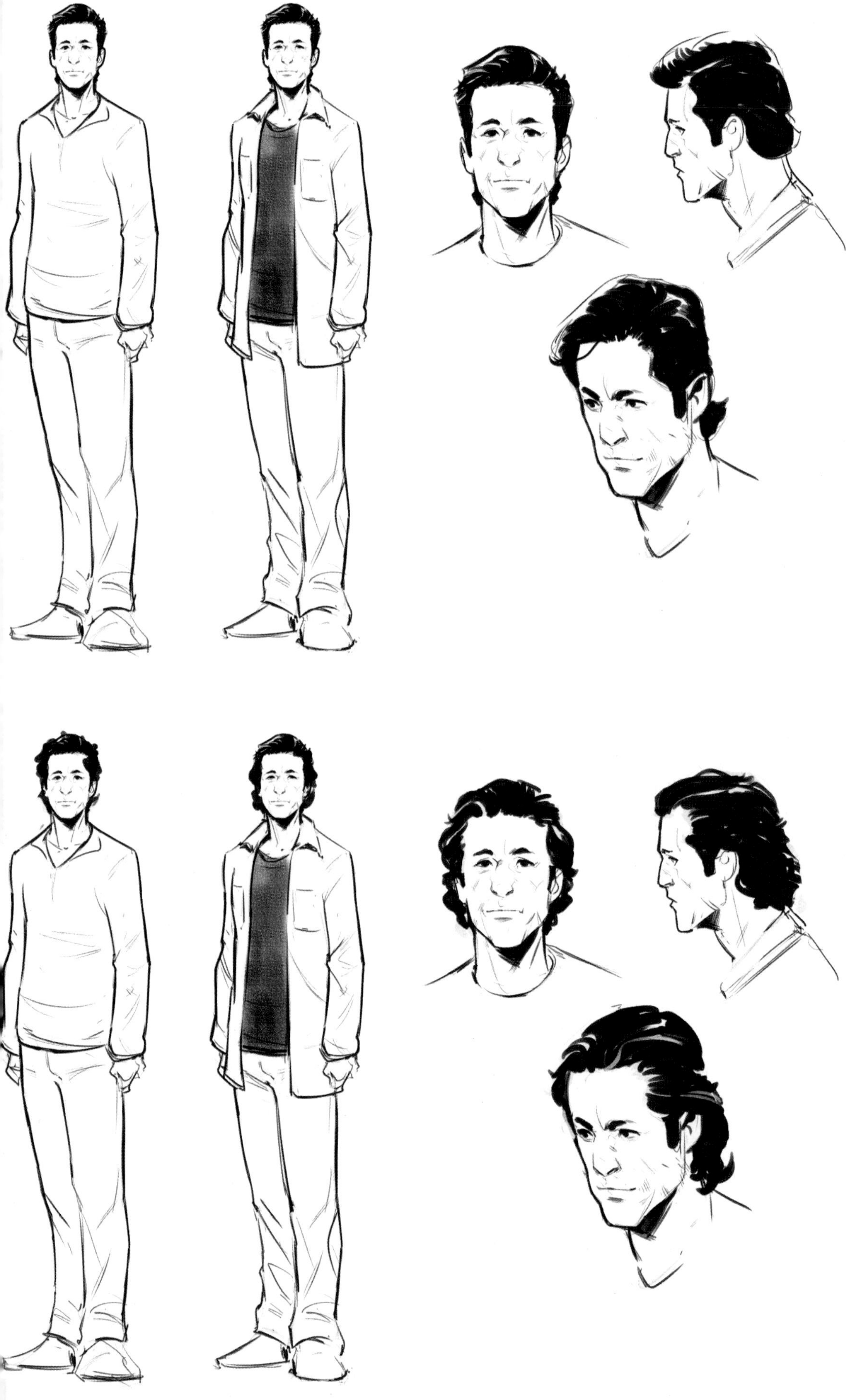

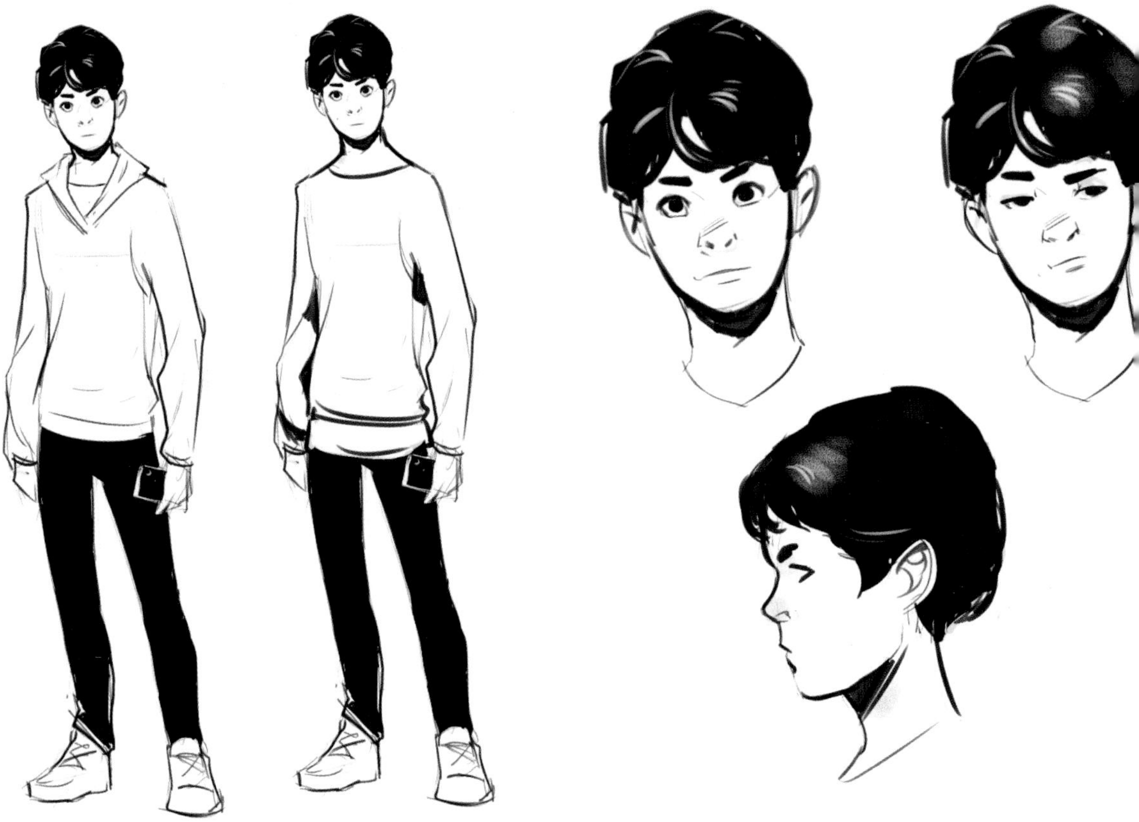

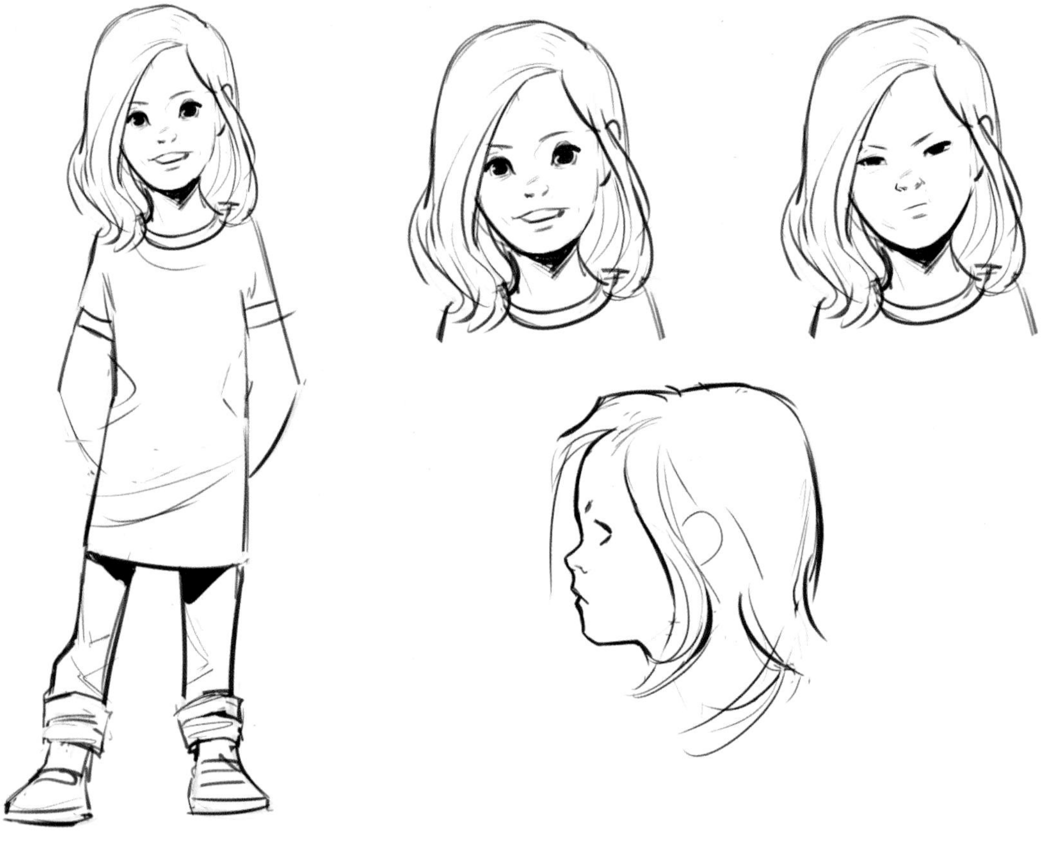

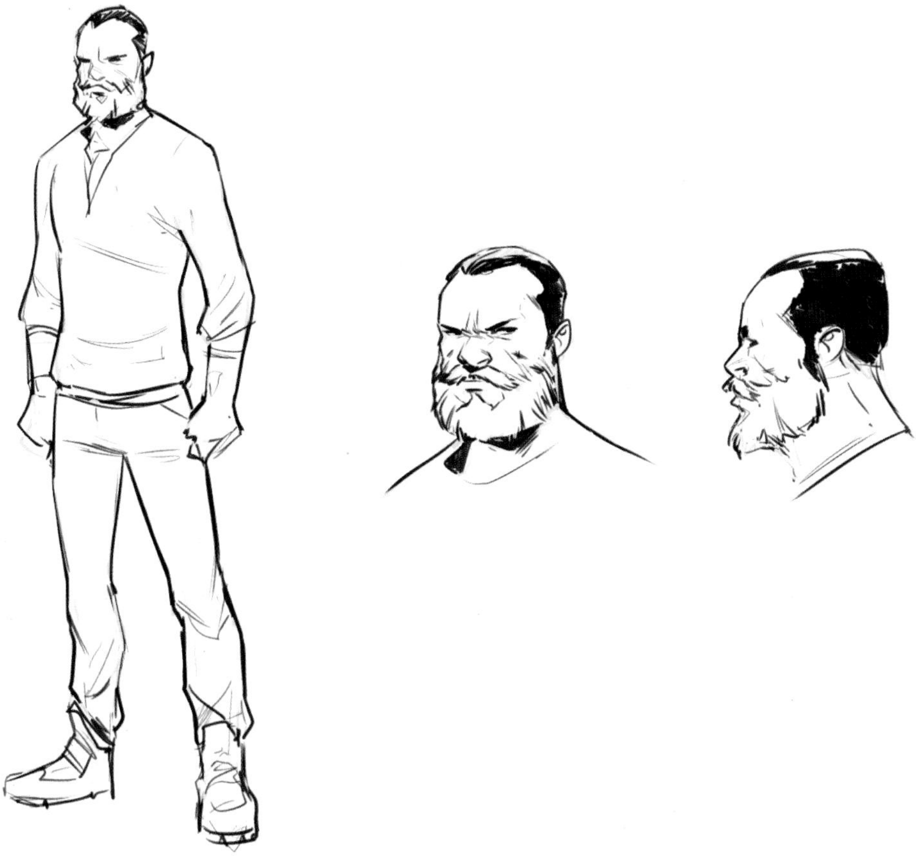

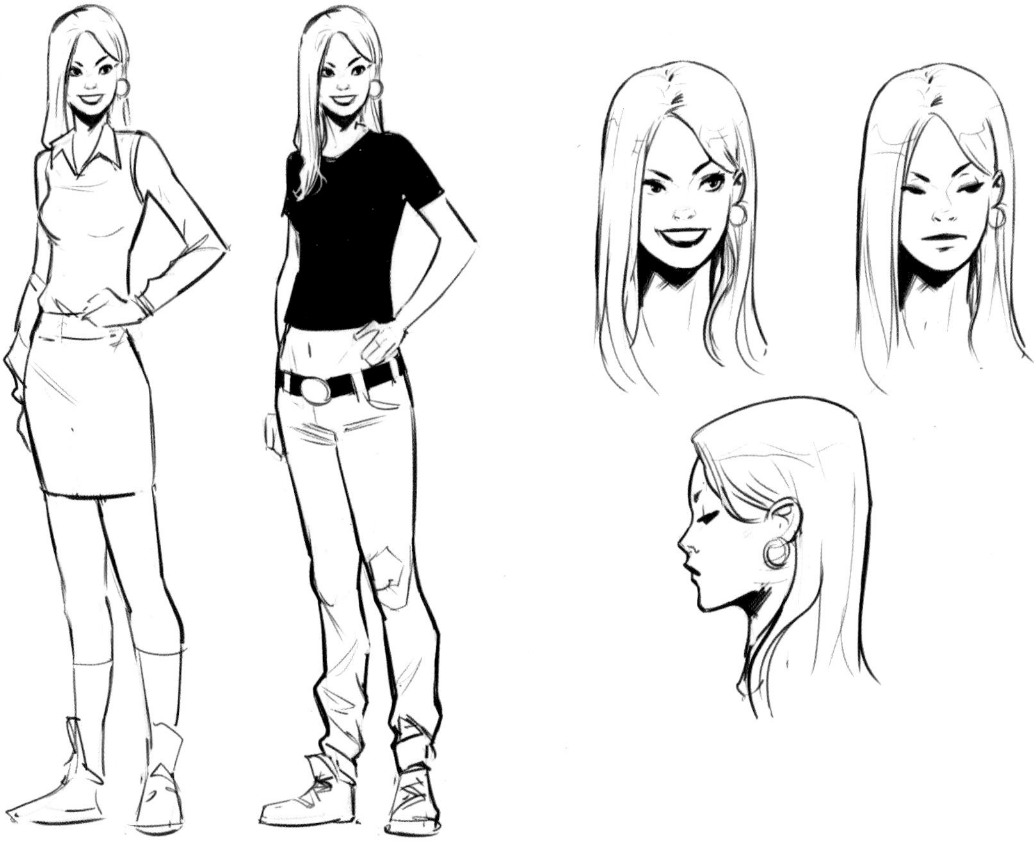

INFORMATION

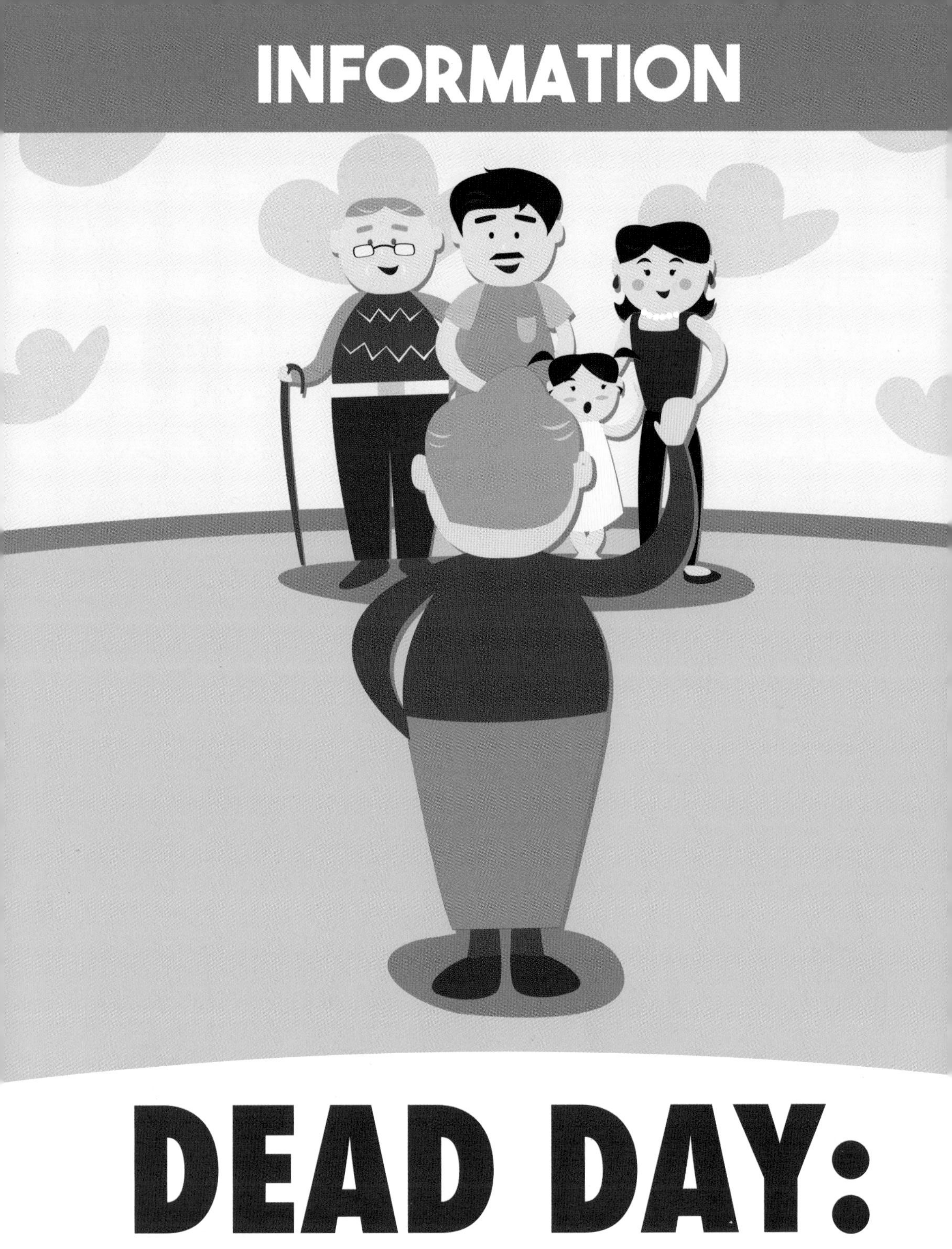

DEAD DAY:

A FAMILY GUIDE TO UNDERSTANDING AND STAYING SAFE DURING THE RETURN OF A LOVED ONE

PREPARE / ENJOY / SURVIVE

THE BUREAU OF POST-LIFE AFFAIRS

DEAD DAY: BASIC INFORMATION AND SAFETY PLANNING

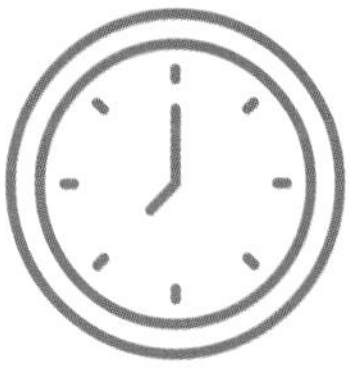

TIMING

The event commonly known as "Dead Day" occurs all around the world, usually beginning at SUNSET and ending at SUNRISE, the next morning.

(Length and duration may depend on your individual timezones.)

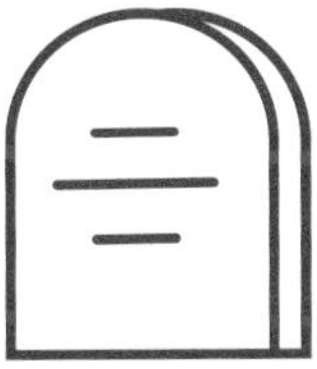

STAY SAFE OUTSIDE

As cemeteries are popular gathering areas on Dead Day, make sure you keep an eye on your belongings and any small children.

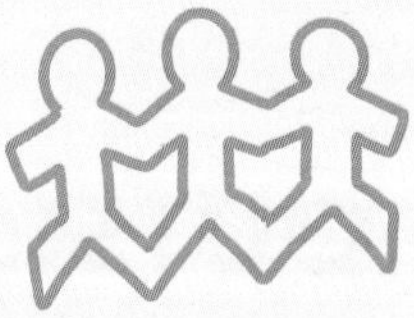

CONNECTION

If you wish to reconnect with a loved one, remember to update your personal contact information at the website for: *THE DECEASED INFORMATION ACT.*

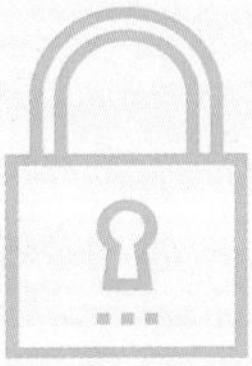

STAY SECURE INSIDE

If you do decide to stay at home on Dead Day, make sure your windows and doors are locked and that your security system is active.

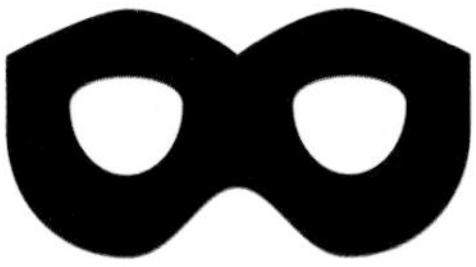

THE DECEASED

It is common for people to don masks or veils in celebration on Dead Day, but if you witness any suspicious activity, please contact your local law enforcement immediately.

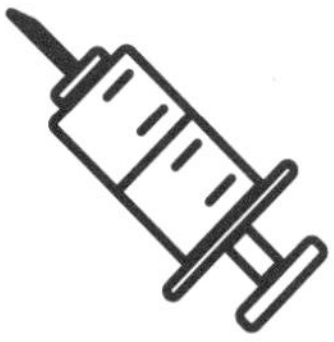

HEALTHY

A deceased body carries a wide array of potential viruses and bacteria. Consult your family physician in anticipation of any prolonged contact.

THE DOs AND DON'Ts OF DEAD DAY!

D DRINK AND EAT RESPONSIBLY

E EXPECT HEAVY TRAFFIC DELAYS

A AVOID HOUSES PERFORMING RITUALISTIC SACRIFICE

D DON'T ALLOW PETS OUTSIDE

D DON'T WEAR FLAMMABLE COSTUMES

A ALWAYS STAY IN CONTACT WITH YOUR FAMILY

Y YIELD TO ANY AND ALL DECEASED

CLOSING

Dead Day is an exciting and family-oriented holiday that can be enjoyed by all ages with just a little forethought and planning. Also, please remember to be kind and courteous to your neighbors who may not be lucky enough to participate in the event.

KEY LOCATIONS

Here is a list of locations to know:

- NEAREST HOSPITALS
- NEAREST LAW ENFORCEMENT
- NEAREST PHARMACY
- NEAREST VETERINARIAN

Here is a list of areas to avoid:

- CEMETERIES
- PRISONS
- LANDFILLS
- MORTUARIES

DEAD DAY IS OVER: NOW WHAT?

If you haven't already, please remember to contact *THE BUREAU OF POST-LIFE AFFAIRS* to schedule any and all potential *BODY RETRIEVALS* and *SECONDARY BURIALS* (some fees may apply.)

PREPARE
ENJOY
SURVIVE

THE BUREAU OF POST-LIFE AFFAIRS

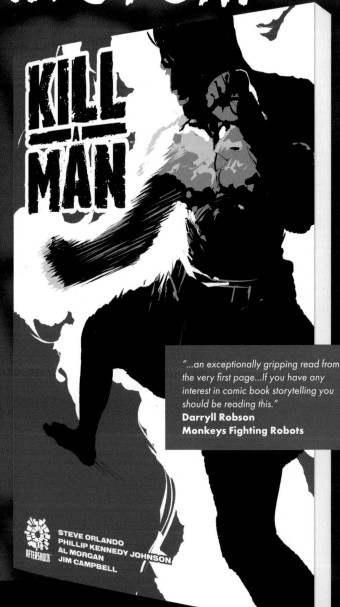

ABOUT THE CREATORS OF

DEAD DAY

RYAN PARROTT writer

@ThatRyanParrott

Ryan Parrott was born in Bakersfield, California but spent the majority of his life growing up in Las Vegas. A graduate of Chapman University, Ryan has worked in television, writing on Hulu's *Chance* and NBC's *Revolution*, as well as in comics, where he has contributed to several series, including Saban's *Go Go Power Rangers*, IDW's *Star Trek* and the New York Time's bestselling *Batman: Gates of Gotham*.

EVGENIY BORNYAKOV artist

@EvgenyBornyakov evgeny_bornyakov

Evgeniy Bornyakov is a Russian artist who started his career working as an illustrator for games, storyboarding and animation. But his love for comic books won. As a comic book artist he began his career at the publishing house Bubble. These days he illustrates for AfterShock Comics.

JUANCHO! colorist

@social_myth socialmyth_studios

Juan Ignacio Vélez, aka JUANCHO! is a comic book colorist/illustrator from Bogotá, Colombia and a Kubert School graduate. His past comic book experience stretches all the way from North American to European publishers. He currently lives in Barcelona, Spain, where he splits his time between eating fuet with guacamole and freelance color duties.

CHARLES PRITCHETT letterer

Brought up on the wrong side of the tracks in a bustling metropolis in Newfoundland & Labrador, Canada, Charles is really terrible at writing epic sounding biographies of his life and times. He enjoys a fine stew from time to time and hates to travel. When he's not working with AfterShock Comics, He can be found currently living in Canada's smallest, but nicest province, outnumbered by powerful women in his own household.